Visual Rhetoric

Series Editor, Marguerite Helmers

Visual Rhetoric
Series Editor, Marguerite Helmers

The Visual Rhetoric series publishes work by scholars in a wide variety of disciplines, including art theory, anthropology, rhetoric, cultural studies, psychology, and media studies.

Other Books in the Series

Ways of Seeing, Ways of Speaking: The Integration of Rhetoric and Vision in Constructing the Real, edited by Kristie S. Fleckenstein, Sue Hum, and Linda T. Calendrillo

Writing the Visual

A Practical Guide for Teachers of Composition and Communication

Edited by
Carol David and Anne R. Richards

Parlor Press
West Lafayette, Indiana
www.parlorpress.com

Parlor Press LLC, West Lafayette, Indiana 47906

S A N: 2 5 4 - 8 8 7 9

Library of Congress Cataloging-in-Publication Data

Writing the visual : a practical guide for teachers of composition and communication / edited by Carol David and Anne R. Richards.
p. cm. -- (Visual rhetoric)
Includes bibliographical references and index.
ISBN 978-1-60235-046-5 (pbk. : alk. paper) -- ISBN 978-1-60235-047-2 (hardcover : alk. paper) -- ISBN 978-1-60235-048-9 (adobe ebk.)
1. English language--Rhetoric--Study and teaching. 2. Report writing--Study and teaching. 3. Visual communication--Study and teaching. I. David, Carol, 1931- II. Richards, Anne R., 1961-
PE1404.W743 2008
808'.042071--dc22

2007051124

Cover Images: "Sacred Sight, Island of Djerba, Tunisia," by Anne R. Richards. Used by permission. "Smooth Sea after Sunset," by AVTG. Used by permission.

Cover design by David Blakesley.
Printed on acid-free paper.

Parlor Press, LLC is an independent publisher of scholarly and trade titles in print and multimedia formats. This book is available in paper, cloth and Adobe eBook formats from Parlor Press on the World Wide Web at http://www.parlorpress.com or through online and brick-and-mortar bookstores. For submission information or to find out about Parlor Press publications, write to Parlor Press, 816 Robinson St., West Lafayette, Indiana, 47906, or e-mail editor@parlorpress.com.

Contents

Illustrations

Acknowledgments

We have relied greatly upon the expertise and dedication of our authors, as well as on editors David Blakesley and Marguerite Helmers. We are also thankful to our families, who encouraged us to undertake this work.

Writing the Visual

If we have once seen,
"the day is ours,
and what the day has shown."

—Hellen Keller, quoting Richard Watson Gilder

1 Introduction
Fields of Vision: A Background Study of References for Teachers

Anne R. Richards and Carol David

Writing teachers hoping to awaken in students a broad understanding of the cultural influences on individuals or of the rhetorical elements influencing the interpretation of discourse do well to acknowledge the importance of the visual: how we live, think, act, and read are all influenced profoundly by images appearing in print and digital media. The authors of the twelve essays published in this collection advocate an enlivened writing pedagogy reflecting the importance of complementary ways of knowing to our students. Teachers will find, in the chapters that follow, useful methods of importing the visual, frameworks informing these methods, and suggested assignments. This introduction summarizes a variety of ways of approaching the visual in the writing classroom, as well as sources that teachers may wish to consult.

"From Analysis to Design: Visual Communication in the Teaching of Writing," Diana George's history of the visual in composition teaching, recognizes the secondary position the visual has taken in our classrooms for the brief time it has been of interest to us: during this period, a sensitivity to the visual has only slowly and tenuously emerged. She observes, however, that new media are revolutionizing composition teaching because "for students who have grown up in a technology-saturated and an image-rich culture, questions of communication and composition absolutely will include the visual, not as attendant to the verbal but as complex communication intricately related to the world around them" (32). James E. Porter, in his account of the ethics of internetworked writing, states flatly that "[w]riting in the 21st century will be electronic" (103). From what we have experienced over the last decade in our ever more complexly networked classrooms, we must agree with him.

Notwithstanding, digital and print media are different and require distinct pedagogical approaches. Recalling Aristotle's concepts of "coherence and perfection of artistic form," which until recently have depended on the existence of a "beginning, middle, and end [. . .] based on fixed texts" (125), Richard A. Lanham observes that these architectonic concepts are being dismantled even as we write. The changes are often bewildering because, as Marshall McLuhan astutely observes, new media change what it means for their users to be human. When "a new technology extends one or more of our senses outside us into the social world," he writes, "[T]hen new ratios among all our senses occur" (41).

Communicators in the age of hypertext are undergoing, in Lanham's words, a "readjustment of the alphabet/image ration." And one of the most transformative potentials of digital technology, according to Lanham, is to "dissolve before our eye [. . .] the disciplinary boundaries that currently govern academic study of the arts" (13). Indeed, "the same volatility" that is shaking rhetoric's edifice "dissolves the boundaries between the arts": the shock we may experience upon encountering new computer technologies suggests the profundity of the change only beginning to occur in the "digital metamorphoses of the arts and letters" (13). Teachers of composition and communication who do not intend to obstruct the transformation that Lanham describes should, ideally, be as skilled in the use of hypertext as the average 18-year-old entering our classrooms. At the very least, we must acquire to the best of our abilities the skills needed to interpret and to create images and sounds and to integrate them electronically with discourse.

Understandably, however, writing teachers may be reluctant to revise pedagogies to reflect a focus on composing in digital environments. We may fear, for instance, that time dedicated to the visual will be time taken from writing—that we may be guilty of "dumbing down" the curriculum if we do not focus exclusively on discourse. That we have been trained to discuss words rather than pictures contributes to our reluctance to introduce images into the curriculum. In *Iconology: Image, Text, Ideology*, W. J. T. Mitchell describes a "fear" that English studies historically has had of images—namely, that their presence will diminish the laboriously constructed superiority of the word as signifier. Yet reading time need not be affected by our including visual texts among the verbal texts we assign students, and writing time need not be affected at all. Our composition students typically are exposed to a wide variety of genres and rhetorical situations, and many of our most widely used writing textbooks, mirroring the texts students encounter in their daily lives, already incorporate images. Our students read, discuss, and write about not only belletristic essays but also visually enhanced advertising, journalism, Internet writing, and, in WAC classrooms, forms of quite specialized communication. Advanced writing classes often focus on such technically complex forms, which conventionally incorporate the visual. Viewed in light of institutional situations, consideration of visual texts in the writing classroom may seem an unremarkable development.

Students are much more likely than we are to be immersed in visual culture and to feel comfortable talking and writing about what they see. As each of the teachers we worked with in creating this anthology has discovered, bringing the visual forward can intensify student engagement with assignments. Teachers of English who make the visual a salient theme may find that students who recognize how an image can persuade may be better able to articulate what constitutes written persuasion or even argument; these students likely will grasp, at the very least, that the distance between visual and written cultures is less vast than they had imagined. Some eventually may intuit that an argument can be conceptualized as an image composed in the mind of the writing subject; for, as Mitchell notes in regard to the discourse-focused epistemological tradition of our discipline, there is a "counter tradition which conceives of interpretation as going in just the opposite direction, from a verbal surface to the 'vision' that lies behind it [. . .], from the linear recitation of the text to the 'structures' or 'forms' that control its order" (*Iconology* 45). Indeed we are all familiar by now with the etymology of *theory.*

What Mitchell's *Art Forum* article labeled the "pictorial turn" is underway. With Porter's forecast and the goals of rhetorical education and critical pedagogy in mind, we offer this anthology in the hope of better equipping colleagues and students to grapple with the diverse texts they encounter in daily life.

Cultural Studies

In 1972, psychologist Rudolf Arnheim asserted in his groundbreaking book *Visual Thinking* that the visual is the "primary medium of thought" (18). The cognitive process, according to Arnheim, begins with identification of familiar objects, and concepts subsequently take form out of the subject's lived experience and knowledge. More recently, Ann Marie Seward Barry examines emotional reactions to the visual and extends Arnheim's work. She explains in *Visual Intelligence: Perception, Image, and Manipulation in Visual Communication* that our reactions to the visual are our *first* reactions—that "we begin to respond emotionally to situations before we can think them through" (18).

Barry indicates not only that visual images automatically evoke a stronger emotional reaction than discourse does, but also that our emotions make us especially receptive to images gratifying our preferences in art and design and in ideology. Attraction to the form of an image may lead us to accept its content indiscriminately because analysis would entail an extended, and at times irksome, process of thought. Hill and Helmers concur (33): "cultural studies," they note, "constitute one type of attempt to understand how visual appeals operate" (26). Not surprisingly, the power of images is of concern to many teachers committed to critical pedagogy.

Art historian E. H. Gombrich argues in *Art and Illusion* a central assumption of visual critique in English studies—namely, that culture influences how we see. His exposition of the history of artistic styles illustrates his thesis regarding the cultural position of the painter: what matters is "not a faithful record of a visual experience but the faithful construction of a relational mode" (78), and the painter's problem is one of "conjuring up a convincing image" (45). Gombrich cites, as one of many examples of the influence of culture on art, the landscape paintings of John Constable, whose familiarity with new methods of studying cloud formation may have made his innovative representations of the sky possible (20). Presumably it was because of his immersion in this cultural change that Constable was able to "break through" the artistic conventions of his day. According to Gombrich, such breakthroughs by "exceptional beings" mark changes in artistic style and tradition and are understood best in their cultural contexts (20). After being introduced to the works of painters such as Joseph Turner, Vasily Kandinsky, or Georgia O'Keefe, students of writing might explore the influence of cultural context and material conditions on the contributions of pivotal artists. Students might also gain insight into these issues by exploring the homelier industrial arts, as Maureen Daly Goggin does in her account of transformations in the situation of embroidery work during the print and Protestant revolutions.

Art critic John Berger's *Ways of Seeing* is a short and highly readable critique of painting and commercial reproductions that is based on his 1970 BBC series on art. The author (and collaborators he names as helping to "make" [5] the book) asks what essential change occurs when original artwork is transformed into a reproduction. His response is "commercialization," and his definition of *image* conforms to his thesis regarding the reproduction of art. Image, for Berger, is a "sight which has been recreated or reproduced" (9).

Ways of Seeing demonstrates that commercialization was a part of the early history of painting in the West, but on a smaller scale than occurs today. Although much of the value of an original painting derives ultimately from its ability to bring viewers close to the (usually dead) artist and the painting's (often recondite) context, paintings have, from the beginning, belonged to the culture of the rich, whose portraits often have featured their material possessions (their clothing, buildings, elaborate gardens and grounds, and the "intimate" rooms of their homes) and evoked mythological themes investing the owners with heroic qualities.

Through reproductions, "great art" has entered the mainstream, but without training or educational support the general public has remained largely uninterested in "high" culture (33). Berger posits that, in its place, advertisements of glamorous lifestyles and locales are consumed by a mass audience that dreams of being rich. In representing wealth and luxury, advertisements often allude to painting styles (138). Fashion and beauty photography, for example, often mimics poses and settings of eighteenth and nineteenth century portrait painting. Such parallels suggest that one of the functions of high art in contemporary society is to feed capitalism.

Berger credits Walter Benjamin's "The Work of Art in the Age of Mechanical Reproduction," published in 1936, as the source of many ideas appearing in *Ways of Seeing*. Benjamin, a Jewish art critic and philosopher writing in Germany in the days leading up to the Second World War, decries mass-produced art for losing the "aura" of the original and for detaching the art object "from the domain of tradition" (223).[1]

Critical Approaches

Berger presents an analysis directed to a broad audience, but images also can be analyzed on the basis of semiotics, which derives from the philosophy of C. S. Peirce and whose concepts icon, index, and symbol, among others, have been appropriated by visual theorists. Loosely, *icon* refers to a sign bearing a resemblance, real or imaginary, to what it is meant to signify (e.g., images of a smiley face or of two hands shaking). *Index* refers to a physical indication that another thing exists (e.g., a jet stream or the howl of a coyote). *Symbol* refers to a sign whose connection to an object is culturally determined (e.g., most verbal language). Peirce, an American pragmatist, did not reject outright the assumption of a correspondence between material world and language, as many postmodernists have.

An alternative to Peirce's semiotics can be found in the structuralist approach of Ferdinand de Saussure, which, as Stuart Hall explains, consists of a system of signs including images, words, and sounds (30). The *signifier* is the form itself, and the *signified* the idea or concept that accompanies it; the relation between them, the *representation,* is created through codes, or culturally agreed upon meanings and judgments (31). Because meaning is never fixed and always in flux, analysis is a requirement for understanding interpretation, and "[t]he reader is as important as the writer in the production of meaning" (33). Hall is a poststructuralist who uses structuralism in a modified and flexible way to highlight the power system of cultural signs (35).

Image-Music-Text, one of French critic Roland Barthes's many works, elaborates a semiological theory to critique a variety of artifacts, both verbal and visual. Barthes argues in this book and in *Mythologies* that, whether in advertising or in other media, representations repeated over time become cultural myths that the public immediately recognizes and responds to in predictable ways. Without either means or motivation to understand their responses, viewers do not consciously notice the strategic character of the message they encounter and so react as its designers have anticipated—positively. To illustrate, *Image-Music-Text* describes a Panzini spaghetti ad incorporating a photograph of packaged pasta, spice mixture, and canned liquid surrounded by fresh tomatoes, onions, peppers, and mushrooms spilling from a string bag, as if just brought from the market. According to Barthes, the greens, reds, and yellows and the name of the product all suggest "Italianicity." The arrangement, which echoes a still-life painting, signifies that the packaged ingredients are both authentically Italian and fresh (33–36). The myth created through the confluence of signs evoking an Italian dinner within the ambiance of a Mediterranean patio Barthes describes as "purified" and "simplified," offered "without contradictions" (*Image* 143).

Authenticity and Exploitation

French sociologist Pierre Bourdieu describes in *Photography: A Middle-Brow Art* how the photo album conveys a narrative of historical unity to the present generation by illuminating the "highest common denominator of the past" (31). Informal photographs of children, often on special occasions or holidays, serve as an authorized "social memory" of family members and good times (31). Family portraits also allow ancestors to be paid due reverence while, and—as often can be the case—by, erasing the accompanying, unpleasant details of their lives. Barthes observes in his treatise on photography, *Camera Lucida,* that in private photography both photographer and subject are aware of the artificiality of their joint activity: "I lend myself to the social game," he muses. "I pose, I know I am posing, I want you to know that I am posing" (11). Moreover, while the image is "motionless, stubborn," the subject is "divided, dispersed" (12). Bourdieu, like Barthes, speaks of the artificiality of the pose, which allows the photographer to impose a concealed gaze on subjects, forcing them into stiff and contrived positions. Subjects, in turn, may respond by attempting to gather dignity through a conventional frontal pose. Bourdieu explains that "frontality is a means of effecting one's own objectification" because it offers "a way of imposing the rules of one's own perception" (83). On the other hand, hopes for creating impressions on our viewers are often unrealistic. In his essay "The Photograph," N. Scott Momaday describes the disgust an American Indian expressed upon viewing a likeness of herself. Her reaction led Momaday to wonder if "perhaps she saw, in a way that we could not, that the photograph misrepresented her in some crucial respect, that in its dim, mechanical eye it had failed to see into her real being" (McQuade and McQuade 291). Figure 1 reproduces an image of and a text by Anh Thuy (Cindy) Dang, a student in one of our classes whose reflections on a photograph taken of her at Georgia's Red Top Mountain during a family outing alludes to the dilemmas attending personal photography.

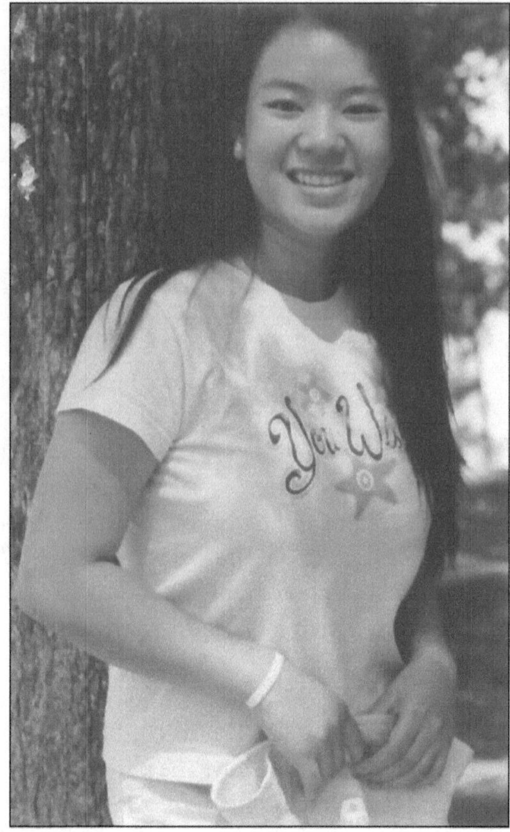

Figure 1. *Anh Thuy Dang at Red Top Mountain.* Dang elaborates: "Well, it's true that everyone must smile when taking pictures. However, what you don't know or can't see is how happy I was at that moment. For me, it was not just a smile, but an expression of happiness, appreciation, warmth, and lovely feelings. I felt that way that day because all of my family members were there. The smile reflects our celebration, [and how] everyone looked up at the sky to sense the wind falling down on our faces." (Courtesy of Anh Thuy Dang.)

Although other postmodern critics have tended to study the problematics of photographic representation (e.g., John Tagg, who takes the commonly held position that no photograph mirrors reality), Barthes considers photographs the quintessential evidence that "the thing has been there" (76). He argues in *Camera Lucida* that, in photographic portraits with personal connections to the reader, authentication of existence is a primary outcome. Susan Sontag, writing before him in *On Photography,* agrees that photography confirms existence—to a point. But, crucially for Sontag, an image is not a transparent copy of reality but a distortion. Sontag is featured in a *New York Times Magazine* article on the Abu Ghraib prison scandals. In this debate, she returns to Barthes's emphasis on the importance of the photograph in affirming that an event did occur. However, the use of a photograph can drastically change its effect. Sontag concludes that "[w]e make of photography a means by which, precisely, anything can be said, any purpose served" (*On Photography* 175). *New York Times* reviewer Michael Kimmelmann describes an art exhibition of the prison photographs held just five months after their publication on the Internet. He expresses surprise at both the multifarious purposes of photography and its potential for almost immediate reinterpretation. However, in her study of cartoon images appearing on the occasion of the death of JFK Jr. and alluding to the historic photograph of the young boy saluting his father's coffin, Janis Edwards asserts that "It is not unusual for iconic images to be appropriated to new contexts, creating analogies that recall past moments and suggest future possibilities" (179).

One of the many purposes to which photography can be put is illustrated by David Perlmutter's *Photojournalism and Foreign Policy: Icons of Outrage in International Crisis,* which describes the process whereby journalistic photographs at times exert so intense a pressure on public opinion that history is altered significantly. Since its inception, documentary photography, which evolved from photo journalism, has featured a series of artistic images that serve as powerful rhetorical instruments for social change. For example, in the early twentieth century, sociologist and photographer Lewis W. Hine created a series of pictures of immigrants at Ellis Island. He illustrated in further photos their miserable living and working conditions, including the exploitation of their children working in factories, documentary images that led to sweeping changes in child labor laws (Newhall 235).

Like the general public, students typically are unaware of the rhetorical strategies that photographers adopt when constructing, for example, angle, lighting, and background. James Curtis reveals in *Mind's Eye, Mind's Truth* that in the 1930s the Farm Security Administration (FSA) hired established photographers to create an image of the rural crisis of the Great Depression that organizers wished to use in convincing the public of the need for their program. FSA photographers Walker Evans, Dorothea Lange, and others posed families in their poverty-stricken surroundings to create images of nobility and courage. "Migrant Mother," a portrait by Lange that has become an icon of the era, features a grouping of small children leaning against the shoulders of a soulful mother, who is holding her youngest baby. The tableau recalls paintings of the Madonna, Christ child, and angels, and not surprisingly, this photograph and many like it in the FSA accounts were posed carefully. For example, four of the older children of the family were excluded from the final portrait for fear of upsetting the cultural norms of the intended audience, who likely would have disapproved of such a large family among the poor (Curtis 53–55). *Let Us Now Praise Famous Men,* the much-loved chronicle of Alabama sharecroppers by James Agee and Evans, also was staged to emphasize its subjects' courage and steadfast character. Evans and Agee, who lived among the sharecroppers, produced conflicting visual and verbal accounts. Whereas Agee wrote of a certain bed as "stale, and moist, and [. . .] morbid with bed bugs, with fleas and, I believe, with lice" (qtd. in Curtis 37), Evans photographed the spare geometric shape of the bed and the contrast of a white bedspread against the dark walls of the room, producing the clean and cared-for interior of poverty that constituted one of his many art photographs in the book.

Recent analysis by John Tagg in *The Burden of Representation* reveals that weighty political and social injustices have been committed by means of what is labeled blandly "documentary photography" when its products are used in institutional recordkeeping. The poor, the weak, and the powerless have, throughout the history of photography, been victimized by prison, institutional, and other bureaucratic photographers. An example of how documentary photography can disempower its subjects is provided by the work of Edward Curtis, who, with the backing of financier John Pierpont Morgan, photographed American Indians in contrived settings and costumes (Newhall 136). More recently, Richard Billingham's photography documents in livid detail the life of his chronically alcoholic father. These images, which have appeared in major art venues including the Royal Academy, by virtue of representing an inebriated subject who likely was not able to give informed consent to having his photographs taken, exhibited, and mass marketed, may also be exploitative. We might add to this list the photography of Abu Ghraib prison torture and ask to what extent the mainstream media, in reproducing the photographs, have further exploited their subjects.

Gender and Women's Studies

Many poststructuralist accounts of women and the visual are available. Berger discusses in his chapter on the female nude the central questions of who looks and who is looked at. Laura Mulvey's useful article on "the gaze" addresses both portraits and film. Carol David offers in "Investitures of Power: Portraits of Women Executives" an account of the representations of women that traces painting styles through the last three centuries. She describes how representations of beautiful women traditionally were objects desired and possessed by men, with the exception of those of a few powerful sitters who demanded they be the subject rather than the object of a viewer's gaze. Queen Elizabeth, for instance, was careful to be painted in imperial settings. Likewise, certain suffragists, accounted plain in their simple black dresses, nevertheless looked directly at the camera—a pose owned by men and the rare powerful woman. The notorious "Madame X," by John Singer Sargent, casts a disdainful gaze at her viewers, a pose that scorned cultural expectations. Despite Sargent's social banishment from France for this scandalous portrait, Madame Gatreaux was an instant sensation and continues to rivet audiences more than a century later. David Blakesley's "Defining Film Rhetoric: The Case of Hitchcock's *Vertigo*" offers psychological insight into "the gaze" by suggesting that it can be read as a sign of the masculine need to identify and to become consubstantial with the feminine. "Pushed to the extreme," Blakesley notes, the male voyeur wishes "to become the other, to inhabit that psychological and physical space" (117).

Julia Margaret Cameron challenged Victorian social hierarchy in her photographic portraits of women. Instead of portraying the rich and famous, she often chose as subjects servants or peasants from her home on the Isle of Wight, dressing them in period costumes to represent religious or classical characters. She also chose as sitters members of her own family, including Julia Stephens, the mother of Virginia Wolfe. Unlike the popular photographs of the day, which depicted women as tranquil and expressionless, Cameron's portraits depicted her sitters as pensive, longing, or suffering (Wolf). Frances Benjamin Johnston flouted the gender norms of the same era by photographing herself with beer mug, cigarette, and petticoats hiked up to her knees, as if engaged in debate with an imaginary partner or with the portraits of men arranged on her fireplace mantel (Figure 2). Contemporary artist Cindy Sherman has photographed herself posing in a variety of settings that depict the restricted roles available to women.

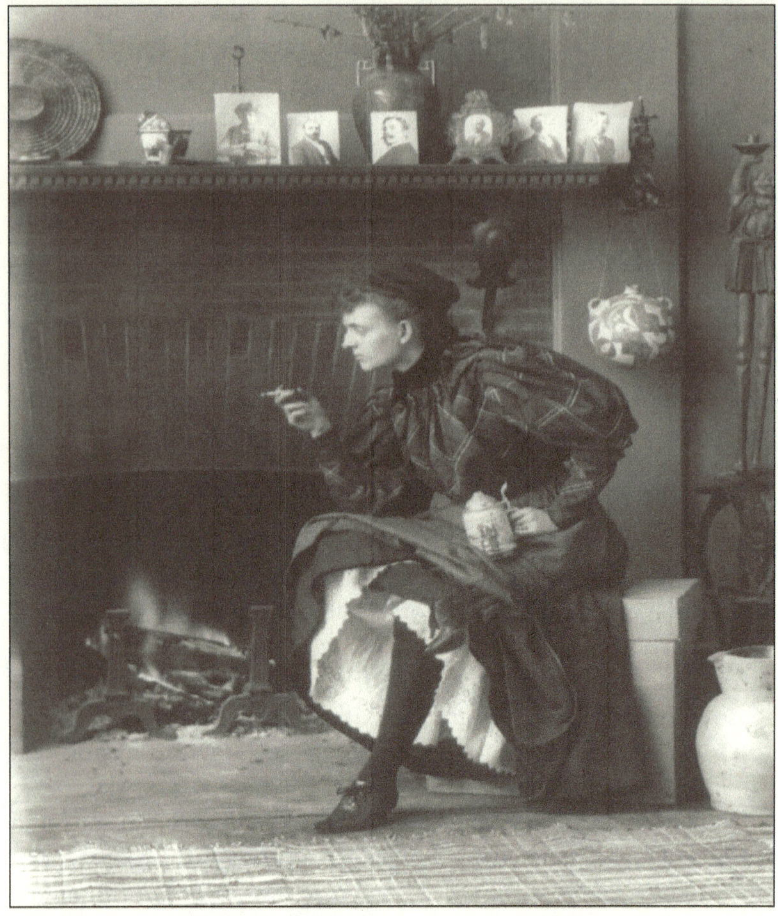

Figure 2. *Self-portrait.* Frances Benjamin Johnston. 1896. (Used by permission of the Library of Congress Prints and Photographs Division, Washington, D.C.)

Current tensions and ambiguities arising from the outworking of women's emancipation are alluded to in J. Cherie Strachan and Kathleen E. Kendall's study of convention films viewed during the 2000 U.S. presidential election. Strachan and Kendall note that the presentation of George W. Bush as a "kinder and gentler" Bush candidate and the choice to downplay his position as Governor of Texas and to focus on Laura and Barbara rather than on George Senior—that is, "to distance [George W.] Bush from stereotypical masculine institutions and activities"—may have been intentional strategies to gain favor with women voters, who had not yet proved a reliable base of support, and to distance him from his father, so that the son would seem "his own man" (150).

As Diane S. Hope explains, "Like verbal rhetoric, visual rhetoric depends on strategies of identification; advertising's rhetoric is dominated by appeals to gender as the primary marker of consumer identity. Constructs of masculine and feminine contextualize fantasies of social role, power, status, and security" (155). Hope's study of advertising images that appropriate feminine (passive, fertile, receptive) and masculine (active, dominating, aggressive) iconographies in natural settings notes that this "rhetoric of gendered environments works to obscure the connections between environmental degradation and consumption" (156). According to Hope, advertising that incorporated natural images before the mechanical revolution tended to present the earth as a powerful mother; later images, on the other hand, presented the earth as a sexualized other awaiting exploitation. Viewers in the United States respond favorably to the latter because so many of us have intent and means to use the earth's resources as we see fit. At the same time, women viewers are disempowered by omnipresent advertising imagery that equates femininity with an idealized physical presence and an undernourished agency (173).

Science Studies

Elizabeth Tebeaux records in "From Orality to Textuality: Technical Description and the Emergence of Visual and Verbal Presentation" that before the explosion of print technology, the visual in technical contexts was much more closely aligned with orality than with discourse. That the usefulness of visual representation to instruction already was recognized helps explain its ready adoption in the earliest print manuscripts on technical subjects. According to Tebeaux, "the increasingly integrated verbal and visual presentation of objects and concepts captured and molded into text" has been a feature of English technical communication since at least the time of Chaucer, and bivocality had emerged as conventional by 1640 (176).

Goggin states that by the late 1600s, the craft of embroidered samplers "was on the cusp of a radical shift from invention to demonstration of knowledge" (101), an observation confirming that utilitarianism was gaining momentum in England with the increasing use of the printing press. At this time, a revolution fueled by the burgeoning need for informative text among newly literate and upwardly mobile readers was occurring in the use and the construction of images. Two centuries before, Leonardo had resurrected the cadaver as an object of scrutiny, and as a result anatomical representations appeared vitalized. As the technology of visual reproduction evolved—as copyists no longer were depended upon to reproduce illustrations; as copper etchings, which allowed for much greater detail work than woodcuts had, became the norm; and as three-point perspective became widely used and understood—the possibility for verisimilitude exploded. As illustrators struggled to create ever-more convincingly realistic representations, a technical culture in which a vast audience of readers relied increasingly on illustrated texts, at the expense of the oral tradition, emerged (Tebeaux, "Emergence," passim).

Bruno Latour and Steve Woolgar argue in *Laboratory Life: The Construction of Scientific Facts* that the scientific method arose not from a new way of thinking, but from a new way of seeing. According to these authors and others, the scientific and technical project, out of which has arisen industrial and now postmodern culture, is profoundly indebted to the reproducibility and, most crucially, the *contrastibility* of visual artifacts forming what these authors consider to be the ultimate basis of scientific claims. Supporting the significance of visual contrastibility to science, Helmers notes "the developing importance of sight, seeing, and *collecting visual objects*" during the Enlightenment (emphasis ours; Pears and Jardine, 71–72).

Scientific representations remain, however, thoroughly constructed, thoroughly rhetorical—a fact all too easy for viewers to forget. Paul Dombrowski records in "Ernst Haeckel's Controversial Visual Rhetoric" how the German naturalist and illustrator of the late nineteenth and early twentieth centuries deliberately misrepresented the embryos of a variety of animals and humans in his line drawings, presumably to substantiate his theory of monism, which viewed science as "including areas of knowledge usually not associated with science, such as religion, ethics, and politics" (305). His broad definition of science appealed to leaders of the Nazi movement because it could be used to promote the idea of national history and identity. Ultimately, Haeckel's work was implicated in the propaganda efforts of the Nazis, who propounded social Darwinism. His theories were debunked, but not before many textbooks in the United States and elsewhere had incorporated his illustrations; recently, they have become evidence for some creationists in their critique of evolutionary biology.

Today, scientist-photographers commonly accept as legitimate an array of rhetorical practices including but by no means limited to colorizing, selecting, and retouching. Anne R. Richards addresses scientific license in "Argument and Authority in the Visual Representations of Science" by deconstructing a series of images appearing in one figure in the *American Journal of Botany:* 19 photomicrographs and, curiously, one line drawing created to replace a photographic image. According to Nels Lersten, her interview subject and former editor of the journal, such a drawing might constitute an instance of "nature-faking" because the original photograph required enhancement if it was to be mustered in support of the author's claim. Just as among the readers of advertising it is understood that photography illustrates a product in an ideal state, among expert readers of science it is understood that photographic images represent a claim in its most persuasively constructed visual form.

Technical and Professional Communication

"A Historical Look at Electronic Literacy: Implications for the Education of Technical Communicators," Cynthia L. Selfe and Gail E. Hawisher's article on the uses of electronic communication at the end of the twentieth century, predicts that rapid changes will continue to occur and that technical communicators will need to learn and to apply the latest advances. But in a review of books he sees as primarily lauding the electronic age, Stephen Doheny-Farina warns that many consequences of this rapid change need assessment, among them the loss of direct communication among individuals. Craig Stroupe emphasizes the need for teachers in the digital classroom to move beyond the instrumental objectives often implicit in institutional initiatives and to guide students towards a "constitutive literacy," one in which dialogue among multimedia voices, e.g., between image and sound, is discernible and the image-word relation is not merely illustrative. Ideally, according to Stroupe, voices will be given reign to "speak to one another" ("The Rhetoric of Irritation," 245) through a "coherent inappropriateness" (251) enabling students to discover the ideological basis of culture. Stroupe's thoughtful critique, however, evidences limited tolerance for the traditionally utilitarian aims of technical writing—that is, for the honing of language enabling "work to get done" in an, or the most, efficient way. It should be mentioned here that because the field of technical communication must concern itself, in part, with technological changes transforming communication in science and industry, it has been among the first specialities within English studies to widely acknowledge the importance of visual rhetoric. Stephen Bernhardt's 1986 article "Seeing the Text" is groundbreaking in its explanation of the importance of design to readability in a range of fields and audiences.

Charles Kostelnick, who has written extensively on the history and theory of visual design, details a rubric for visual design in "A Systematic Approach to Visual Language in Business Communication." Recently, he describes in "Melting-Pot Ideology, Modernist Aesthetics, and the Emergence of Graphical Conventions: The Statistical Atlases of the United States, 1874–1925" a history of graphics beginning in the early nineteenth century, when the U.S. government published statistical atlases of census data on immigrants. The designers of these atlases developed conventions that still influence the graphical presentation of data.

Jacques Bertin applies a semiotic approach to the creation of graphs, maps, and diagrams. He differentiates between *monosemic* systems, where meanings are specified and clearly understood, i.e., the graphic meaning, and *polysemic* systems, in which readers choose from a group of similar signs, making signification comparatively subjective (2). His discussion of size, value, texture, color, orientation, and shape in graphic design provide a useful framework for analysis and discussion of visual artifacts.

Edward R. Tufte, coiner of the term *chartjunk,* complicates the discussion of graphic displays in *The Visual Display of Quantitative Information* by addressing the dangers of uncritically accepting visual representations of data. Likewise, Carlos Salinas reprimands technical communicators for approaching the visual primarily as a vehicle for disseminating truth and for failing to exploit its many potentials, especially for cultural critique. His article "Technical Rhetoricians and the Art of Configuring Images" describes Punk Ska's 1998 anti-Nike website, which reconfigures the swoosh as a "modified swastika" and adds the slogan "Nike: Made by Kids in Sweat Shops" (178) to illustrate how multimedia texts can be reread.

Donna Kienzler applies in "Visual Ethics" general ethical principles to the selection of material for visual displays in professional communication documents as well as to their design and identifies criteria for evaluating visual data. Nancy Allen's "Ethics and Visual Rhetorics: Seeing's Not Believing Anymore" provides instruction and examples for the ethical construction of visuals, and lists visual rhetoric sources that would be helpful to professional communicators working on visual design. David critiques the ethics of the elaborate visuals placed in corporate annual reports, asserting that the "reports" are mythmaking documents rather than objective summaries of the year's activities ("Mythmaking").

Among those writers who have lamented the slow incorporation of a broader rhetorical focus into technical communication curricula are Richards and David. We point out in "Decorative Color as a Rhetorical Enhancement on the World Wide Web" that the widely circulated advice to avoid color in technical documents unless for logical purposes is anachronistic, for color obviously commands the attention of readers of technical information in hybrid documents, both in print and on the Web. Thus, we encourage colleagues to reconsider the assumptions that the decorative is irrelevant to students of technical and writing, or that attempts to study the decorative are doomed to be "non-rigorous" (Helmers and Hill 2), and to conduct research into the pathos of technical writing. We agree with Helmers' assessment that theories of visual rhetoric provide opportunities to "unhing[e] the traditional dynamic of pleasure/expressiveness and function/persuasiveness in favor of a dialogic, transactional viewing" (65).

Pedagogical Approaches

Several books have been published recently that respond to the burgeoning interest in visual and verbal intersections in the writing classroom. Charles A. Hill and Marguerite Helmers's anthology, *Defining Visual Rhetorics,* offers a rich menu of visual genres useful to teachers and scholars in rhetoric and communication disciplines; the text has generated thoughtful discussion in our graduate document design courses, and this introductory chapter has cited numerous essays from the text. Charles Kostelnick and David D. Roberts's textbook *Designing Visual Language: Strategies for Professional Communicators* covers visual theory and application for advanced college students in business and technical majors. Nancy Allen's *Working with Words and*

Images: New Steps in an Old Dance constructs a broadly interdisciplinary context for the visual. Donald and Christine McQuade's *Seeing and Writing 2* provides provocative images, texts, and assignments for students of first-year writing. Christine Alfano and Alyssa O'Brien's *Envision: Persuasive Writing in a Visual World* teaches these same students to analyze and to understand visual texts as essential to effective writing. And Lester Faigley, Diana George, Anna Palchick, and Cynthia Selfe's *Picturing Texts* provides suggestions for students evaluating and producing visual artifacts.

In our classrooms, when we have offered discussions and assignments invoking painting, architecture, sculpture, and photography, most students have accepted these subjects readily. When creating writing assignments and discussion topics for classes in composition, rhetorical analysis, cultural studies, and professional and technical writing, we have supplied students with materials from art books and from museum websites. Arnheim's *Art and Visual Perception* offers chapters on the elements of visual composition and contains many examples that could be of use to teachers contemplating assignments along similar lines.

Titles of books on women, both as artists and as models, are included in David's article "Investitures of Power." Paintings of women by the Pre-Raphaelites (who worshipped female beauty while treating their beautiful wives and models carelessly), as well as other well-known portraits and their contexts, will interest students, as we have found, and may motivate them to bring in favorite reproductions of their own. Assignments drawing on the history of portraiture style might ask students to find family pictures, old and new, in order to analyze the expressions and configurations of sitters, or to examine the styles of portraiture in different cultural and historic contexts. Figure 3 presents very different photographic representations of couples from the mid-eighteenth through the early twenty-first centuries; these juxtapositions suggest that popular styles of intimate portraiture are influenced by artistic conventions.

Helpful sources for teachers conducting discussions and creating writing assignments around photography are Lemagny and Ruille's *A History of Photography: Social and Cultural Perspectives* and *The History of Photography* by Beaumont Newhall, both of which present a history of photographic styles. And many early images now are available on the Web. As Institutional Repositories (such as Emory University's

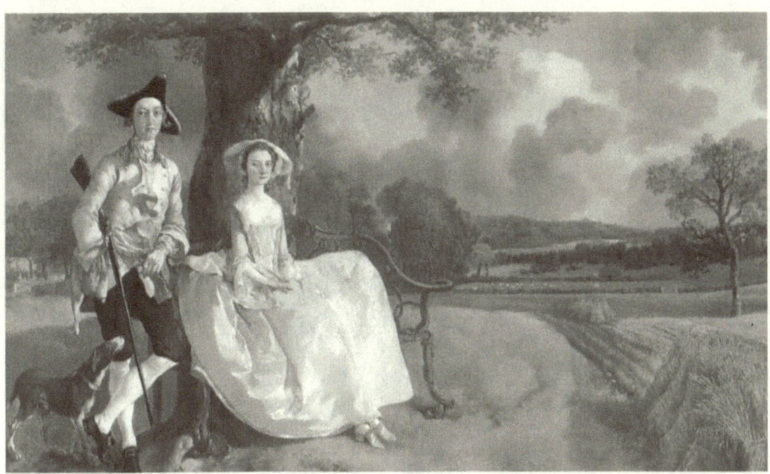

Figure 3a.

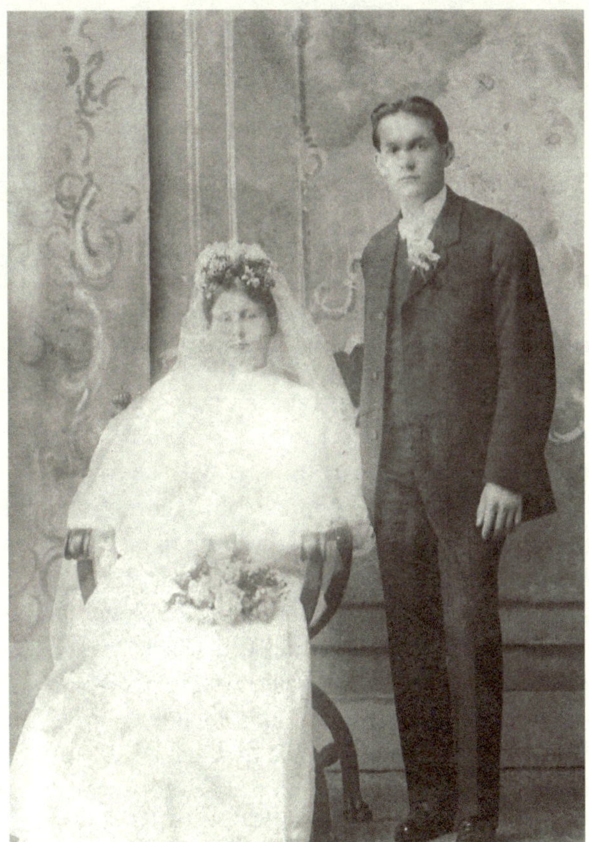

Figure 3b.

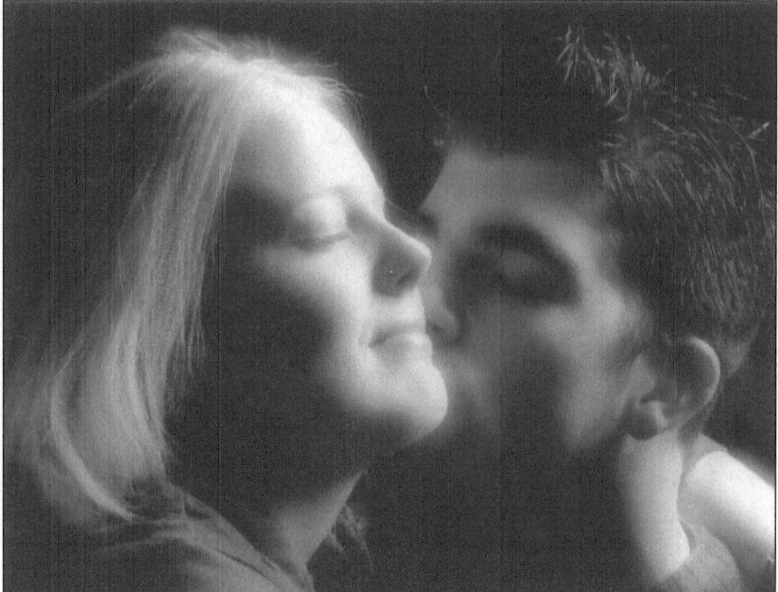

Figure 3c.

Figure 3. These three images suggest a feminist framework for considering the representation of couples over the centuries. (a) *Mr. and Mrs. Andrews*. Thomas Gainsborough. 1727. (© National Gallery, London); (b) *Laura and Walter Rypstat*. 1910. (Courtesy of Anne R. Richards.); (c) *Shannon and Ben*. 2004. Consider how the contemporary image echoes popular film images. (Courtesy of Shannon Sellars and Benjamin Workman.)

Library-of-Congress-funded Meta-Archive of Southern Culture) go online, students with access to the Internet will have virtually limitless accessibility to the gamut of photographic genres. In addition to researching such archives, students might bring in pictures from their own "galleries" to analyze.

Recently, one of us taught a special-topics first-year composition course focusing on visual rhetoric. Students discussed and wrote about images including those that appeared in traveling photography exhibits, which many postsecondary institutions, including our own, house regularly. The WebCT post appearing in Figure 4 reproduces text written by Katie Jezghani after a visit to the Kennesaw State University campus exhibit "Beggars and Choosers: Motherhood is Not a Class Privilege in America." Jezghani and her classmates had been assigned to choose one photograph in the exhibit to describe and to analyze in terms of Ryan Jervings's rubric "Thirteen Ways to Read a Black-and-White Photograph," which appears later in this book.

Message no. 6
Author: Katie Jezghani (kjezghan)
Date: Wednesday, September 8, 2004 1:35 p.m.

Katie Jezghani
Photo Response

I analyzed a photograph taken in 1996 by Amy Toensing called "Waiting." It is a black and white silver-gelatin print. The photo was taken through a set of mesh curtains, into a kitchen of a pregnant woman. She is not looking at the camera, which gives it a third-person stance. She seems to be almost nine months pregnant with a very round stomach and possibly has a hard time walking through the kitchen. Her clothes are simple and look as if they were bought right off of the clearance rack of the nearest Goodwill store. The kitchen is set up tidily with every pot and pan in what seems to be its usual place. The floor appears to be cheap vinyl with a typical seventies looking pattern. The table and chairs look like they could be folded up and taken outside for a picnic. They are probably made of aluminum and light-weight materials. This shows me that the pregnant woman probably has a family and a low income to take care of them. Even though it looks as if the family lives in poverty, it is obvious that the mother takes care of everything nicely as if it were worth more. The woman is a mother bird, building her nest of twigs and leaves.

Looking through the old curtains gives the photography a depth-of-field effect. The photo is mostly out of focus except the mother walking past the camera. This makes her seem important and shows me that she is the subject and focal point of the photograph. The print is framed in a shiny black frame with white matte board around it. This creates a balanced and not distracting setting. The photo is not cropped as well as it could have been because there is a lot of unnecessary negative space in the background. The kitchen distracts me from focusing on the woman, although it gives the photograph the mood of poverty and lets you know that the pregnant woman is not very well off.

Next to the photography in the exhibit, there was a page long caption on the wall. It explained how the woman actually was struggling. She and her family lived in a mobile home and had very little money. She worked in a café at night and was losing her welfare money from the government. She said that she soon would have to get another job in the day time to add to the money from her waitressing job at night. It is obviously hard for her being pregnant and having very little money with a family and a small home. She mentioned her daughter saying that she wished they could all be together at home on the weekends. It broke her heart. She knows that her family needs her there and she can not be. This woman works hard at everything, even though she has almost nothing, besides her family, low-paying jobs, and her mobile home.

Figure 4. Katie Jezghani's response to an online discussion prompt illustrates how a rhetorical rubric focusing on images can elicit in-depth critical responses from first-year composition students. (Courtesy of the author.)

Students can also benefit from opportunities to write about the visual as part of a more materially complex and paratextually informed situation, that is, as signs appearing in grocery stores (Dickinson and Maugh), gardens (Lambert and Martinez), homes (Tange), suburbs (Robbins), and a great variety of public and private spaces.

Drawing extensively on the tradition of the ancients, the first chapter of our collection, Nancy Allen's "Seeing Rhetoric: A Foundational Approach," highlights the complementarities between verbal and visual modes of communication. Using a variety of professional examples to support her explanation, Allen catalogues the visual applications of the rhetorical appeals, canon, and triangle and provides a solid working model for writing teachers who wish to introduce students to the elements of visual rhetoric.

"Mediated Memory: The Language of Memorial Space" describes how L. J. Nicoletti's students studied a site that was of special interest to them and then designed and wrote a text justifying the creation of a new memorial. Nicoletti focuses on the fourth canon of rhetoric by deconstructing the "seeming rhetorical sanctity" of this architectural form and asks students to consider issues such as rhetorical purpose, context, and audience in light of memorial architecture, as well as the goals of inclusiveness (remembrance) and originality. Developed in the aftermath of 9/11, her approach demonstrates how writing projects incorporating the visual can resonate in students' lives.

Barbara Worthington and Deborah Rard's "Visual Rhetoric for Writing Teachers: Using Documentary Film in Classroom Instruction" describes the authors' film-based methods for teaching the principles of rhetorical analysis to first-year students. By thoughtfully viewing a documentary containing a narrative of a fatal drunk-driving accident, students develop awareness of rhetoric's terms and functions. The chapter includes an analysis of student discussions of visual arguments arising from and directed at viewers in different socioeconomic contexts.

C. Richard King's chapter, "Envisioning Justice: Racial Metaphors, Political Movements, and Critical Pedagogy," describes an advanced writing unit on race, social justice, and culture. Asserting that white supremacy is a "structured field of vision no less than systems of economic, political, and social relations," King examines how "metaphors, analogies, and juxtapositions" buttress racialization. His chapter also highlights the complexities raised by the images, slogans, and advertisements of social organizations invoking victimization.

Jane Davis wrote "Seeing the Unspeakable: Emmett Till and American Terrorism" in response to the fiftieth anniversary of the lynching of Till, a 14-year-old African-American who was gruesomely tortured and murdered by white men for whistling at one of their wives. Horrific photographs of Till maimed in his coffin brought home the reality of racist violence and outraged people across the United States, helping give force to the nascent Civil Rights Movement. Davis illustrates both the power of visual media and the role of images in perpetuating and combating racism.

"A Study of Photographs of Iran: Postcolonial Inquiry into the Limits of Visual Representation," by Iraj Omidvar, notes that in the United States visual representations of Muslims generally and of Iranians specifically have been ubiquitous—and negative—since 9/11. Yet countering these visual stereotypes without resorting to an objectivist stance requires a commitment to teacher-student dialogue in the spirit of Socratic *elenchos.* Omidvar suggests that teachers and students trace the roots of racist images by engaging in research designed to illuminate the material bases of stereotyping.

Yong-Kang Wei's chapter, "Ethos on the Web: A Cross-Cultural Approach," highlights differences between rhetorics of "East" and "West." After identifying key concepts of classical Western rhetoric and providing an overview of classical Chinese rhetoric as it occurs in speech, architecture, landscape, and document design, Wei demonstrates how Chinese hypertext reflects its cultural and rhetorical traditions. His chapter has served as a provocative starting point for courses addressing cross-cultural professional communication.

Jean Darcy describes in "Christopher Columbus's Maps: Visualizing Discovery" a project exemplifying Mitchell's analysis of the verbal-visual relation. Her assignments for courses, from beginning to advanced, require students not only to use maps and textual sources in extrapolating the critical thinking processes of Columbus in his "New World" voyages but also to investigate their own methods of learning and knowing. Her original assignment is open to a variety of artifacts and could be adapted easily to technical writing syllabi.

Alyssa O'Brien describes in "Drawn to Multiple Sides: Making Arguments Visible" an assignment for which students choose images and create texts to explore alternative viewpoints. The Feature Articles

Multiple Sides Project elicits from students rhetorical analyses, new perspectives, innovative approaches to visual layout, and stylistic experiments in voice. This chapter provides examples of student writing and offers a companion webpage.

Ryan Jerving's rubric "Thirteen Ways to Read a Black-and-White Photograph" identifies key compositional elements in black-and-white photography and highlights their potential influences on interpretation. Jerving also presents an activity that will help students of writing develop a rhetorical appreciation for the photograph as a designed object by considering the key issues of its subject matter, camera work, scene of representation, and institutional location.

Mark Mullen's chapter, "Collapsing Floors and Disappearing Walls: Teaching Visual and Cultural Intertexts in Electronic Games," recommends that teachers import electronic games as objects of analysis into the writing classroom. While preparing teachers for the challenges that can attend analysis of this genre in typical wired classrooms, Mullen explains how the visual elements of games can require interpretive strategies as complex as those applied to traditional literary texts. His analysis of *American McGee's Alice* demonstrates that electronic games can be sophisticated texts suited to college-level analysis.

Kristin Walker Pickering's "Revising for Activity Purposes: Improving Document Design for Reader-Oriented Activities" considers the relevance of activity theory to the human factors of website design. Focusing on the effective integration of text and graphics from a user-design perspective, Pickering discusses work her students have undertaken in revising workplace documents. To illustrate how complex the analysis of users and stakeholders can be as well as the usefulness of activity theory in facilitating analysis, Walker focuses on the efforts of a student to make a state government website more readable.

In the Western tradition, the value of sense data to inquiry was a driving question 2,600 years ago among the presocratics. Heraclitus concluded that "sight tells falsehoods" (McKirahan 118) although the eyes are yet "more accurate witnesses than the ears" (119). Parmenides claimed that mortals were benighted because they accepted as reality what they saw; Anaxogoras's paradox of color illustrated this same point. But Empedocles articulated an ancient rationale for triangulation, enjoining the inquirer to allow the mind to question the certainties of the senses, and the senses to destabilize the mind's cherished beliefs:

> Look with every means of apprehension, in whatever way each thing is clear, Not holding any sight more in trust than [what comes] through hearing, Or loud-sounding hearing above the things made clear by the tongue, And do not hold back trust in any of the other members, Whatever way there is a channel for understanding, but Understanding each thing in whatever way it is clear. (McKirahan 235)

Empedocles's point was not to privilege any one of the senses, but to utilize each as fully as possible. From this perspective, an interest in the visual and in the study of alternative theories, methodologies, tools, and worldviews that such an interest entails, would advantage the inquirer-writer. We believe that by cultivating new approaches to thinking, knowing, and communicating, our students may find themselves making a habit of the wonder that formed the daily diet of those remarkable inquirers who puzzled through reality in a less fragmented time.

Note

1. Because Benjamin committed suicide on meeting resistance during an attempt to leave Paris during the occupation and emigrate to the United States, most of his work was published posthumously, writes Hannah Arendt in the introduction to *Illuminations,* which reprints "The Work of Art" from *Zeischrift für Sozialforschun (Journal for Social Research)* V 1936.

Works Cited

Agee, James, and Walker Evans. *Let Us Now Praise Famous Men: 3 Tenant Families.* Boston: Houghton Mifflin, 1941.

Alfano, Christine L., and Alyssa J. O'Brien. *Envision: Persuasive Writing in a Visual World.* New York: Longman, 2005. Companion website: http://wps.ablongman.com/ long_alfano_envision_1.

Allen, Nancy. "Ethics and Visual Rhetorics: Seeing's Not Believing Anymore." *Technical Communication Quarterly* 5.1 (1996): 87–105.

—, ed. *Working with Words and Images: New Steps in an Old Dance.* Westport, CT: Ablex, 2002.

Arnheim, Rudolf. *Visual Thinking.* Berkeley: U of California P, 1969.

—. *Art and Visual Perception: A Psychology of the Creative Eye.* Berkeley: U of California P, 1965.

Barry, Anne Marie Seward. *Visual Intelligence: Perception, Image, and Manipulation in Visual Communication.* Albany: SUNY P, 1997.

Barthes, Roland. *Camera Lucida: Reflections on Photography.* Trans. Richard Howard. New York: Hill and Wang, 1982.

—. *Image-Music-Text.* Trans. Stephen Heath. New York: Hill and Wang, 1977.

—. *Mythologies.* Trans. Annette Lavers. New York: Hill and Wang, 1972.

Benjamin, Walter. "The Work of Art in the Age of Mechanical Reproduction." *Illuminations: Essays and Reflections.* Ed. Hannah Arendt. New York: Harcourt, Brace and World, 1968: 219–53.

Berger, John et al. *Ways of Seeing.* London: British Broadcasting Company and Penguin Books, 1977.

Bernhardt, Stephen. "Seeing the Text." *College Composition and Communication* 37.1 (1986): 66–78.

Bertin, Jacques. *Semiology of Graphics: Diagrams, Networks Maps.* Trans. William J. Berg. Madison: The U of Wisconsin P, 1983.

Blakesley, David. "Defining Film Rhetoric: The Case of Hitchcock's *Vertigo.*" Hill and Helmers, 111–34.

Bourdieu, Pierre, and Luc Boltanski, Robert Castel, Jean-Claude Chamboredon and Dominique Schnapper. *Photography: A Middle-brow Art.* Trans. Shaun Whiteside. Stanford: Stanford UP, 1990.

Curtis, James. *Mind's Eye, Mind's Truth: FSA Photography Reconsidered.* Philadelphia: Temple UP, 1989.

David, Carol. "Investitures of Power: Portraits of Professional Women." *Technical Communication Quarterly* 10.1 (2001): 5–29.

—. "Mythmaking in Annual Reports." *Journal of Business and Technical Communication* 15.2 (2001): 195–222.

Dickinson, Greg, and Casey Malone Maugh. "Placing Visual Rhetoric: Finding Material Comfort in Wild Oats Market." Hill and Helmers, 259–76.

Doheny-Farina, Stephen. "Reviews" [*City of Bits: Space, Place, and the Infobahn* by William J. Mitchell; *The War of Desire and Technology at the Close of the Mechanical Age* by Allucquie're Rosanne Stone; *Culture on the Brink: Ideologies of Technology.* ed. Gretchen Bender and Timothy Druckery]. *Technical Communication Quarterly* 5.2 (1996): 183–87.

Dombrowski, Paul M. "Ernst Haeckel's Controversial Visual Rhetoric. *Technical Communication Quarterly* 12.3 (2003): 303–19.

Edwards, Janis L. "Echoes of Camelot: How Images Construct Cultural Memory Through Rhetorical Framing." Hill and Helmers, 179–94.

Faigley, Lester, Diana George, Anna Palchick, and Cynthia Selfe. *Picturing Texts.* New York: W. W. Norton and Co., 2004.

George, Diana. "From Analysis to Design: Visual Communication in the Teaching of Writing." *College Composition and Communication* 54.1 (2002): 11–39.

Goggin, Maureen Daly. "Visual Rhetoric in Pens of Steel and Inks of Silk: Challenging the Great Visual/Verbal Divide." Hill and Helmers, 87–110.

Gombrich, E. H. *Art and Illusion: A Study in the Psychology of Pictorial Representation.* London: Phaidon, 1960.

Hall, Stuart. "The Work of Representation." *Representation: Cultural Representations and Signifying Practices.* Ed. Stuart Hall. London: Sage: 15–64.

Helmers, Marguerite. "Framing the Fine Arts Through Rhetoric." Hill and Helmers, 63–86.

Hill, Charles A., and Marguerite Helmers. eds. *Defining Visual Rhetorics.* Mahwah NJ: Lawrence Erlbaum Assoc., 2004.

Hope, Diane S. "Gendered Environments: Gender and the Natural World in the Rhetoric of Advertising." Hill and Helmers, 155–78.

Kienzler, Donna. "Visual Ethics." *The Journal of Business Communication* 34.2 (1997): 171–87.

Kimmelman, Michael. "Abu Ghraib Photos Return, This Time as Art." *The New York Times* 10 Oct. 2004: AR 29.

Kostelnick, Charles. "Melting-Pot Ideology, Modernist Aesthetics, and the Emergence of Graphical Conventions: The Statistical Atlases of the United States, 1874–1925." Hill and Helmers, 215–42.

—. "A Systematic Approach to Visual Language in Business Communication." *The Journal of Business Communication* 25.3 (1988): 29–48.

Kostelnick, Charles, and David D. Roberts. *Designing Visual Language: Strategies for Professional Communicators.* Boston: Allyn and Bacon, 1998.

Lambert, Bernadette, with Sylvia Martinez. "What a Garden Can Teach Us." Winter and Robbins, 45–48

Lanham, Richard A. *The Electronic Word: Democracy, Technology, and the Arts.* U Chicago P, 1993.

Latour, Bruno and Steve Woolgar. *Laboratory Life: The Construction of Scientific Facts.* Princeton: Princeton UP, 1979.

Lemagny, Jean-Claude, and Andre Rouille. *A History of Photography: Social and Cultural Perspectives.* Trans. Janet Lloyd. Cambridge, UK: U of Cambridge P, 1987.

McKirahan, Richard. *Philosophy Before Socrates: An Introduction With Text and Commentary.* Indianapolis: Hackett Publishing Co., 1994.

McQuade, Donald, and Christine McQuade. *Seeing & Writing 2.* New York: Bedford/St. Martin's, 2003.

Mitchell, W. J. T. *Iconology: Image, Text, Ideology.* Chicago: U of Chicago P, 1986.

—. "The Pictorial Turn." *ArtForum* 30.7 (Mar. 1992), reprinted in *Picture Theory: Essays on Visual and Verbal Representation:* Chicago: U of Chicago P, 1994.

Momaday, N. Scott. "The Photograph." The Man Made of Words. St. Martin's, 1997. 191.

Mulvey, Laura. "Visual Pleasure and Narrative Cinema." *Screen* 16.3 (1975): 6–18.

Newhall, Beaumont. *The History of Photography.* New York: The Museum of Modern Art, 1982.

Perlmutter, David D. *Photojournalism and Foreign Policy: Icons of Outrage in International Crisis.* Westport, CT: Praeger, 1998.

Porter, James E. *Rhetorical Ethics and Internetworked Writing.* Greenwich, CT: Ablex Publishing Corp., 1998.

Richards, Anne R. "Argument and Authority in the Visual Representations of Science." *Technical Communication Quarterly* 12.2 (2003): 183–206.

Richards, Anne R., and Carol David. "Decorative Color as a Rhetorical Enhancement on the World Wide Web." *Technical Communication Quarterly* 14.1 (2005): 31–48.

Robbins, Sarah. "'Writing Suburbia,' in Image and Print Text." Winter and Robbins, 166–69.

Salinas, Carlos. "Technical Rhetoricians and the Art of Configuring Images." *Technical Communication Quarterly* 11.2 (2002): 165–83.

Schriver. Karen A. *Dynamics in Document Design: Creating Texts for Readers.* New York: John Wiley and Sons, 1997.

Sontag, Susan. "Regarding the Torture of Others." *The New York Times Magazine.* 23 May 2004: 24–29+

—. *On Photography.* London: Penguin Books, 1979.

Strachan, J. Cherie, and Kathleen E. Kendall. "Political Candidates' Convention Films: Finding the Perfect Image—An Overview of Political Image Making." Hill and Helmers, 135–54.

Stroupe, Craig. "The Rhetoric of Irritation: Inappropriateness as Visual Literate Practice." Hill and Helmers, 243–58.

Tange, Andrea Kaston. "Envisioning Domesticity, Locating Identity: Constructing the Victorian Middle Class Through Images of Home." Hill and Helmers, 277–302.

Tagg, John. *The Burden of Representation: Essays on Photographies and Histories.* London: MacMillan Education, Ltd., 1988.

Tebeaux, Elizabeth. The *Emergence of a Tradition: Technical Writing in the English Renaissance, 1464–1640.* Amityville, NY: Baywood Publishing Co., 1997.

—. "From Orality to Textuality: Technical Description and the Emergence of Visual and Verbal Presentation," *The Emergence of a Tradition*, 175–236.

—. "The Voices of English Women Technical Writers, 1641–1700: Imprints in the Evolution of Modern English Prose Style." *Technical Communication Quarterly* 7.2 (1998): 125–53.

Tufte, Edward R. *The Visual Display of Quantitative Information.* Cheshire, CT: Graphics, 1983.

Winter, Dave, and Sarah Robbins. *Forging Communities: Interdisciplinary Lessons and Reflective Models for Exploring American Culture.* Kennesaw, GA: Kennesaw Mountain Writing Project, 2002.

Wolf, Sylvia. *Julia Margaret Cameron's Women.* New Haven: Yale UP, 1998.

2 Seeing Rhetoric

Nancy Allen

It's safe to say that rhetoric—as an approach to using words to inform, deliberate, and persuade—has been tested by the ages. Uses of rhetoric reach from the classical period of Greek civilization to modern writing classrooms, policy determinations, and political campaigns. Explanations of and guidelines for using rhetoric in written and oral communication abound.

We live, however, in a visually oriented time. According to Arthur Berger, author of numerous books on culture and media, "We live in a world of things seen, a world that is visual [. . .]. Like fish, we 'swim' in a sea of images, and these images help shape our perceptions of the world and of ourselves" (1). Ann Marie Seward Barry, author of *Visual Intelligence,* concurs, observing, "Visual communication dominates every area of our lives" (3). We now recognize that effective communication includes more than words.

Imagine yourself about to read an essay or listen to a speech. Your first impressions begin with visual elements. Before we read the opening sentence or hear a speaker's first words, we have already begun to form impressions from the setting, the medium, and the speaker's appearance. These features fall within the domain of visual rhetoric. We bring a different set of expectations to reading a magazine, comic book, or the Web, to comments by a sequined rock star or a white-coated doctor, to a lecture in a museum or a chat in a coffee bar or online. Even the look of a piece of writing sets up expectations that influence how we will interact with it.

When words spread across a page
Or are in short centered lines,
We recognize

We're in a creative space,
And our past experiences
With poetry
Influence our reading.

Visual rhetoric refers to the visual features of communication and the effects they have on readers/viewers. When we become sensitive to the visual features of our communications, we can begin using them to help us achieve our goals in writing and speaking. We also become more aware of how these features are being used to influence us.

Yet, as important as visual rhetoric is to our lives, teaching students to recognize its features and effects and to use them in achieving their own communicative purposes is a complex and difficult task. This volume is dedicated to helping with that task, and in this chapter I argue two points:

1. Visual representations can help us understand rhetorical principles. Sometimes a picture may be worth more than a thousand words—or at least a few hundred words—of explanation.
2. Visual rhetoric can be an effective tool for presenting information and persuading an audience. Examples included here will demonstrate the effectiveness of visuals in specific communications.

This chapter is not organized around assignments, nor does it describe any specific assignment in detail, as other essays in this book do. Instead, I discuss general guidelines for using visual representations for two purposes: to teach rhetorical principles and to present information in a manner intended to persuade or to inform.

Issues in Teaching Visual Rhetoric

Teaching students how to use visual rhetoric is as challenging as teaching them to use written language effectively. One reason for the difficulty stems from our educational system. As children, we are visually oriented, learning to draw before we learn to write. When we enter school, however, language, math, and science are emphasized. Development of our visual skills is usually relegated to art class, which is a small part of the school day or week; in some schools, visual training may not be included at all. Most of us lose our sensitivity to the effects visual elements have on our perceptions. Teaching visual rhetoric, then, isn't so much teaching a new set of skills as reawakening our visual skills and developing our ways of seeing. In Marcel Proust's words, "The real voyage of discovery consists not in seeking new landscapes but in having new eyes" (qtd. in Barry, 1).

In teaching visual rhetoric, the term *rhetoric* can itself be an issue. Rhetoric has an ancient lineage and is inexact, an art rather than a science. These very strengths of long history and versatility, however, raise questions for students, who are immersed in their own times and live quite differently from the way citizens in fifth century B.C.E. Athens did. Many students wonder how such an old theory can have anything to do with the issues they face and the documents they'll be called upon to write in the academy or on the job. Students may find assignments requiring rhetoric to be boring or amusing, but few of them see a reason to take such an ancient process seriously. Rhetoric's versatility is also a problem. Students may wonder how this system can be useful when it is so variable—when there is no set of rules for using it. Rhetoric's heuristic strategies are broad and malleable, permitting application to various situations, but this versatility can make rhetoric confusing to writers who are being introduced to its principles.

The visual examples included in this chapter are drawn from current publications and websites to help with both problems—the understanding of rhetoric as language and visual representation, and rhetoric's relevance to current forms of communication. These visual examples of rhetorical principles at work will connect with current communication practices, thus supporting rhetoric's importance to today's writers. In addition, because visual presentations aid understanding and learning, they will show how the principles of rhetoric can operate visually. Citing neurological research, Barry tells us that, "It is no longer possible to divide the process of seeing from that of understanding" (44).

Though Plato may have raged against visuals because he perceived them to be related to emotion rather than to logic, people today are comfortable with and more sophisticated in their interpretation of visuals. We know about Photoshop's functions for mutating pictures or for morphing one image into another: We know, for example, that people can be added to or taken from a group photo for personal (divorce in a family) or political (a shift in power) reasons. What we see in images may not be factual. Yet images can be very powerful in creating responses in viewers, and they can be very helpful to understanding concepts. As Donald Norman tells us, "The easiest way to make things understandable is to use graphics or pictures" (199).

Visual Representations of Rhetorical Principles

The elements of rhetoric that can be so important to effective communication are defined in many texts, but they can also be presented visually. Visual representation may, in fact, clarify a point about a rhetorical function better than language can for some people. Here, I will focus the discussion on those rhetorical elements often used for effective communication: the persuasive appeals and the rhetorical canon. The samples described below will show how visual rhetoric can incorporate these elements in communications.

Persuasive Appeals

Three rhetorical appeals—logos (the appeal through reason), ethos (the appeal through values and the speaker/writer's character, credibility, and integrity), and pathos (the appeal through emotions)—undergird Aristotelian rhetorical analysis (Corbett 15). We'll begin here with logos, which generally gets the most attention and respect in writing classes.

Logos. Aristotle established in *The Rhetoric* that good arguments are based on good reasons, reasons that are valid, appropriate to the topic discussed, and valued by the audience. It is common practice to articulate those reasons substantially through words. However, in our attempts to inform or to persuade we miss an opportunity if we limit ourselves to words alone. We're familiar with visuals in their supporting roles, through which they organize and emphasize information. We see examples in colored maps, such as those representing states as red or blue depending on the outcome of their presidential vote; and in line graphs, such as those showing the rise and fall of the stock market. But visuals can play an even more persuasive role, as in the following examples.

To show how information can be carried and developed within a design, Anne Frances Wysocki describes differences in her interactions with two CD-ROMs about art collections: "The differences between the visual presentations of these CDs are differences of assertion and thought" (224). She further explains that various features of the design "might conventionally be called form, and yet clearly they too have carried significant argumentative weight" (231). These design differences influenced Wysocki's impressions of the collections, one collection being focused, she believed, on the collector and other focused on the works of art. Such impressions influenced the understandings that she formed as she viewed the images and textual information of the collection. Such an in-class analysis and comparison of CD-ROMs or of websites on similar topics might help students begin to see ways in which the design of information influences their opinions.

Visuals can also add information and nuances that serve as elements of the argument itself. In an interview, lawyer Fred Steingold explained how he sometimes uses visuals in making arguments in court. He described a case in which his client was being sued by a neighbor for damages that might or might not have been caused by the client's sewer during a backup. The lawyer created a poster six feet long, with the client's property represented on one end and his neighbor's on the other. The lawyer wanted the length of the poster to illustrate to the jury the long distances involved in the case, which would allow for the possibility of another cause. Though the actual distances were much greater than six feet, the long poster in the courtroom gave the impression of length that the lawyer needed for his argument. He also added small cleaning buckets at each end of his poster to minimize the interpretation of the clean up required. These visuals weren't designed simply to get attention or act as interesting diversions; they provided content, information for the jury to interpret that contributed to the lawyer's argument. In another case in which a man fell from a roof, the lawyer first had photos taken of rivets sticking up on the roof. Because the photos didn't show clear distinctions between the rivets and the roof, he hired an artist to draw the roof, showing the rivets more clearly. When the rivets could be seen protruding from the roof, the risk they could present became more understandable. In both of these instances, the visual representations contributed to the logical reasoning of the arguments being offered. The facts didn't change, but the visual representations influenced how they were interpreted. Similar techniques can be practiced in the classroom. For example, in writing their own persuasive reports, students can look for instances in which "seeing" the situation can add to and help clarify the information provided in their reports.

A third example occurs as an illustration in a professional journal. After several years of work, a group of geneticists and biochemists prepared an article for the February 16, 2001 issue of *Science* to explain the sequencing of the human genome (Venter et al.). Illustrations formed an important part of the logos of their presentation. The article ran from page 1304 to 1351 and included 16 figures and 19 tables to clarify readers' understanding of the genome's very complex structure and the scientists' painstaking reasoning in determining it. Several of the figures included subparts, but one was extraordinary. The first figure, the annotation of the genome assembly, was a chart inserted into the February issue. It measured 39 3/4" by 56 1/2", yet it still required very small print to document each chromosome in tracks, displayed as a nucleotide scale and color coded to define the structure. Though it would require extensive education to read the chart accurately, any viewer is immediately aware of the immense complexity of what is being illustrated. The chart's size and detail impress viewers with the careful and thorough work that must have been required to produce the data represented there. As pointed out by Saho Tateno, a student in one of my classes who researched visual rhetoric's uses in this article, the chart itself presents an argument for the importance and likely accuracy of the content presented. "When people unfold such a large map, they feel as if they explore the world of the human genome" (12), she wrote. The visual rhetoric of the outsized first figure was crucial to achieving the writers' goals of providing detailed information and persuading readers of its credibility and importance. These goals would not have been achieved as well with words alone.

Ethos. The appeal through ethos, that is, through the speaker or writer's character, credibility, and integrity and through community values, is often subtly indicated by clues rather than direct statement—for example, through a professional or governmental title under the author's name, the source (e.g., professional journal or e-zine) in which a piece is published, or the stylish clothing or haircut sported by a speaker. Clues such as these encourage us to attribute certain qualities of education, authority, or sophistication to individuals. (Titles such as "The Military" and "Business Cut" given to haircut styles in Figure 1 illustrate that relating hair-style cues to ethos is an old idea.) Although we

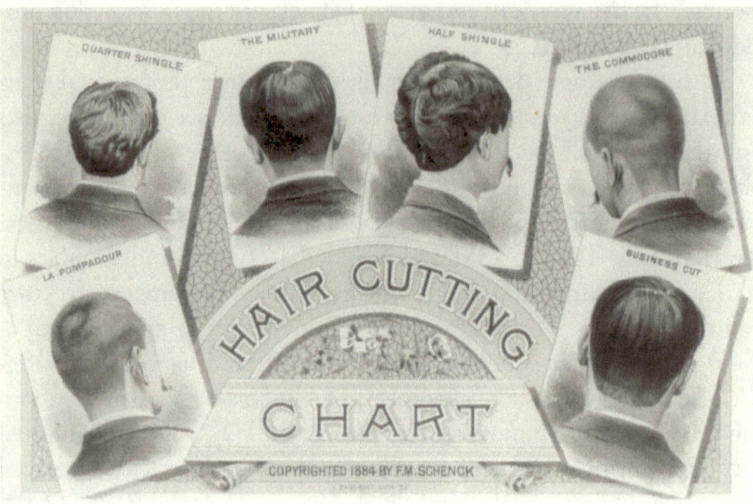

Figure 1. Styles of haircut reflect the character of the individual. *Haircutting chart*. A. L. Bancroft and Co. 1884. (Used by permission of the Library of Congress Prints and Photographs Division, Washington, D.C.)

all recognize that images are being created by such visual cues, we may not be aware that they are being used to persuade us of something. When President George W. Bush wanted to show his commitment to the environment, he toured Sequoia National Park for photo ops beside the big trees. When Michael Dukakis needed to bolster the toughness of his image during his presidential campaign, he had his picture taken in a tank. (Ironically, because Dukakis was shown in a helmet that was much too big for him, the image backfired.) University websites include pictures of students involved in campus activities to show the school's dedication to students, and clinics are careful to append *MD* or *DO* after names on the medical staff to assure us of the value of the care and advice offered there. The clinics could save money on ad space by leaving the degree information out, but that wouldn't achieve the same effect. We use visual design to enhance ethos and personal image; Susan Hilligoss and Tharon Howard, however, warn that "inappropriate format or jarring visual choices may make the document less credible" (2). To use visual rhetoric effectively, then, we must be careful to consider each item's appropriateness to our audiences and purpose.

In searching websites for interesting uses of rhetoric, Sara Maurer, a student in one of my classes, found a complex use of ethos in the images used to present a new medication, Seasonale. The website, describing the medication and its uses, featured the image of "a smiling, well dressed woman who represents as many consumers as possible with one image. The woman has dark hair, dark eyes, and a medium complexion. Her ambiguity is intentional: she could be Caucasian, Latin, Middle Eastern, etc.; she could be as young as twenty and as old as forty; she could be single or married; rich or middleclass" (4). No matter what group she represented, she was definitely vibrant and attractive. Maurer also reported the uses of color and authority on the site that contributed to the image of the drug and the manufacturing company. "Whereas the rest of the page comprises purples and pinks, 'FDA-approved' is yellow. And where the rest of the text is horizontal, this insertion is at a 20-degree angle. [. . .] Approval by the FDA, as a federal regulating agency, provides Seasonale instant credibility" (4). To support the credibility, the site also included images of medical experts.

A good source for finding examples of the appeal through ethos is personal websites. In a recent *Wired* article about websites for presidential candidates Kerry and Bush, Adam Penenberg commented, "In the end, it may not matter what kind of information appears on the candidates' websites, as long as they have a cool design" (1). He referred to the results from a 2002 Stanford study on website credibility and reported, "Nearly half of the study's participants—about 46 percent—rated a site's credibility based primarily on its design or look" (2). Personal websites are developed to illustrate and sometimes to promote the author's ethos or image, which is presented first through the visuals that meet us when we open the appropriately named Splash page or the homepage. The colors and graphics chosen and the sizes of graphics and words create an immediate impression of the personal image, thus carrying the appeal through ethos. To learn more about this use of visual rhetoric, students can investigate a variety of personal websites, such as those for professionals, their favorite entertainers, and some contemporaries whom they may or may not know (if an appropriate website for a professional is a little difficult to find, a good one to check is <http://www.a2.com>, the site for a marketing consultant). After analyzing a variety of sites, students might try to design their own personal website, on a computer or on paper. Their experiences analyzing the ethos of other people's sites should encourage them to think closely about the items they add to their own site, how they design the layout, and what messages these images and the design convey to viewers.

Pathos. Visuals are most often associated with pathos, the appeal to our emotions. Photos can evoke sympathy, and films can frighten. For instance, television news programs were prohibited from showing film of flag-draped coffins being unloaded from transport planes returning from Iraq because of the dismay that viewing large numbers of dead soldiers might have on the public. Such a focus on the human cost of war could weaken viewers' support for the war effort. In contrast, images of the twin towers destroyed on September 11 are shown to arouse our anger toward our perceived enemies and reinforce our fear of what could happen to anyone. Of course, visual representations aren't always connected to international issues. Through their joyous colors, balloons tied to a mailbox signal a celebration at a nearby household.

Visuals and the emotions they invoke can be put to positive use in building arguments. It is pathos, the appeal to our emotions, that is credited with adding motivation to persuasive discourse. While good reasons and the credibility of the author work to convince us of the rightness of a cause, we are often swayed more by our passions or emotions (Corbett 34), and it is emotion that inspires us to take action (99). A group of medical students at the University of Michigan has appealed visually to the emotions of their institution's policymakers through "photovoice," a technique used in "advocacy efforts from China to Flint to San Francisco for more than a decade" (Rueter E1). The medical students photograph patients in ways that emphasize the patients' unmet needs and use the photos in presentations made to medical center administrators and community leaders. These students also used photovoice to argue their own need to work in outpatient clinics serving people without health insurance. As a result, medical school officials are now forging a partnership with such a clinic, in which interested students can do rotations, learning about loan-forgiveness programs and low-cost clinics.

Rhetorical Canon

In addition to providing useful tools for presenting our ideas to others, rhetorical theory also provides help for guiding us in the development of those ideas into coherent essays, articles, and presentations. Classical theory breaks the process into five steps, which together are referred to as the rhetorical canon. Each step can be illustrated through visuals to help us understand the procedure more clearly and incorporate it into our work.

Invention (*inventio*). We've all suffered from paralysis of the blank page. Before we can present a persuasive discussion, we need something to say, but what? We need to develop ideas that will help to make our case. In rhetorical theory, that process is called invention, but of course we don't just make up imaginary facts, as the term may imply. What we invent, or develop, are topics (*topoi*) related to our purpose. Visual representation can be especially helpful with this step of rhetoric.

Because it is hard to come up with ideas, writing teachers have developed heuristic strategies, such as brainstorming, to stimulate our thinking, but we don't all think in the same ways. Some people rely on manipulating language to generate ideas whereas others rely more on the right side of the brain, which is associated with our visual processes. For these individuals, visual heuristics and the overall process of visual thinking can help spark creative ideas. We can, for example, create mind maps, matrices, storyboards, and sketches as we develop our way of approaching a problem. Through these visual thinking activities, we may discover relations among the parts of a problem and use them to create new directions in our thinking. When students in my classes are developing ideas, with the goal of preparing a recommendation report, I ask them to create visual representations of the problem as part of the development process. In fact, I ask them to create two or three representations so that they get beyond the more linear matrices and flow charts to sketches and visuals based on freer types of associations. One year, my students decided to investigate the problem of insects in their residence halls and to send recommendations to the housing staff. In preparation, they created idea maps and sketches to represent their thought processes. Representations such as these give students a wide range of ideas to draw on that can help them see connections among issues as they begin writing (Figure 2).

The lawyer mentioned earlier, who described using visuals in his court presentations, also uses visuals to aid his invention process in preparing arguments. While thinking about a case, he makes a literal or schematic drawing of the scene or situation to help him develop a general approach; for some cases, he also hires a photographer to help

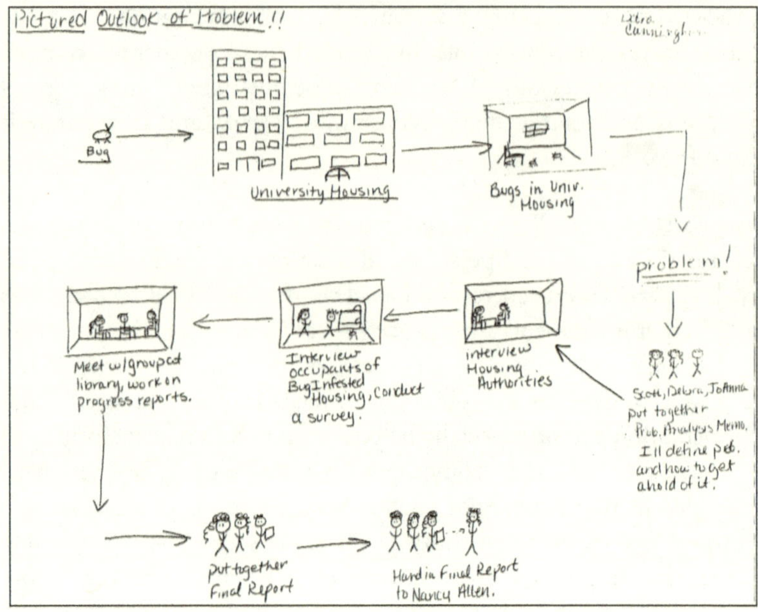

Figure 2. Visual narrative of research and report writing process.

him get a clearer view of a setting. These visual representations help him to clarify and to organize his thinking on a case, to absorb the whole, and to see relations among the parts. He feels that the visuals translate relations over time into relations in space so they can be comprehended and evaluated more easily. Visuals, he believes, can cut through the murkiness sometimes created by words and help him see features of an issue more clearly (Steingold). (Figure 3 shows paper mill workers using graphic models in a similar way, to help them understand a production problem.)

Scientists have long used the Internet to exchange information. The advent of browsers added the power to exchange visuals as well as text, and the World Wide Web has relatively recently become a valuable resource for many of us seeking information. A great deal of information is available there on almost any topic, and it's easily accessible to anyone with a computer connection. Online search tools have become tools of invention, and these tools are themselves becoming more visual. Not only can they display graphics, but search engines such as Vivisimo and Grokker show the results of a search as a visual representation rather than as a list. Results are sorted into categories

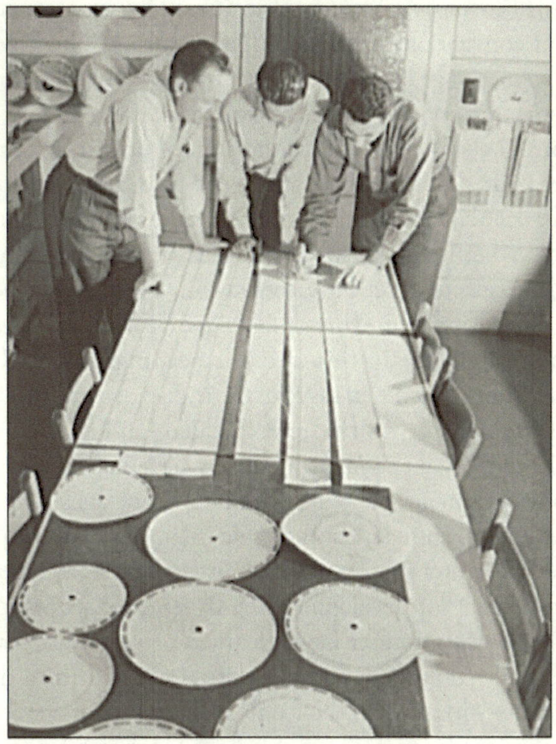

Figure 3. *Workers at Southland Paper Mill consult organizational charts in order to understand production timelines*. John Vachon. 1943. (Used by permission of the Library of Congress Prints and Photographs Division, Washington, D.C.)

and then mapped into a display, for instance, as a set of labeled geometric shapes. The software uses a combination of linguistic and statistical analyses to determine categories that fit the subject matter and then maps search results visually into colorful circles of information that allow a viewer to zoom in for detail. An article about these new search tools describes a search for "Paris Hilton" as an example. A textual search tool like Google would return a long list that includes items on a celebrity named Paris Hilton as well as on a Hilton Hotel in Paris. The visual search tools group the responses into categories, such as booking sites, maps, celebrities, etc., making it easier for us to select a circle with the information we need (Bergstein).

Arrangement (*dispositio*). The visual features of a page are more than simply print conventions; they are full of meaning. The headings and indentations of a page layout indicate a hierarchy of meaning, the order of importance for the points being made. For example, headings in the center are more important than those on the side, and items in a list are related. Through arrangement of information on a page, we make particular points stand out and take on importance in our presentation, whether it's persuading reader/viewers to purchase a particular toothpaste, to accept the conclusions of an experiment, or to pass legislation. As Karen Schriver explains, "The visual organization of the rhetorical cluster (in this case, the headings, subheadings, and listed items) should make it easy to see the structure; that is, to see which lists are related, which are embedded, and so on" (400). We can think of the visual cues of arrangement as a map for a reader's trip through our document, showing where to go next as well as which items should be taken together and which will come afterward.

Standard design principles of proximity, contrast, etc. are also rhetorically important for developing Web pages, new spaces for writing that the Greeks would never have dreamed of. In addition to typical highlighting and alignment cues, websites involve a third dimension of arrangement—hyperlinks. Not only can we indent a section of information that needs to be set apart, we can move it to a different location. In addition to preparing a list of items that go together, we can group them on their own page. Visual proximity or virtual separation reinforces the strength or weakness of connections among different pieces of information on a topic and allows us to feature what we find most important. What should we do with those unimportant but still necessary details? Put them two links deep in the website's structure.

Style (*elocutio*). The visual rhetoric of style can be subtle and is often found within the text itself. The font we choose, for example, presents a personality to our readers. Times New Roman gives a businesslike quality to reports whereas Comic Sans catches our attention in a party invitation, and Nuptial Script says we're invited to a wedding. In addition, the density or openness of the lettering and words in a text conveys an attitude and helps to set our expectations about the subject matter of the text. In the introduction to this chapter, for example, I referred to text placed in short, centered lines as often indicating poetry, which brings with it specific expectations. (For an extended discussion of the personality qualities of various fonts, see Eva Brumberger's articles in *Technical Communication.*)

The letters themselves also constitute a design element (Figure 4). As Wysocki says about one of the CD-ROMs she analyzed, "The

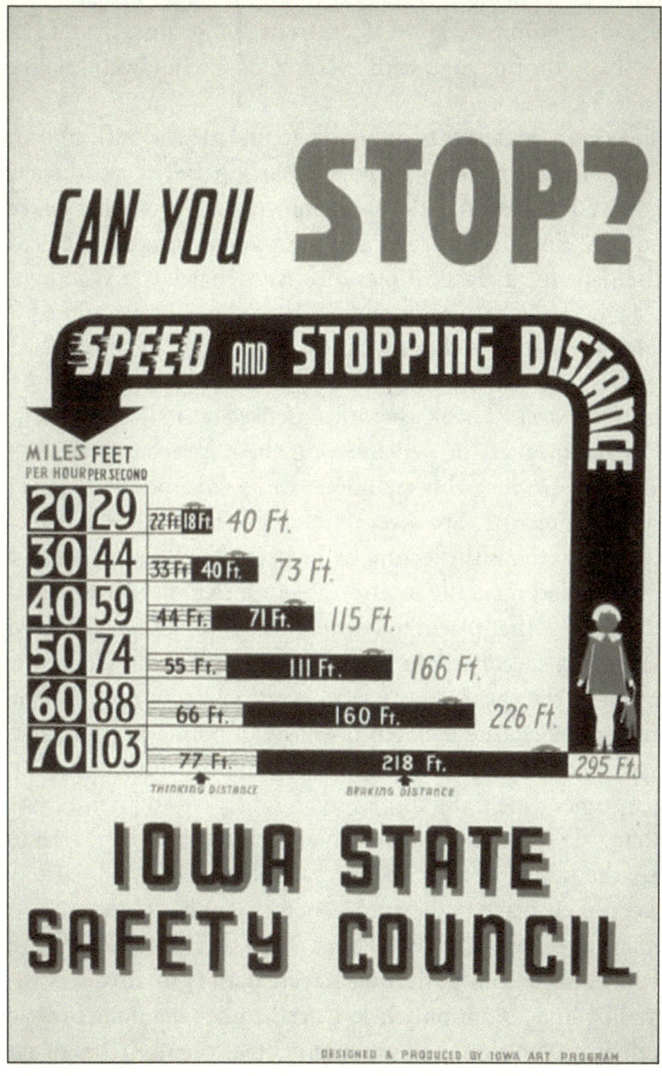

Figure 4. In this poster from the Iowa State Safety Council, key words have taken on design functions. (Used by permission of the Library of Congress Prints and Photographs Division, Washington, D.C.)

words have been designed to be as much a part of this screen as the art and the photographs, making the words and photographs and paintings equally visual and equally visually weighted" (223). When text becomes art, it is sometimes laid out in a pattern on a page, which we refer to as iconistic text layout. In a newspaper article predicting who would be nominated for Oscars from 2003 films, the text formed Oscar's shape on the page with pictures of likely nominees lined up along side it (Turan).

Which graphic elements we choose to include also reflects our style. One person may select strong colors in block patterns; another chooses wispy, curved pastels. A rock poster showing a singer with spiked hair and multiple rings in eyebrows and nose sets a different tone from an advertisement for a classical piano concert that has a shadowy schematic of a piano in the background. These choices set a tone as well as conveying information about what sort of concert each will be.

Memory (*memoria*). Greek rhetoricians used visualization as a technique to aid speakers in remembering their speeches. As Cicero described in *De Oratore,* this technique was a mnemonic of association based on architecture. Speakers were taught to envision a place, such as a house or perhaps the lecture hall where the planned speech would be delivered, and mentally to associate each section of a speech with a room or item in that place, to create, in a sense, a mental map of images. Parts of a speech might be envisioned as laid out along the steps leading up to the speaker's platform or associated with a row of windows lining the lecture hall. An overview of points to be made could, in the speaker's mind, be resting on the podium, and the major points of the argument mentally displayed among a row of statues standing along one side of the hall. Such visual techniques helped speakers remember the points of their speeches and their order, and also helped them keep their place as they proceeded through a speech.

Today's speakers use PowerPoint. The images have moved out of our minds and onto a projection screen thanks to advances in technology. The images not only help us remember the points we wish to make, they also help our audiences remember them. Access to external memory supports is one of Donald Norman's principles of designing for usability (34–80). In describing memory's role in usability he says, "Don't underestimate the power or importance of simple mental aids [. . .]. They reduce memory load by providing external memory devices (providing knowledge in the world instead of requiring it to be in the head)" (192–93).

Delivery (*pronuntiatio*). The fifth rhetorical canon, delivery, has changed and continues to change dramatically through advances in technology. Once, when we wanted to persuade someone of our ideas, our only instrument for delivering the message was our voices. With the development of writing and its technologies, we moved through scratching with sticks or rocks, painting with brushes, writing with pen and ink, typing on paper, and now, though usually still at a keyboard, creating virtual electronic communications with computers. Each technological advance has brought new opportunities for delivering our messages to listeners/readers/viewers until today we have an array of options, many of which involve visual elements and, therefore, visual rhetoric.

Much of our writing to inform and to persuade occurs today through the media and on the World Wide Web. We get much of our news from television, which is by name a visual medium that often gives us information through multiple means simultaneously. An interview, for example, might have a crawl line of text running below it for us to read while we are also able to watch the speakers in the interview, gaining information from their facial reactions as well as the questions and answers, and to hear other events occurring in the background. Mitchell Stephens has said that moving images will become how we write in the twenty-first century (201). We saw evidence of that in the summer of 2004. Michael Moore's film *Fahrenheit 9/11,* which is clearly a message and not a fictional story, set attendance records. Apparently many people wanted to see the film in order to evaluate his message for themselves. Today's communicators would be wise to learn the techniques of these media for conveying their ideas and for putting the rhetorical principles described here to use.

Visual Representation as a Rhetorical Tool

Visuals can be very persuasive, carrying information as well as appealing to our emotions. J. Carl Ganter, Jr., a journalist and photographer, told me of a photo exhibit that played a part in developing history. This exhibit was shown in the early 1990s when events were occurring in Yugoslavia that would result in breaking that country apart, but few people in the United States were yet interested in what was happening so far away. Pictures of events in Yugoslavia were not being printed in the news magazines they had been intended for. Ganter's picture editor in New York at the time "had heard about all these images coming back from Yugoslavia, and these pictures weren't being published. They were pictures by very famous photojournalists who were risking their lives to cover important stories of atrocities that were going on" (Interview). The editor had a connection with an administrator at the United Nations and gained permission to show the photos in the main entrance of the UN building. He had the pictures enlarged and framed, and a writer added captions and an introduction. The show was placed at the UN entrance, where it could be viewed by everyone entering or leaving. "Suddenly Yugoslavia was on the map because the pictures, some of them were so strong that people were brought to tears." Ganter also makes the point that, as powerful as images may be, for him pictures don't tell the whole story. "A picture tells a thousand words, but there's always more [. . .]. There's always a context to put it in [. . .]. I want to know the story behind the picture" (Ganter). For the pictures of Yugoslavia, the introduction and captions served that purpose.

People in all fields are beginning to realize the importance of visual elements and the rhetorical effects they carry. As Felice Frankel has written in an article on "Visualizing Data,"

> I am convinced that to develop the much-needed new approaches to representing data, scientists must begin to embrace ideas from those who have not necessarily made a career in science but who have a serious interest in visual thinking and communication. In the process we will learn that making intelligent and communicative representations will clarify the complicated ideas that are the data.

The same is true of all our writing to inform or persuade. Visual thinking during our writing process expands our reservoir of ideas. Visual rhetoric in our documents helps us carry our messages to our readers and viewers more effectively.

Works Cited

Aristotle. *The Rhetoric and The Poetics of Aristotle.* Trans. W. Rhys Roberts. Ed. Friedrich Solmsen. New York: Modern Library, 1954.

Barry, Ann Marie Seward. *Visual Intelligence.* Albany, NY: State U of New York P, 1997.

Berger, Arthur Asa. *Seeing Is Believing: An Introduction to Visual Communication.* Mountain View, CA: Mayfield, 1989.

Bergstein, Brian. "Consumer/Technology: Seek and Ye Shall Find." *Tucson Citizen,* 16 Jan. 2004. 30 Jan. 2005 <http://www.tucsoncitizen.com/index.php?page=business&story_id=011604b1_search>.

Brumberger, Eva R. "The Rhetoric of Typography: The Persona of Typeface and Text."*Technical Communication 50*.2 (2003): 206–23. See also: *Technical Communication Online* (2003) <tc.eserver.org/publisher/Technical_Communication_Online>.

—. The Rhetoric of Typography: The Awareness and Impact of Typeface Appropriateness. *Technical Communication* 50.2 (2003): 224–31.

Cicero. *De Oratore, Books I and II,* Trans. E. W. Sutton and H. Rackham. Vol. 348 of Loeb Classical Library. Cambridge, MA: Harvard UP, 1996. Reprinted in *The Rhetorical Tradition: Readings from Classical Times to the Present.* 2nd ed. Ed. Patricia Bizzell and Bruce Herzberg. Boston: Bedford/St. Martin's, 2001. 289–339.

Corbett, Edward P. J. *Classical Rhetoric for the Modern Student.* 2nd ed. New York: Oxford UP, 1971.

Frankel, Felice. "Visualizing Data." *American Scientist Online,* 19 Feb. 2004. 30 Jan. 2005 <http://www.americanscientist.org/template/AssetDetail/assetid/31222>.

Ganter, J. Carl, Jr. Personal interview. 27 Sept. 1998.

Hilligoss, Susan, and Tharon Howard. *Visual Communication: A Writer's Guide.* 2nd ed. New York: Longman, 2002.

Maurer, Sara. "Rhetoric. Period. An Analysis of Seasonale.com <http://www.seasonale.com>" Unpublished Report. 25 Nov. 2003.

Norman, Donald A. *The Design of Everyday Things.* New York: Basic Books, 2002.

Penenberg, Adam L. "Unleashing the Web Police." *Wired News,* 26 July 2004. 30 Jan. 2005 <http://www.wired.com/news/print/0,1294,64319,00.html>.

Rueter, Anne. "Cameras Give Future Docs New Perspectives on Health Care. U–M Students Try Documentary Technique to Explore Problems and Sway Policy Makers." *Ann Arbor News,* 22 Feb. 2004: E1–2.

Schriver, Karen. *Dynamics in Document Design: Creating Texts for Readers.* New York: John Wiley & Sons, 1997.

Steingold, Fred. Personal interview. 19 May 1990.

Stephens, Mitchell. *The Rise of the Image the Fall of the Word.* New York and Oxford: Oxford UP, 1998.

Tateno, Saho. "Rhetors and Rhetorical Principles in the Two Articles about the Human Genome Project." Unpublished Report. 25 Nov. 2003.

Turan, Kenneth. "A Critic's Best Guess: Reviewer Predicts Who'll Be on Tuesday's Oscar Nominee List." *Ann Arbor News.* 24 Jan. 2004: B1–B2.

Venter, J.C., et al., "The Sequence of the Human Genome." *Science* 291.5507 (Feb. 2001): 1304–51.

Wysocki, Anne Frances. "Impossibly Distinct: On Form/Content and Word/ Image in Two Pieces of Computer-Based Interactive Multimedia." *Computers and Composition* 18.3 (2001): 209–34.

3 Mediated Memory: The Language of Memorial Spaces

L. J. Nicoletti

Our cities, as well as our campuses, are memorial landscapes begging analysis. Architectural historian Andrew Shanken pointedly asks, "who has not visited a memorial playground or memorial hall? And who has not driven on a memorial highway?" (132). A 1990s study by Heritage Preservation (The National Institute for Conservation) documented 32,000 works of outdoor sculpture in the United States—many of them memorial monuments—with North Dakota claiming the fewest works, at 76, and Pennsylvania the most, at 2,570 ("Statistics" & "Distribution"). Then there are historic markers, generally 50 to 2,000 per state according to cultural critic James W. Loewen, although certain states (like Texas, which registers 12,000 [455]) have radically more. From roadside crosses and commemorative plaques to international projects such as Berlin's "Memorial for the Murdered Jews of Europe," we routinely confront—and at times ignore—the way a monument-saturated landscape can work on us, visually (re)constructing both experience and memory.[1] In our classrooms, these "material commemorative rhetorics" (Blair 23) can be enlisted to reveal slant, audience, persuasion, effective design, and our students' at-times uncritical consumption or cynical rejection of authoritative images or texts. By examining how events with contested histories are memorialized, students plainly see the versatility of language and its supporting visual design to appear monolithic or to say nothing at all.

Static Structures, Shifting Rhetoric

Since Roland Barthes's "Rhetoric of the Image" (1964) and John Berger's *Ways of Seeing* (1972), rhetoricians have become increasingly interested in how language in two- and three-dimensions functions. Marita Sturken reminds us how "an image can substitute for a memory. The distinction between the image and the memory, between the screen and the real, becomes imperceptible" (22). And Carole Blair uses memorial sites to support her hypothesis that rhetoric itself may be inherently material: "Rhetoric's materiality constructs communal space, prescribes pathways, and summons attention, acting on the whole person of the audience" (48). It may surprise us to find that visual rhetoric is as slippery as its verbal counterpart.

Our indoctrination into the seeming rhetorical sanctity of memorial space begins when we are children and we visit museums and monuments and stop to read markers on family road trips. Secure in the past, the stories these sites tell seem fixed, inviolable. Having grown up in Minnesota, I remember much plaque-speak about Indian massacres, heroic soldiers, the untamed prairie, and brave explorers, traders, and settlers. Preserved sites, such as Fort Snelling, the Sibley House, and the Laura Ingalls Wilder homesite stressed the veracity and primacy of these narratives. James Mayo describes their import:

> While restored forts from the American Indian wars are simple in design and have little aesthetic merit, they do convey the sense of visiting the locker room for the home team. Being on federal turf rather than Indian land, visitors are spatially conditioned to identify with the United States rather than the Indians. American Indians and people empathetic to them can consciously reject this conditioning, but others may find that the immediate experience awakens or reinforces their selective patriotism. (147)

Only as an adult did I begin to realize what these histories excluded. Culturally, the terms used to describe the others (the "Indians," the "Sioux") who once impeded Euro-American desires became unpopular. Manifest Destiny became synonymous with genocide, clearly illustrated by the provocative title of David Stannard's book, *American Holocaust: The Conquest of the New World.* The spaces, however, kept speaking an earlier generation's narratives, and little existed to challenge the exclusiveness of this memoryscape until activist-artist Hachivi Edgar Heap of Birds installed his project *Building Minnesota* along the Mississippi River in 1990. Its forty official-looking signs memorialized the individual Dakota resisters and fighters publicly hanged by the Army in Mankato in 1862 and 1865. History had not been shown this way before, and by employing the physical rhetoric of official memorialization (materials and fonts that mimicked state signage), Heap of Birds staged a coup against Minnesota's grand narratives.

Sometimes, only such a shift in our visual fields will cause us to take note of the excluded histories within memory spaces, especially those sites that are government sanctioned. We are not typically educated to notice how "monuments may not remember events so much as bury them altogether beneath layers of national myth and explanation" (Young, *At Memory's Edge,* 94). We are raised, instead, to be in awe of and respectful towards memorial spaces, to trust their rhetoric, to embrace their stories as our own (Figure 1). Which educator among us, trying to impress upon our students that it is imperative to quote accurately and to use sources with integrity, is not startled to read in James W. Loewen's *Lies Across America: What Our Historic Sites Get Wrong* that the Jefferson Memorial "juxtaposes fragments from widely scattered writings of Thomas Jefferson to distort his ideas and policies" (327)? Dwight Pitcaithley, Chief Historian of the National Park Service, reminds us, "Public or collective memory is inherently related to public forgetting. Monuments, memorials, and anniversaries often are designed not to help us understand the past, but to generate support or evoke empathy with one view of the past to the exclusion of often competing views" (51). But in the face of awe-inspiring memorial architecture, and given the absence of an on-site counternarrative, who can remember?

Scholars and theorists now agree that although a moment may be "written in stone," to borrow Sanford Levinson's title, the public's understanding and reception of that history will perpetually change. Anthropologist Elizabeth Hallam and gender studies scholar Jenny Hockey claim that "[m]emory practices and experiences shift over time as perceptions of the past are reworked in the context of the present and in anticipation of the future" (3). As art historian Erika Doss distills from Pierre Nora's theories on memory, "sites of memory exist because of their capacity for metamorphosis [. . .]. Sites of memory are, at their core, sites of struggle, with stakes in larger cultural struggles over national collective identity" (69).

Rhetoric's materiality is mutated not just by memory but even by weather: "Even the bare materiality of a memorial site does not guar-

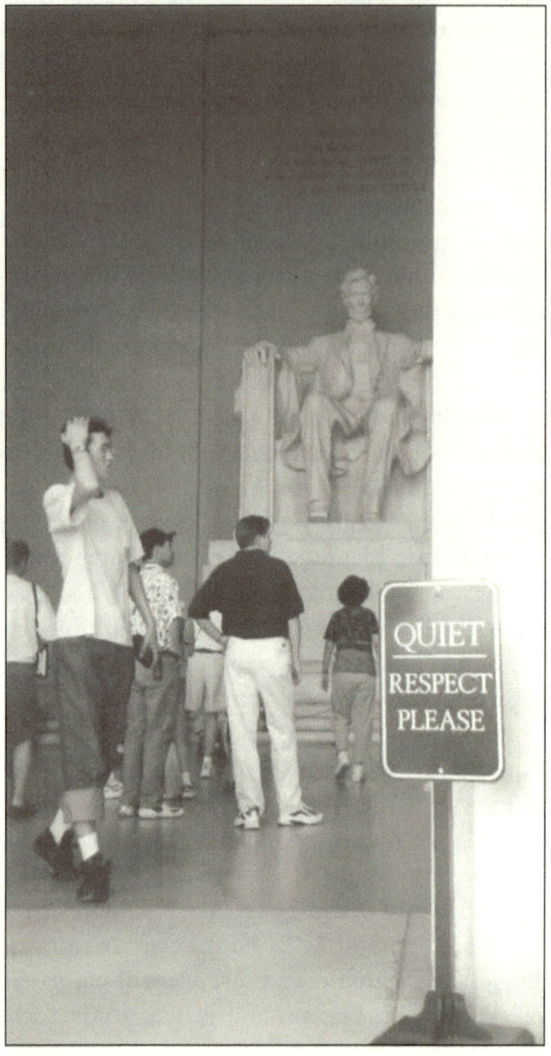

Figure 1. Monuments mediate our memory of history and direct our experience through their design *and* the rhetoric surrounding them. (*Lincoln Memorial, Washington, D.C.* 1001. Courtesty of the author.)

antee that it is the same text on a cloudy day as on a sunny one, on a crowded day as when almost deserted, at dawn as at midday" (Blair 38–39). A vivid example of monuments' "extreme mutability" (Blair 39) appears in the debates surrounding New Orleans's memorial to the "Battle of Liberty Place," discussed fully by Levinson (45–52) and Loewen (214–19). The memorial, erected in 1891 by white supremacists, commemorates the 1874 coup against the state's mixed-race Restoration government. As the demographics of New Orleans changed and the historical memory of white supremacists has become increasingly marginalized, the monument has been removed, relocated, censored, vandalized, reinscribed, protested, and even re-celebrated. Loewen, a specialist in race relations and an educational reformer, calls the monument "the most overtly racist icon to white supremacy in the United States" (214). A constitutional lawyer, Levinson diplomatically refrains from scathing judgments and considers how the Constitution can be enlisted to resolve the social conflict. Composition or communication instructors can examine not only the rhetoric of that visual culture, but also the rhetoric that visual culture engenders through this single monument.

The study of memorials provides for experiential learning in the form of field trips, biographical and historical research, and the creation of design proposals. Every instructor and student has easy access to memoryscapes, from named buildings on campus, local cemeteries, and plaques or sculptures relating regional history, to international memorial competitions. Reproductions of many memorials are found easily on the Web. Assigning students to design a memorial teaches them to consider how visitors interact with these spaces and requires the use of descriptive, analytical, and argumentative writing in stating its purpose, portraying its appearance, defining its audience, justifying its materials and placement, and explaining how it promotes remembrance, not forgetting. It also makes students more astute visual consumers, allowing them to see how their experience of a space or understanding of an event can be manipulated through visual rhetoric.

Re-Visioning Our Memoryscapes

In the semester including September 11, 2001, the composition assignments I had planned for my English 101 students at Centenary College of Louisiana became trivial. The first-year students, having lived away from home just three weeks at the time of the attacks, seemed especially traumatized, vacillating between subdued panic and numbness. Our campus is just a few minutes away from Barksdale Air Force Base, where President George W. Bush landed after being whisked out of Florida on Air Force One, and where he gave his first public statement after the attack. We knew that American bombers would fly over our community as soon as the U.S. began to retaliate. We, too, felt like potential targets. Students' grades began to plummet. Their focus was decidedly on the present, so I could not easily employ the argument that in the future they would be thankful for having dedicated themselves, that semester, to learning better writing and communication skills. They were consuming political rhetoric and visual forms of memorialization as never before—from Manhattan's impromptu memorials, TV news special reports, and commemorative pins, bracelets, buttons, t-shirts, stamps, and magazines. They welcomed assignments that helped them process and respond to this input, including the prospect of envisioning a new memorial landscape or, potentially, designing it.[2]

To introduce them to the memorial design assignment, I helped them see how familiar they already were with the language of memorial spaces. Because memorials are omnipresent, even on small campuses, students quickly become versed in the ingredients of effective memoryscapes. Although there is no foolproof formula, the following design elements needed their immediate consideration: symbolism, setting, audience, scale, permanence, and inscriptions. I'll briefly explain why.

Symbolism. Students saw that certain emblematic elements were so rarefied or commonplace they were ineffective or clichéd. Cultural geographer Kenneth E. Foote notes, "Despite their popular appeal in moments of loss, teddy bears, hearts, flags, and ribbons, as well as angels, crosses and other religious symbols, can be divisive when used as generalized emblems of a tragedy or disaster. They can alienate people as easily as they can comfort them" (344). The diversity of those killed on 9/11—thousands of individuals with varied religious beliefs representing dozens of countries—creates a design challenge that may be addressed best through open narratives instead of iconic, pre-determined signs. A minimalist or abstract aesthetic may further prevent a painful reconstruction of the loss.[3]

Setting. We witnessed that properly situating a memorial in a protected space could add to the historic moment's idealization. Architects like Philip Johnson implored would-be memorialists after the second World War not to show the backsides of horses and soldiers but to keep them covered: "The rear end of General Sherman's horse [in Manhattan, by Augustus St. Gaudens], for example, is neatly shielded by a semi-circle of sycamores" (24) while, in contrast, a Pennsylvania statue of a World War I doughboy posed a "traffic hazard" by "present[ing a] realistic rear view of [the] sculpture to at least half its beholders" (9).

Audience. What part of the story, which viewpoints are silenced by scale and stone? Human memory is fluid, human experience diverse. In contrast, memorials typically are static and monolithic. Their designs often exclude multiple (or unpopular) perspectives, and their location may make them more accessible to one memory-group than another. It is important, therefore, that students analyze the silences at any given public space, to ask whose voices are disenfranchised there, and whether that omission is justified. A Civil War memorial created by a private group, such as the United Daughters of the Confederacy, will represent a narrower constituency than one created by a federal commission. One does not expect Maya Lin's *Civil Rights Memorial,* which stands in front of the Southern Poverty Law Center in Montgomery, Alabama, to record the opinions of racists and the Ku Klux Klan, though their historical presence occasioned the memorial. One may rightly expect that the grounds of the Oklahoma City National Memorial, a National Park Service site, would instruct the public about Timothy McVeigh's motivations—regardless how misguided—to destroy the Alfred P. Murrah Federal Building and 168 lives on April 19, 1995 (Doss 79), or at least the significance of the date he chose (Linenthal 6). It doesn't. This story is partly given to visitors who pay for admission to the adjacent Memorial Center. This is equivalent to the forthcoming World Trade Center memorial site leaving out a discussion of the U.S.'s connection to and one-time support of Osama bin Laden and Al-Qaeda. By examining intended audience, students may start to determine a memorial's rhetorical slant and whether controversy or special interests influenced its design or placement.

Scale. Students learned that excessive size could mar the chance for personal reflection or even recall the visual rhetoric of 20th-century fascism. (Consider, for example, the Third Reich's large-scale projects—sculptures, parades, stadiums—that supported myths about German history and supremacy.) As Andreas Huyssen summarizes,

The monumental is aesthetically suspect because it is tied to 19th-century bad taste, to kitsch, and to mass culture. It is politically suspect because it is seen as representative of 19th-century nationalisms and of 20th-century totalitarianisms. It is socially suspect because it is the privileged mode of expression of mass movements and mass politics. It is ethically suspect because in its preference for bigness it indulges in the larger-than-human, in the attempt to overwhelm the individual spectator. (198)

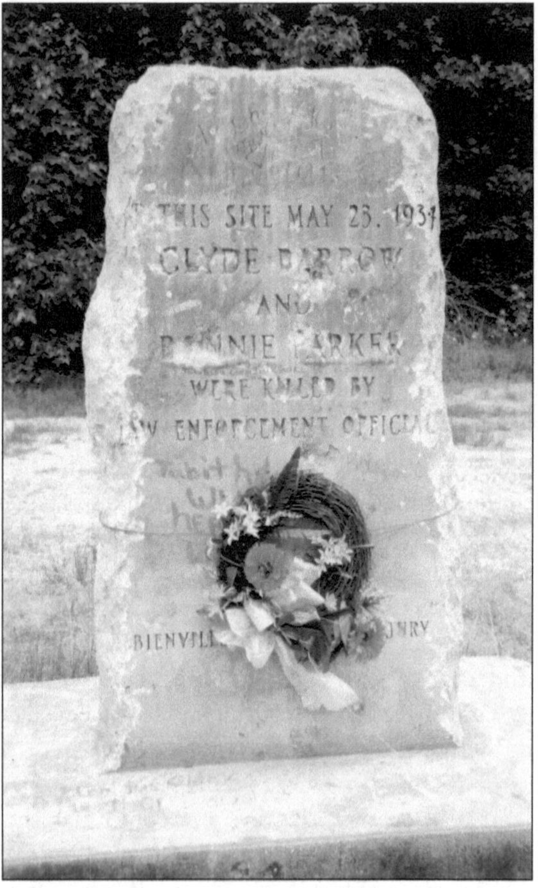

Figure 2. Marker at death site of Bonnie & Clyde. (*Bienville Parish, Louisiana*. 2000. Courtesy of the author.)

Antidotes to monumental excesses, namely temporary or vanishing memorial projects, have become popular, such as the beams of light illuminating the space of the destroyed World Trade Center towers, and Jochen Gerz and Esther Shalev-Gerz's infamous *Monument against Fascism* erected in Harburg, Germany in 1986. The Gerzes lowered this "countermonument" (Young, *Texture* 27)—a lead-coated pillar that could be easily tagged by the community—into the ground at the rate it became covered with graffiti, until it was fully buried in 1993.

Permanence. We noticed a number of memorial projects that were not designed to disappear, but had outlived their materials, if not memory itself. Some, due to remoteness or popularity, attracted destruction (Figure 2). Students considered the effect that time or vandalism could have on their chosen medium.

Additionally, we saw that memoryscapes may need the flexibility to change. While memory is selective and exclusive, monumental projects can stimulate inclusiveness, and this remembering may stress an existing design. For example, on the Vietnam Veterans Memorial, names are ordered by death date. When errors or omissions are discovered, they are inscribed in the nearest space remaining. According to the National Park Service, "When the memorial was dedicated [. . .] officials listed the war's first death as 1959. Later, a 1957 death was discovered, and that name was inscribed out of order. Hundreds of names, inscribed after the memorial was completed, could not be inserted chronologically" (Allen 242).

Inscriptions. Students observed that plaque-speak often consists of poor punctuation and grammar.[4] An inscription on the aforementioned Liberty Place monument in New Orleans concludes with the following sentence fragment: "A CONFLICT OF THE PAST THAT SHOULD TEACH US LESSONS FOR THE FUTURE." Passive voice, unclear referents, faulty parallelism, and misused abbreviations are commonplace in plaque-speak. Students may be directed to uncover examples of poorly presented memorial language and discuss what happens when such officializing rhetoric canonizes common writing errors that a composition instructor would be quick to note.

Once the designs of physical monuments have been analyzed, one may more astutely examine the rhetoric produced before and after them in the form of mission statements, official dedications, and commemorations that direct history and cultural response. Volumes were written in response to President Reagan's controversial decision in 1985 to visit and lay a memorial wreath at Bitburg Cemetery in Germany, where Waffen-SS and Wehrmacht soldiers are buried. He reasoned "those young [Wehrmacht] men are victims of Nazism also, even though they were fighting in the German uniform [. . .]. They were victims, just as surely as the victims in concentration camps" (qtd. in Hartman 240). Although such a conflation of perpetrators with victims is unusual, many memoryscapes must address the issue of how to tell the story of the complete tragedy. At Columbine High School, debates raged over how or whether the two student-shooters should be memorialized (Doss 71). Even without calls to memorialize the 9/11 hijackers, the Lower Manhattan Development Corporation understood the group they planned to memorialize was complicatedly diverse. Their Memorial Mission Statement reveals a sensitive rhetorical tightrope walk:

> Descriptive words were carefully considered for their meaning and implications for the statement: "murdered, killed or lost," "senseless, horrific or devastating," "sacrifice," "hero," "Islamic or Muslim terrorists." All of these words raised issues that were debated and decisions were made that best reflected the intentions of the committee. The draft mission statement contrasts the darkest depths of humanity and the bright light of human compassion and bravery. (par. 8)

The design competition for the World Trade Center site memorial reflects well the process by which rhetoric is physically manifested to connect diverse victims and viewers and mediate a common memory. After exploring various memorial spaces and examining what memorial projects said (and what they didn't or couldn't), students began to present their own 9/11 memorial designs. Their assignment (now expanded to include any commemorative project) is appended at the end of this chapter.

Re-Absorbing Our Memorial Saturation: Learning the Syntax of Visual Rhetoric

Shanken rightly claims that a plethora of memorial civic building projects in the wake of World War II turned our memorial landscape into "an invisible and unremarkable part of daily life" (140), but it also produced a public capable of intertextual (mis)readings. Civil rights memorials, such as those in Montgomery or Birmingham, Alabama, can enhance our engagement with Martin Luther King, Jr.'s rhetoric, which conceptually drives the former's design. Likewise, Maya Lin's apolitical memorialization of the Vietnam War in Washington, D.C. illuminates an era's controversies and the literature and film it spawned. Now, high-profile memorial competitions routinely familiarize us with the syntax of visual rhetoric—effective design principles, the construction of identity, the intersection of text and image, etc.—allowing students to theorize on our memorial saturation, a state they may cease to question. When students tackle the complex task of designing a memorial and writing the visual, however, common writing problems materialize in 3-D.

Just as argumentative theses and organization may be lacking in undergraduate essays, student memorial proposals do not always ensure the design is a unified, readable whole. They may opt for bells and whistles over simplicity or clarity and may not always question whether their audience will be able to decipher potentially esoteric symbolism. To demonstrate these pitfalls in advance, the Oklahoma City National Memorial can be used as an interesting case study, for it demonstrates the collision of totalistic memory projects and democratic process through its competing components. Its "Gates of Time," "Rescuer Orchard," "Survivor Tree," "Children's Tile Wall," "Memory Fence" (Figure 3), "Field of Empty Chairs," "Memorial Center," "Reflecting Pool," and "Children's Area" were the result of a broadly composed selection committee, which Edward Linenthal reveals was more democratically than aesthetically motivated (188). This committee, along with designers Hans and Torrey Butzer, created a densely emblematized memoryscape; many of its complex metaphors are comprehensible only through adjacent and lengthy didactic panels. Consider an on-site plaque's explanation of the symbolism behind the Rescuer Orchard:

> The Orchard symbolically "rushes in" from both east and west on the Memorial Grounds toward the Survivor Tree. This placement was selected as a tribute to the Rescue workers who rushed in to help following the disaster. Three tree varieties were selected: Oklahoma Redbud, Amur Maple and Chinese Pistache.

> The Oklahoma Redbud is nearest to the Survivor Tree in honor of the Oklahomans first on the scene.

While the Oklahoma redbud trees with their distinctive heart-shaped leaves make good sense in this iconographic simulation of memory, they lead one to expect a similar metonymic function of the maples and pistaches, which more likely were selected for their colorful leaves, blooms, or fruit. Without this legend, the Rescuer Orchard's rhetoric remains largely illegible.

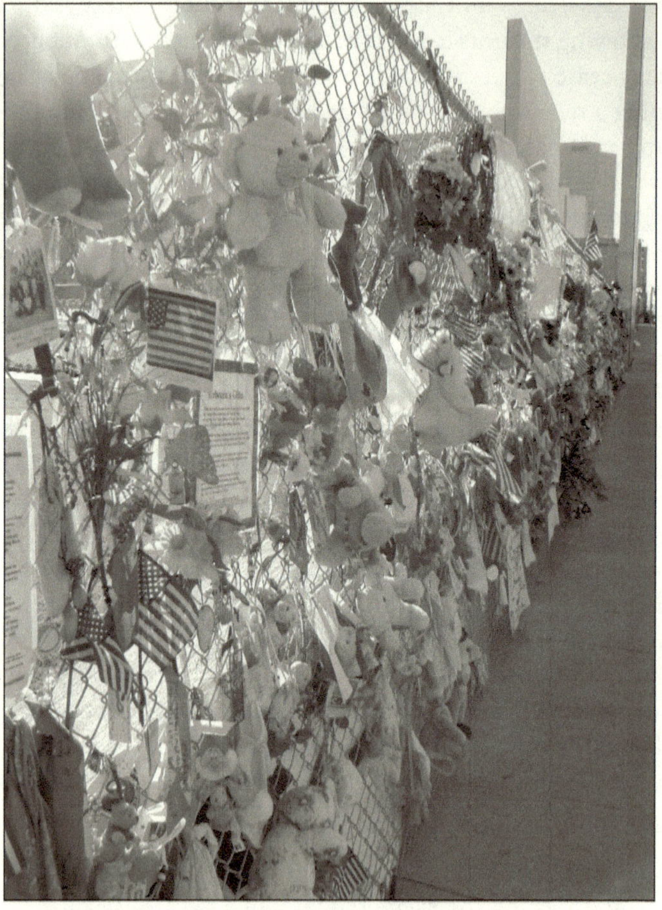

Figure 3. Spontaneous memorials demonstrate the implausibility of monolithic memory projects in democracies. (*Memory Fence, Oklahoma City National Memorial*. 2001. Courtesy of the author.)

Albeit popular and visually compelling, Oklahoma City's memorial serves an example of "the additive form of conventional memorialization after World War II" discussed by Andrew Shanken (142). Although Shanken's phrase describes how a memorial space changed or could be reconceived over time into a "living memorial"—one that serves a utilitarian function, the Oklahoma City National Memorial embodied this additive rhetoric from its inception. It demonstrates the legacy of World War II memorials, which "introduc[ed] an uneasy pluralism into American strategies of memorialization" (Shanken 142). The fusion of designs planned for the new World Trade Center landscape is one more reminder that today's memorials, except perhaps for those in our cemeteries, must serve many constituencies and support diverse needs.

Historical memory is exclusive and culturally biased. Memorials may focus our attention on one group, tragedy, accomplishment, or injustice, thus redirecting us from recognizing or commemorating others. They may even serve as propaganda. As Loewen has said, "Who controls the present controls the landscape. Who controls the landscape controls the future" (197). And history will be rewritten to better suit contemporary agendas. Reflecting upon the Oklahoma City National Memorial, Linenthal worries that it transformed "mass murder into patriotic sacrifice": "its location among the pantheon of national historic sites has engendered what I think of as another insidious preferred narrative, one that situates the bombing within a comforting national narrative of patriotic sacrifice" (234). At its dedication, politicians including President Clinton, compared the disaster site to both Civil War and civil rights battlefields (234)! Similarly, when a monument attempts to be neutral or polysemous, to use Barthes's term, "various techniques are developed intended to *fix* the floating chain of signifieds in such a way as to counter the terror of uncertain signs" (39). For example, Lin's minimalist Vietnam Veterans Memorial (1982)—a reflective, black, low-to-the-ground granite wall whose horizontal format and color problematized for some our nation's demand for personal sacrifice in wars—"reject[ed] the architectural lineage of monuments and the aesthetic codes of previous war memorials" and "refuse[d] to sanction the closure and implied tradition of those structures" (Sturken 51). Hence, critics have sought "anchorage" (Barthes 38 ff.) of its rhetoric by the addition nearby of figurative sculptures, as Erika Doss explains:

> Unlike Lin's design, [Frederick] Hart's superficial sculpture [*Three Fightingmen*] [. . .] uncritically affirms the neo-conservative position that the Vietnam War was an honourable episode in US history. Likewise, sculptor Glenna Goodacre's Vietnam Women's Memorial [,] [. . .] featuring bronze figures of wartime nurses and wounded infantrymen, also stands as a thoroughly right-wing recuperation of the war, sentimentalized as an altruistic, innocent and unfinished American adventure. (65)

In July 2004, yet another memorial was added near the site: a commemorative plaque honoring all veterans who died due to their service in Vietnam—from Agent Orange exposure, post-traumatic stress disorder, and other causes. The memorial cacophony surrounding Lin's austere Wall illustrates that whether or not monuments enshrine grand historical narratives, their very presence may imply omission and the absence of dissenting viewpoints.

Rhetorically or symbolically embedded in every memorial structure, whether large or small, is a thesis, usually highly condensed. A tombstone may literally argue through inscription that the deceased is "beloved" or was a devoted child, spouse, or parent. Its form and placement, however, encapsulates additional arguments: that survivors respect and remember the deceased, that it is personally and/or culturally important to memorialize the dead, that others should take note of this loss. A war memorial commissioned by military veterans may or may not make the claim that the war's cause was just, but will always show to passers-by that the soldiers' personal losses were significant and memorable, their services honorable, and their sacrifices made for a greater good, including those future visitors to the memorial. Uncovering these explicit and implicit arguments in monuments will strengthen the ability of students to recognize and to structure their own rhetoric.

Appendix: Memorial Design Project

Preparation

First, for a vivid example of major design and selection processes at work, watch the Academy Award-winning documentary *Maya Lin: A Strong Clear Vision* (dir. Freida Lee Mock, American Film Foundation,

1994). The film outlines the creation of the Vietnam Veterans Memorial, the Montgomery Civil Rights Memorial, the Yale Women's Table, and the Juniata Peace Chapel, illuminating design considerations and controversies.

Second, do research on memorials whose designs and/or subjects interest you. Before embarking on selecting a 9/11 memorial, the Lower Manhattan Development Corporation visited 19 memorial sites across the nation to analyze their designs and see how they function. (Their PowerPoint slideshow of this research trip is available on the Web; see resources below.) You can also view on the Web the winning World Trade Center memorial design by Michael Arad and Peter Walker, and all the 5,201 submissions entered. This research will make you more fluent in contemporary memorial design and introduce you to standard proposal formats.

Objective

Using your growing knowledge of the language of effective memorials, design and describe a contemporary memorial for any event or person. Justify its location and intended audience, explain what purposes it serves, why it is needed, how it is distinguished from existing memorial projects, and how viewers will interact with it. You may design it from any medium, and it need not be static. The final product you submit should consist of both a written and a visual component.

Your memorial should serve a clear purpose; educate the public and sensitively promote community understanding (the memorial shouldn't polarize one group against another); be appropriate to its location and audience; encourage remembrance, not forgetting; preferably address an overlooked history, people, or event; be unique; and not employ memorial clichés (angels, urns, religious figures, etc.) without justifying their inclusion.

Your proposal should consist of both a well-written description and rationale justifying the need for this memorial (1000+ typed words) and a visual component (a simple sketch, a computer generated image, a model, etc.—images may be simple but shouldn't look hastily produced); clearly explain how visitors will interact with it; provide a rationale for its design; incorporate a comparative analysis of at least one other memorial; cite at least three sources (at least two must be from books) on memorials to support your design; and be formatted and documented according to MLA style.

Website Resources

National Memorial Spaces

http://www.renewnyc.com/memorial/MemorialTripPresentation.ppt

A downloadable PowerPoint presentation examining 19 national memorial spaces, created by the Lower Manhattan Development Corporation as part of their memorial planning process

Memorial Competition Site

http://www.wtcsitememorial.org/submissions.html

The official memorial competition site containing a "Virtual Exhibit of all 5,201 Submissions"

9/11 Manitoba Memorial Design Competition

http://www.mala.net/911_Competition/body_911_competition.html

Provides sample submission guidelines and ideas for visually presenting your proposal

Virtual Museum for Center for Holocaust and Genocide Studies

http://www.chgs.umn.edu/Visual Artistic Resources/visual_artistic_resources.html

University of Minnesota site containing links for public Holocaust memorials near bottom of page

Holocaust Memorials in Hamburg

http://www.rrz.uni-hamburg.de/rz3a035/holoham_welcome.html

Holocaust Memorials in Amsterdam

http://fcit.coedu.usf.edu/holocaust/resource/gallery/amster1.htm

Oklahoma City National Memorial Official Website

http://www.oklahomacitynationalmemorial.org

Tolerance.org

http://www.tolerance.org/pt/index.html
Contains a link to the Virtual Civil Rights Memorial by the Southern Poverty Law Center, modeled on Lin's design

Books

Bogart, Michele H. *Public Sculpture and the Civic Ideal in New York City: 1890–1930.* Chicago: U of Chicago P, 1989.

Doss, Erika. *Spirit Poles and Flying Pigs: Public Art and Cultural Democracy in American Communities.* Washington, DC: Smithsonian, 1995.

Dubow, Neville. *Imaging the Unimaginable: Holocaust Memory in Art and Architecture.* Cape Town: U of Cape Town, 2001.

Gillis, John R. ed. *Commemorations: The Politics of National Identity.* Princeton: Princeton UP, 1994.

Hass, K. A. Carried to the Wall: American Memory and the Vietnam Veterans Memorial. Berkeley: U of California P, 1998.

Linenthal, Edward T. *Preserving Memory: The Struggle to Create America's Holocaust Museum.* New York: Viking, 1995.

—. *Sacred Ground: Americans and Their Battlefields.* Chicago: U of Illinois P, 1993.

Mills, Cynthia, and Pamela H. Simpson, eds. *Monuments to the Lost Cause: Women, Art, and the Landscapes of Southern Memory.* Knoxville: U of Tennessee P, 2003.

Senie, Harriet F. *Contemporary Public Sculpture: Tradition, Transformation, and Controversy.* Oxford: Oxford UP, 1992.

Young, James, ed. *The Art of Memory: Holocaust Memorials in History.* New York: Prestel, 1994.

Acknowledgments

The 2003 Holocaust Literature Seminar through the United States Holocaust Memorial Museum's Center for Advanced Holocaust Studies, as well as Cornell University's 2003 Interdisciplinary Seminar in German Studies, sponsored by Deutscher Akademischer Austausch Dienst, contributed significantly to the research for this article. The insights and hospitality of Erika Doss, Michelle Glaros, Michael Laffey, Dwight Pitcaithley, and Pam West, Director of the National

Park Service's Museum Resource Center, further stimulated the creation of both assignment and article.

Notes

1. As this essay primarily concerns memorial structures, I will generally use *monument* and *memorial* as synonyms. James Young provides clarification, defining "all memory-sites as memorials, the plastic objects within these sites as monuments. A memorial may be a day, a conference, or a space, but it need not be a monument. A monument, on the other hand, is always a kind of memorial" (*Texture* 4).

2. After all, Maya Lin was an undergraduate when she submitted her handwritten winning proposal for the Vietnam Veterans Memorial.

3. Consider Aren Almon-Kok's intense objection to an Oklahoma City memorial statue based on the photograph of fireman Chris Fields cradling her dead daughter Baylee (Linenthal 145–64). Nonetheless, this icon has been translated to other memorials, including the Fallen Fire Fighters' Memorial in Jackson, MS.

4. As described by Loewen, a great number also botch the histories they purport to tell.

Works Cited

Allen, Thomas B. *Offerings at the Wall: Artifacts from the Vietnam Veterans Memorial Collection.* Atlanta: Turner, 1995.

Barthes, Roland. "Rhetoric of the Image." *Image-Music-Text.* Trans. Stephen Heath. New York: Noonday, 1977.

Berger, John, et al. *Ways of Seeing.* New York: Penguin, 1972.

Blair, Carole. "Contemporary U.S. Memorial Sites as Exemplars of Rhetoric's Materiality." *Rhetorical Bodies.* Ed. Jack Selzer and Sharon Crowley. Madison: U of Wisconsin P, 1999: 16–57.

"Distribution of Outdoor Sculpture and Monuments in the United States." *SOS! Self Guide.* 13 April 2004 <http://www.heritagepreservation.org/nic/htdocs/sos/sos2000/selfguide/statis-map.html>.

Doss, Erika. "Death, Art and Memory in the Public Sphere: The Visual and Material Culture of Grief in Contemporary America." *Mortality* 7.1 (2002): 63–82.

Foote, Kenneth E. *Shadowed Ground: America's Landscapes of Violence and Tragedy.* Austin: U of Texas P, 2003.

Hallam, Elizabeth, and Jenny Hockey. *Death, Memory and Material Culture.* Materializing Culture. Oxford: Berg, 2001.

Hartman, Geoffrey H., ed. *Bitburg in Moral and Political Perspective.* Bloomington: Indiana UP, 1986.

Huyssen, Andreas. "Monumental Seduction." *Acts of Memory: Cultural Recall in the Present.* Eds. Mieke Bal, Jonathan Crewe, and Leo Spitzer. Hanover: Dartmouth, 1999: 191–207.

Johnson, Philip C. "War Memorials: What Aesthetic Price Glory?" *Art News* 44 (Sept. 1945): 9–10; 24–25.

Levinson, Sanford. *Written in Stone: Public Monuments in Changing Societies.* Public Planet Books. Durham, NC: Duke UP, 2001.

Linenthal, Edward T. *The Unfinished Bombing: Oklahoma City in American Memory.* Oxford: Oxford UP, 2001.

Loewen, James W. *Lies Across America: What Our Historic Sites Get Wrong.* New York: Touchstone, 2000.

Lower Manhattan Development Corporation. "Memorial Mission Statement and Memorial Program." 2002. 11 Feb. 2005 <http://www.renewnyc.com/Memorial/ memmission.shtml.htm>.

Maya Lin: A Strong Clear Vision. Dir. Freida Lee Mock. Videocassette. American Film Foundation, 1994.

Mayo, James. *War Memorials as Political Landscape: The American Experience and Beyond.* New York: Praeger, 1988.

Pitcaithley, Dwight T. "The American Way of Memory." *CRM (Cultural Resources Management)* 21.11 (1998): 51–52.

Shanken, Andrew. "Planning Memory: Living Memorials in the United States During World War II." *Art Bulletin* 84.1 (Mar. 2002): 130–47.

Stannard, David E. *American Holocaust: The Conquest of the New World.* New York: Oxford UP, 1993.

"Statistics: What is the Profile of America's Collection of Outdoor Sculpture and Monuments?" *SOS! Self Guide.* 1997. 13 April 2004. <http://www.heritagepreservation.org/nic/htdocs/sos/sos2000/selfguide/statistics.html>.

Sturken, Marita. *Tangled Memories: The Vietnam War, The AIDS Epidemic, and the Politics of Remembering.* Berkeley: U of California P, 1997.

Young, James E. *At Memory's Edge: After-Images of the Holocaust in Contemporary Art and Architecture.* New Haven: Yale UP, 2000.

—. The Texture of Memory: Holocaust Memorials and Meaning. New Haven: Yale UP, 1993.

4 Visual Rhetoric for Writing Teachers: Using Documentaries to Develop Student Awareness of Rhetorical Elements

Barbara Worthington and Deborah Rard

In "Dancing with Bigotry: The Poisoning of Racial and Ethnic Identities," Lilia I. Bartolomé and Donaldo P. Macedo write that "more public education is done by the media than by teachers, professors, and anyone else" (66). As teachers of first-year composition, we have developed a method of introducing rhetorical theory that centers on the use of film, a medium that helps our students understand the somewhat bewildering terms of rhetoric.

Students in Our Program

In our program, the goal of writing instruction is to help students think rhetorically by looking at message, purpose, and audience as well as authorial appeals to ethos, logos, and pathos. At California State University, Hayward, an urban university, we have students with native, dialect, and second-language English abilities who come from all parts of society and who differ greatly in terms of age and ethnicity. If we add to these elements their serious lack of preparation for academic writing, we find many students who have inadequate scaffolding for the necessary critical thinking, reading, and writing they will do in college. Students come to the university from a literature-driven curriculum and often find non-fiction text difficult. According to CSU student profiles, nearly half of the first-year students are not prepared to write at a college level. These data are supported by the

2002 California State University Focus on English that states, "40,000 first-time freshmen are tested each year. Of those students enrolling in the fall of 2001, approximately 54 percent demonstrated proficiency in reading and/or writing skills needed to succeed in college level work" (30). Forty-six percent of first-year students required some type of remedial instruction before they could confidently attempt first-year composition courses. Combine these facts with a ten-week quarter system, and it becomes imperative to find methods of instruction that quickly bring students to a level of critical thinking that encompasses the rhetorical skills they require.

In the following chapter we will show how we have used documentary film to develop a rhetorical scaffold for our students that will aid them not only in bridging rhetorical analysis from film to text but also in analyzing all visual and textual messages. To that end, we accompany the film with topical essays and appropriate news articles. Students make connections first through the topics and ultimately through the rhetorical elements they have come to understand. We believe this works for students because, as Ann Marie Seward Barry writes, "we are a nation of watchers rather than discriminating readers, of instant believers rather than reflective, visually aware critics" (2).

Theoretical Framework

In his introduction to *The Rise of Rhetoric and Its Intersections with Contemporary Critical Thought,* Omar Swartz defines rhetoric for today's academic requirements. He writes, "a very simplistic, but useful contemporary definition of rhetoric is that it is the strategic use of language [. . .]. The measurement of persuasion, then, is not its end, but the product itself [. . .]. The measurement of rhetoric, in the new sense of the term, is not success, but competency" (9). Rhetoric and the ability to persuade have moved away from the Socratic ideal of One Truth and toward the contemporary view that the skill of the rhetorician is significant. Swartz implies that this process of argument is grounded in understanding the rhetoric of persuasion, not discovery (9). Students should be fluent in rhetoric to comprehend and converse in the academic dialogue. More than simply identifying the parts of an argument, they should see the intersection and overlay of the various elements to adequately use language as they engage texts, teachers, and other students.

The dichotomy that writing instruction presents—whether it is contained within the traditional paradigm of the university or interacting in an on-going contextual conversation with the greater world—has been intensely discussed in the literature. We do, however, find resonance in John Clifford's assessment of Kenneth Burke's view of the "need to work within, not outside, established discourse conventions" (224). Students must have the power derived from understanding an academic writing based on rhetorical analysis. If they watch an expository documentary such as "Looking for Answers" from PBS's *Frontline* in the post-9/11 American environment, they might be tempted to react with emotional and patriotic fervor and miss the most important information in the film—reasons that explain the deadly attack. As Barry explains, audiences respond first to the emotional impact of visual images before they consider the logical argument. However, if these students have rhetorical tools that encourage dispassionate viewing and analysis of the film, they will begin to question this and other forms of discourse they encounter daily. This skill would echo Clifford's remarks about writing instruction:

> [Burke] does not hope to transcend what some might view as regimented discourse. Instead, he wants to unmask the neutrality of rhetoric, to alert us and our students to the need to be active, critical rhetors, conscious that the struggle that inheres in academic discourse is not merely over neutral academic conventions, but the power, the power to make meaning and interpret experience. (225)

Documentary Film

Documentary film provides an excellent source for composition students' analysis. The genre evolved from early photographers' production of a series of photographs illustrating social conditions or news events. Lewis W. Hine was a pioneer in photographing both topics, including, for example, the living conditions of immigrants in 1930s New York, and the construction of the Empire State Building, with the workers' dizzying acrobatics on the high girders (Newhall 235). Well-known photographers such as Walker Evans and Dorothea Lange participated in the government's Farm Security Administration (FSA) project, where they shot thousands of photographs to publicize the plight of rural America during the Great Depression; and Margaret Bourke-White, among other distinguished photographers, contributed in the documentary genre to *Fortune* and *Life* magazines (Newhall 244–45). The mission of the institutions that published the photos and the artistry of the photographers combined to produce emotional picture stories, sometimes carefully posed. What bias was embedded in the message often went unnoticed.

Out of these picture documentaries came documentary film, its first examples showing news features with voice-over commentaries explaining events that viewers would accept as facts. But these representations of reality were from the beginning, as Bill Nichols writes, "part and parcel of the discursive formations, the language games, and rhetorical stratagems by and through which pleasure and power, ideologies and utopias, subjects and subjectivities receive tangible representation" (10). As a background study for documentary film, Nichols explains that this genre can be analyzed through its four modes of representation: expository, reflexive, observation, and interactive (32).

Recognition of the common areas for bias inherent in each mode can help students in writing rhetorical analyses of documentary film. For instance, according to Nichols, the *expository* mode features a speaker directly addressing the viewer. It "emphasizes the impression of objectivity and of well-substantiated judgment" (35). News feature programs allow the anchor or other known personality to represent authority; however, the speaker may have little expertise on the topic. Furthermore, the producers of the film may have created the documentary to argue for their favored viewpoint without signaling this intent to viewers.

In the *reflexive* mode, the filmmakers themselves appear and comment on the topic, speaking directly to the viewer. Although the message seems less hidden than in the expository mode, its bias is always in question. Many documentaries contain a mixture of techniques, but the expository and the reflexive modes are the closest in form to a written essay.

In the *observation* mode, filmmakers become observers of events and film the story as it unfolds. The product is similar in form to fictional films and at times even creates the events photographed. When the participants are filmed unaware and do not provide permissions or explain their points of view, their motivations are implied by the photographer's skill and intent.

The *interactive* mode juxtaposes action with interviews and commentary from the subjects. A narrator provides coherent exposition to the film. This mode is subject to the weaknesses of the expository and observational modes, and interviews are problematic. For example, who directs the topics and the time allotted to each speaker? Where does the interview take place and how are the interviewees presented? (Nichols 32 ff).

Our students (and many viewers) are typically not aware of the bias of documentary film, but using this genre in classes makes good sense because students are more comfortable with images than with text. Their greater ease with the medium of film over text is explained by Vincent Ruggiero, who writes, "[b]y the age of eighteen the average teenager has spent 11,000 hours in the classroom and 22,000 hours in front of the television set. He or she has done perhaps 13,000 school lessons yet has watched more than 750,000 commercials" (5). Taking advantage of the students' eagerness to view films over reading texts allows us to find a negotiated area of instruction that will bring the students to an academic level. And it is important to select documentaries that will strike a note with students, films such as the *Frontline* productions "The Marketing of Cool" or "The Jesus Factor." Each film combines elements of the expository, observational, and interactive modes. Michael Moore's *Bowling for Columbine* and *Fahrenheit 9/11* are also strong candidates for the composition classroom; however, Moore's films are much more in the interactive and reflexive modes, with some critics feeling that Moore dominates his films too much to let them stand alone as unbiased views of their topics. All of these films have a strong emotional appeal. Students must look beyond the emotions to carefully evaluate the message and must be aware of the narrators, producers, and production locations, which all contribute to each film's strengths or weaknesses.

Another benefit of using film in this instructional process is that students can more quickly articulate their personal experiences as they connect to the classroom discussions. For example, in *Contemporary Perspectives on Rhetoric,* Foss, Foss, and Trapp discuss how the author bell hooks "proposes two primary ways in which marginalized rhetors can use rhetoric to challenge and transform the ideology of domination—critique and invention" (275). These authors point out that hooks would have those who are from the marginal groups in education interact rhetorically by critiquing traditional perspectives. "In this rhetorical option, hooks explicates and recommends the production or invention of nondominating cultural forms" (279). In other words, the students who predominate in our own multicultural classes are better served by access to the friendlier medium of film. As we discovered through a lesson with the *48 Hours* film, *Binge*, students from different perspectives within society saw the rhetorical process of the film with very different eyes.

Evolution of the Film Unit

But how did we come to use this process of rhetorical instruction in the first place? As with many composition programs, ours has shifted to a primarily critical thinking pedagogy, with emphasis placed on reading and writing arguments through processes. One common form of argument instruction uses Stephen Toulmin's terms of analysis (claim, reason, warrant, backing, grounds, qualifier), the rhetorical triangle (writer, message, reader), and the Aristotelian concepts of ethos, pathos, and logos. These, we feel, are rhetorical elements that students must learn before they can write effective academic arguments.

First-year composition students are frequently intimidated by what they perceive as new and somewhat provocative terms, as we discovered when assigning a first essay for the quarter. We asked the students to summarize and analyze an essay on alcohol consumption and abuse, expecting them to identify the author's thesis and main ideas while responding to the author's viewpoint and method of presentation. We assumed the assignment was fairly simple, but it was a serious challenge for the students. Although we provided a handout with specific rhetorical questions, some students were completely committed to their own perspectives based upon their experiences and personal convictions and could not recognize perspectives that seemed to challenge their own beliefs. Conversely, other students quickly accepted the author's opinion while abandoning their own critical thinking process, failing to engage in any questioning process. Even the most ambitious student focused primarily on the topic or subject matter but was incapable of recognizing more subtle rhetorical elements. We needed better methods for getting students to engage rhetorically with the material as we had only ten weeks in which to help the students reach a higher ability of rhetorical analysis.

We determined that the *48 Hours* documentary *Binge* might be an efficient means to the desired end. The film uses the expository and interactive modes, and there are similarities between it and the essay that had presented such a challenge to the students. As we introduced the film as a critical thinking tool, the students would become familiar with the rudimentary elements of argument, helping to clarify unfamiliar terms such as ethos, logos, and pathos. Students then could move beyond reacting to the subject of the film and text toward an appreciation of the rhetoric as a method for meaningful discussion. The various correspondents, one for each segment of the film, would interview students, teachers, and parents and also comment on what the audience sees, providing appropriate and pertinent statistics and facts. Unlike a persuasive essay that uses an accumulation of data or anecdotes to persuade the reader, the filmmaker can layer all of the information over the visual images that frequently reinforce the pathos of the presentation. Students could begin to see how exposition frames the facts so that they can appeal to the emotions of the reader/viewer. As students began to isolate each rhetorical element, they could also see these same elements at work in the essay.

Steps in the Assignment Process

Breaking this learning process into manageable steps in the beginning allows students to acquire a rhetorical awareness while maintaining a level of comfort. To this end, we have designed and implemented a unit for teaching rhetoric that uses film in combination with non-fiction reading. Encountering two genres can help students analyze text rhetorically, and, ultimately, to employ a keener rhetorical awareness in their writing. After introducing the film to the class, we saw that it would be necessary for us to provide specific viewing guidelines. Experience had taught us that most students tended to be passive viewers. Before watching the program, we asked the students to begin the critical thinking process by engaging in a "pre-viewing" writing assignment. They first debated the merits of changing the legal drinking age to 18 years by freewriting two paragraphs, the first a "believing" statement in support of this change and the second a "doubting" statement that supported the opposite view. Students now had a vested interest in analyzing the film's message. We then separated the students into five groups and distributed colored handouts that contained five specific rhetorical tasks (See "Brainstorming Session" in the appendix). Each student was required to focus on the task that corresponded to one particular group assignment. In previous film viewings, we had required students to take notes during a film, but we found that if the program captured their attention, they frequently abandoned the task, or they attempted to take extensive notes, most of which had little rhetorical value. More often, however, students disengaged because they found the tasks too demanding. By focusing on one task and being able to rely upon two or three group members to help collect the same information, students found they could handle the amount of information in the film.

Identifying the Target Audience

The first group attempted to identify the program's target audience. While viewing each segment, they also considered who might be omitted from the discussion and how the various segments might change if the target audience changed. By identifying a specific type of audience, the students began to draw parallels between visual and written messages and suggest how each might affect certain audiences.

Identifying Logos

Acting as the class statisticians, the second group identified the logos by noting various types of statistical data and considered the effects that such numbers might have on the viewer. This task helped the students question the validity of written evidence as they evaluated data.

Identifying Pathos

The third group considered ways that the producers used emotional appeal, or pathos, to influence the viewers. After noting several examples from each segment, they discussed their own reaction. By identifying emotional examples from the various segments, they began to recognize the persuasive power of these appeals as part of their viewing, reading, and writing experience.

Identifying Ethos

The fourth group, in an effort to understand ethos, listed examples of professional people that the commentators interviewed in each segment. They also considered ways that such interviews might influence an audience. This task provided an opportunity for discussion of the significance of ethical appeals and how professional opinions also influence written arguments.

Identifying Purpose

Finally, group five's exercise introduced key Toulmin terms as the students focused on the program's primary purpose. They identified the producers' claims and any counterarguments. After the students received their assignments, they were finally ready to enjoy an active viewing experience.

Synopsis of Film

Binge is produced by Susan Zinisky and introduced by Dan Rather. The correspondents Susan Spencer, Harold Dow, Bill Lagatuta, Erin Moriarty, and Troy Roberts each present one segment of the film, interviewing high school and college students, educators, parents, and law enforcement personnel. The use of young people gives the film a stronger ethos for young viewers, such as our students, while the interviews of parents and other responsible adults appeal to the more typical audience of *48 Hours.* The "Target Audience" segment by Bill Lagattuta shows a recovering alcoholic traveling across New Mexico to demonstrate the persuasive methods of beer makers in marketing their products. It is a chance for our students to see the on-screen students echoing, in effect, what we are doing in our classroom.

As the students discussed the emotional aspects of the *Binge* presentation, they noted the use of the various rhetorical tools to carry the producers' message. The first segment emphasizes the tragic effects of binge drinking by reporting the deaths of two college students from midwestern universities. Each scene is described in graphic detail accompanied by photographs of the teens and tearful interviews with family members and friends. In another segment, the tone is lighter but no less serious as the *48 Hour*s team film the wild antics of teens who abuse alcohol in Tijuana, Mexico, and follow the campaign of a concerned parent who voluntarily patrols the border to report underaged drinkers to authorities. The team then visits a small town to applaud the success of a young girl who manages to recover from alcohol addiction by attending Sobriety High, a school designed to meet the needs of young alcohol abusers. In the fourth segment, the producers emphasize the impact that commercial advertisements have on children by following a recovering alcoholic as he visits schools to educate students and help them to avoid the lure of alcohol advertisements through early intervention. The program ends somberly with a middle-aged African-American male charged with drunk-driving and ultimately killing a bright young college student. In an emotion-packed courtroom scene, the prosecuting attorney graphically describes the fiery crash and the devastation that it caused the victim's family. Before the defendant receives his sentence, the victim's mother offers a tearful appeal for justice accompanied by a moving video of key moments in her son's life.

Reaction of the Students

As the class prepared for group discussions by compiling their information and sharing their ideas, the spirit of collaboration was impressive, as was their eagerness. A spokesperson for each group presented information to the class. The initial findings were fairly predictable. Several students concluded that the target audience included "all viewers" and all statistics and professional references were "great" and affected "everyone" who viewed the program. Such vague responses gradually led to incorporating rhetorical language into the discussion. We suggested that the students qualify their responses by avoiding generalizations and encouraged them to question their original assumptions by delving more deeply into the social implications in the presentation. Our hope was that students would comprehend the layers of social implications in this film, and they were, in fact, coming up against their own emotional reactions to the class and race undercurrents of the film.

The class agreed that the producers' goal was to educate teens about the perils of binge drinking and alcohol abuse. We prompted the class to apply deeper critical thinking to the rhetorical aspects of the presentation by considering possible social implications and carefully analyzing the producers' method for convincing their audience. Several of the class statisticians reviewed their findings and concluded that the producers presented numerous statistics but the viewer was unaware of the source of the information or how the data were collected. Also, the many doctors, psychologists, college administrators, and other professionals that appeared in each segment were impressive, but once again such appearances were more likely to appeal to a white, middle-class viewer. One student also pointed out that such evidence might appear to logically support the producers' claim; however, the film was actually using subtle forms of emotional appeal to influence viewers. This student's observation led to a lively debate regarding the media in general and its ability to influence viewers by triggering a range of emotional responses through the use of statistics (logos) and experts (ethos).

While the students agreed that each part of the film undeniably used strong emotional appeal to reinforce the message that binge drinking can kill, it was the last segment that triggered an intense debate, resulting in the highest level of critical thinking for the class and the instructors as well. The rhetorical skills the students learned became most apparent. In her essay "Teaching Resistance: The Racial Politics of Mass Media," bell hooks pinpoints an unease similar to what students began to feel, possibly subconsciously at first, as they viewed the *48 Hours* film. She states, "[f]or the most part television and movies depict a world where blacks and whites co-exist in harmony although the subtext is clear; this harmony is maintained because no one really moves from the location white supremacy allocates to them on the race-sex hierarchy" (246). We saw students begin to demonstrate such critical insight on this point.

Some students noted that, with the exception of the final segment, most individuals in the program were young, fairly affluent white teens who engaged in binge drinking. The class then concluded that the target audience could be teens in general, but was most likely educated, middle-class white parents who were concerned about their children's drinking habits. This led to a more in-depth debate regarding viewers who might feel marginalized or left out of the program's discussion. One older African-American student pointed out that she found it disturbing that her teenaged sons were not represented in the program. As a mother and educated professional, she should have been able to relate to the program's message, but after viewing each segment, she sensed that the producers implicitly omitted people of color and less educated viewers. The student's candid comments caused some discomfort, but most were encouraged by her frank assessment as the discussion moved from surface responses to more critical analysis. A rather intense debate followed on the significance of the program's concluding scene. Finally, one student who had been relatively quiet during the discussion pointed out that this scene introduced serious issues related not only to race but also to class. He reminded the class that the defendant appeared to be poor, and after attempting to defend himself, appeared somewhat illiterate compared to the victim's family. He further asserted that the producers purposely used that particular case as an emotional ploy to move their target audience. Surprisingly, the African-American mother and several other black students felt little sympathy for the defendant, claiming that race and class issues were insignificant, while several young white students felt the last segment bordered on racism and should have been omitted. Other members of the class agreed that the last segment came dangerously close to perpetuating the media's negative image of black males in general.

As the discussion continued, we were amazed at the responses. Students not only were actively engaged in the discussion, but many appeared comfortable using rhetorical terms that were initially quite foreign to them. We suggested that they continue their discussion in writing by describing ways that the producers used rhetorical appeals, especially in the last segment. The students were able to transfer these skills to other assignments and could now view their world with a more critical eye, reflecting an awareness of subtle forces within both obvious and implied messages.

This is a gateway skill to a lifetime of critically thinking, viewing, reading, and writing the subtleties of cultural assumptions. Indeed, we have gone on to use this approach to media critique with other combinations of readings and documentaries. For example, Michael Moore's *Bowling for Columbine* can be used in conjunction with some of the many excellent readings on media influence or gun control, including "Columbine: Whose Fault Is It?" by Marilyn Manson. The film is expository and reflexive, with Moore demonstrating his thesis that America is a culture obsessed with fear and pointing the finger of blame when young people are violent. He uses humor, interviews, and his own experience as a gun owner, comparing it to the experience of people in other countries, such as Canada, where residents have the guns but not the fear. Manson's essay echoes Moore's presentation and is all the more surprising because it lays out Manson's refutation that he and other "rebel" musicians are not responsible for the actions of a few. Another excellent source, previously mentioned, for timely and appropriate documentaries is the PBS program *Frontline*. This PBS news program has a sound reputation of investigative reporting, using highly credible interviews and knowledgeable interviewers. Their mode is both expository and interactive. Almost all of these videos are now available for $20–$30 at the program websites, such as PBS.org.

Also, many are also available in larger library collections, allowing instructors free access to this varied and valuable resource.

Appendix

Visual Rhetoric Lesson Handouts and Assignments

Essay Assignment #1: Summary/Rhetorical Analysis Essay

The purpose of this essay is to create an argument based on an analysis of a written textual argument. You will write a summary/strong response essay that includes: (a) a summary (approximately 150–250 words) and (b) a strong response to that reading. As you formulate your own response, consider both the author's ideas (subject matter) and rhetorical choices concerning audience, purpose, genre, and style.

General Assignment

Write a three- to four-page summary/rhetorical analysis essay in response to "The Drug that Pretends It Isn't" by Anne Quindlen. Your summary should be approximately 150 words. The remainder of your essay should be devoted to a rhetorical analysis of Quindlen's argument. Remember that you are not only responding to what the author discusses but how she presents her argument. Remember to follow the guidelines presented in chapters one to three and chapter six in Allyn and Bacon. Also, there is a model available on page 124.

Organization/Format

Your first paragraph should consist of a summary that includes the author's thesis and main points (the author's thesis may be stated or implied). Your summary should lead to your own thesis, which should include your purpose for writing the essay and what you will discuss. The remainder of your essay should be devoted to your analysis of the author's text. To avoid plagiarism, remember to enclose all original language in quotes. Direct quotes and the author's original ideas must be followed by a parenthetical citation. All drafts should be neatly typed and double-spaced in MLA format (we will discuss formatting in class). Each page of your essay should include your last name and the page number in the upper-right corner of the page. Your heading should be double-spaced and should appear in the upper-left corner of the first page.

Brainstorming Session

Carefully read the essay selection and respond to the following guide questions:

Author's Thesis/Claim: What is the author's *main* purpose for writing this essay? Remember that the author's thesis may be openly stated (explicit) or implied (implicit). What reasons does the author offer to support the main claim?

Audience: Who is the target audience? What individuals or groups are omitted from the author's discussion? How might the essay change if the author's target audience changed?

Evidence/Support: What evidence does the author use to support his or her assumptions? Consider different types of support (examples, statistics, case studies, etc.). How are you affected as a reader?

Emotional Appeal (pathos): Does the author use emotion to persuade the reader? If so, find examples in the text. How were you personally affected by such appeals?

Professional Sources (ethos): What sources does your author use to strengthen his or her ethos or credibility? Provide specific examples. How do such references influence you as the reader? How might such references influence the target audience?

Author's Tone/ Overall Balance: How would you describe the tone of the essay (angry? concerned?). Is the author convincing? Explain why. Does the author include opposing points of view? If so, how does this affect the overall argument?

Writing a Strong Response: Strategic Questions

—How is the author trying to change his or her intended readers' view of the topic?

—What rhetorical strategies does the author use to influence the intended audience?

—How has the author changed your view of this topic? What do you have to give up or lose in order to change your view? What do you gain? How do the author's rhetorical strategies affect you?

—What is excluded from this author's text? All writers must select certain details to include in their texts and others to exclude. By looking at what is omitted from a text, you can often ascertain something about the author's value system.

—How can you question this author's data, evidence, and supporting arguments? If you are not persuaded by the author's data and evidence, why not? What is missing? What can be called into question?

—How can you question the author's values, beliefs, and assumptions, both stated and unstated?

—How can you use this author's ideas for your own purposes? What new insights have you gained? What new ways of thinking can you apply to another context?

Group Activity for 48 Hours' *Binge*

—Review the "believe/doubt" paragraphs that you completed in response to the following prompt:

> "The legal age for consuming alcoholic beverages should be lowered to 18."

—Watch the 48 Hours presentation *Binge.*

—As you view the presentation, focus on your assigned question (#_____).

—Meet with fellow group members to discuss your question. (Note: questions are color coded by group and question number.)

—Select a scribe to record your responses and a spokesperson to share your results with the class.

—Journal Entry: How did the presentation influence your thinking about teen alcohol consumption or about alcohol consumption in general?

Group Assignments

Group One: Who is the target audience? Who was omitted from the discussion? How might the presentation change if the target audience changed?

Group Two: What statistics do the producers include in the 48 Hours presentation? What possible effect might statistics have on the viewer?

Group Three: How do the producers use emotional appeal to influence the audience? Consider at least three examples. How were you personally affected?

Group Four: What professional people do the producers interview or refer to in the presentation? How might such interviews and references influence the audience?

Group Five: What is the primary purpose or the presentation? What might be the producers' positions on under-age drinking? Do the producers present opposing points of view? If so, provide examples.

Works Cited

Barry, Ann Marie Seward. *Visual Intelligence: Perception, Image, and Manipulation in Visual Communication.* Albany: State U of New York, 1997.

Bartolomé, Lilia I., and Donaldo P. Macedo. "Dancing with Bigotry: The Poisoning of Racial and Ethnic Identities." *Critical Ethnicity: Countering the Waves of Identity Politics.* Ed. Robert H. Tai and Mary L. Kenyatta. New York: Rowman and Littlefield, 1999. 65–91.

Binge. 48 Hours. Host Dan Rather. CBS News. New York, 23 Jan. 1999.

Bowling for Columbine. Dir. Michael Moore. 2002. DVD. Columbia Tristar, 2004.

Clifford, John. "A Burkean Critique of Composition Praxis." *Pedagogy Is Politics: Literary Theory and Critical Teaching.* Ed. Maria-Regina Kecht. Urbana: U of Illinois P, 1992. 215–29.

Fahrenheit 9/11. Dir. Michael Moore. DVD MGM, 2004.

Foss, Sonja K., Karen A. Foss, and Robert Trapp. *Contemporary Perspectives on Rhetoric,* 3rd ed. Prospect Heights, Il: Waveland, 2002.

Harrington, Mary Kay, et al. *The California State University Focus on English.* 2002. 15 Jan. 2004 <http://www.calstate.edu/as/EPT.PDF>.

hooks, bell. "Teaching Resistance: The Racial Politics of Mass Media." *Readings in Contemporary Rhetoric.* Ed. Karen A. Foss, Sonja K. Foss, Robert Trapp. Prospect Heights, Il: Waveland, 2001. 243–49.

The Jesus Factor. Frontline. Narr. Will Lymon. Written, Produced, and Directed by Raney Aronson. PBS. WGBH, Boston. 29 April 2004.

"Looking for Answers." *Frontline.* Correspondent Lowell Bergman. Written and Produced by Martin Smith and Lowell Bergmen. PBS and *The New York Times,* New York. 9 Oct. 2001.

Manson, Marilyn. "Columbine: Whose Fault Is It?" 2003. 9 Feb. 2005 <http://www.gothcentral.com/gothcentral/testfiles/manson.asp>.

"The Merchants of Cool." Frontline. Narr. Douglas Rushkoff. Prod. Barak Goodman and Rachel Dretzin. PBS. WGBH, Boston. 27 Feb. 2001.

Newhall, Beaumont. *The History of Photography.* New York: The Museum of Modern Art, 1997.

Nichols, Bill. *Representing Reality: Issues and Concepts in Documentary.* Bloomington: Indiana UP, 1991.

Quindlen, Anna. "The Drug That Pretends It Isn't." *Newsweek.* 10 April 2000: 88.

Ramage, John D., John C. Bean, and June Johnson. *Allyn and Bacon Guide to Writing.* 3rd ed. New York: Longman, 2003.

Ruggiero, Vincent Ryan. *Beyond Feelings: A Guide to Critical Thinking,* 7th ed. Boston: McGraw Hill, 2004.

Swartz, Omar. *The Rise of Rhetoric and Its Intersections with Contemporary Critical Thought.* Boulder: Westview, 1998.

5 Envisioning Justice: Racial Metaphors, Political Movements, and Critical Pedagogy

C. Richard King

The media campaigns of People for the Ethical Treatment of Animals (PETA) simultaneously delight and repulse me. As a vegetarian I sympathize with the group's ambitions and enjoy the reactions it evokes from readers alienated from the conditions and processes that bring food to their tables. But I find myself troubled by the group's tactics, such as its reliance on scantily clad young models, who, like *NYPD Blue* star Charlotte Ross, "would rather show their buns than wear fur" (PETA), to promote its vision. These distinct feelings collided in the summer of 2003 when PETA unveiled "Holocaust on a Plate." In press releases, a traveling installation, and on the World Wide Web, the group made explicit comparisons between the treatment of animals in factory farms and the experience of Jews in Nazi Germany. Most striking are the digital images online (<www.masskilling.com/>). A slideshow cycles through a sequence of visual comparisons: dead human bodies gathered together in a chaotic stack beside a heap of animal carcasses; then a group of emaciated, bare-chested Jews in their death camp barracks alongside a group of chickens at a factory farm. Together, they juxtapose animals and people, suggesting that the routine processing of animals for human consumption, considered acceptable if not desirable by most in North America, is equivalent to the systematic killing of more than six million Jews, gypsies, gays and lesbians, and other Europeans. It was hard for me to look at these images and not be moved. They raised questions that continue to haunt me: Why make such comparisons? Does the argument advanced belittle the historic realities of the Holocaust? Is this a sign of creative critique or critical exhaustion?

If "Holocaust on a Plate" were an isolated event, we might label it a media stunt cynically designed to garner attention; however, glancing around struggles over culture, history, and power, we see that the use of racial metaphors has become commonplace. Increasingly, movements for social justice invoke the experiences, position, or treatment of racial groups to call attention to inequity, oppression, and mistreatment. Racial analogies, juxtapositions, and metaphors allow such groups to speak to a broad audience about pain, power, and praxis. Powerful images often anchor their arguments about injustice, animating their efforts to effect change. My understanding of racial analogies used to advance social justice echoes my reaction to PETA's media campaigns. Indeed, as I argue in this paper, the racial metaphors employed by animal rights advocates and opponents of anti-Indian imagery in athletics offend and inspire; they claim injury and victimization even as they potentially injure and victimize others; they critique through shock but may have little lasting significance. In short, their visual rhetoric is conflicted and context dependent: at once, it scripts great political theater with powerful evocative force, exposing both the contradictions and limitations of critical thought in post-civil rights America.

With this argument in mind, I have designed a module on racial metaphors, social identities, and cultural critique for a senior-level writing intensive course: Social Justice in American Culture. In this chapter, I set out a theoretical framework for approaching the visual rhetoric of race and then outline the specific assignment that highlights the social and pedagogical significance of racial metaphors in struggles against anti-Indian imagery in athletics and in movements to advance animal rights. I endeavor to make sense of the use of racialized images and experiences, namely slavery and the Holocaust, in efforts to end Native American mascots and factory farming. On the one hand, I strive to unpack the imagery through which activists draw parallels between slavery and the treatment of animals or between imagery of Jews in Nazi Germany and imagery of indigenous peoples in contemporary American popular culture. On the other hand, I outline ways in which the examination of metaphors can and should be brought into the classroom to talk about visuality, race, and cultural politics. I conclude by discussing the implications of studying visual rhetoric, for the formulation of antiracist pedagogy.

Theoretical Background

Perhaps the most fundamental thing I hope my students take away from my class is an understanding of racialization, an appreciation that race is not natural or inert, but a sociohistorical construct, emergent through specific relations and conditions of possibility. How do people do race? What do they do with race? How do they give life to specific identities, communities, and hierarchies through racialized practices? How and why do these change over time? In other words, race moves. It moves peoples. It is made active by individuals and institutions as they make claims about history, identity, rights, and responsibility. Individuals use race to make arguments about self and society. And racial images are among a culture's most powerful signifying practices.

I come at racial representation and visual rhetoric from what might be best described as a cultural studies framework, deeply influenced by poststructural approaches. I have found Stuart Hall's work on representation to be especially helpful for addressing the complexities of images. Hall reminds us that symbols are not flat or simple vehicles through which individuals easily or intentionally exchange messages with one another. Instead, symbols are active, put into action by individuals and institutions as they encode and decode cultural texts (Figure 1).

For me, this approach means first recognizing that visual communication hinges on signing, on linking together culturally meaningful symbols to convey messages to audiences. In unpacking these signs, we are not interested in the intention of the author, but what individually and collectively the signs say, claim, or insist. As socially situated practices governed by accepted forms and norms, visual representation, moreover, is deeply implicated with history and power. An analysis of this representation requires an understanding of context and connections: Where did the image come from? What other images is it referencing? How is the image supposed to be understood; that is, what are the preferred readings? What grand ideas about personhood, difference, gender, freedom, and the like does it invoke? Moreover, this analysis entails thinking about effects: How do an image's claims resonate with broader political struggles? How does the image shape understandings of self and society? How does it reconfigure affect and action? All representations are texts that are encoded and decoded by multiple constituencies and toward multiple ends: like all languages representations can be read.

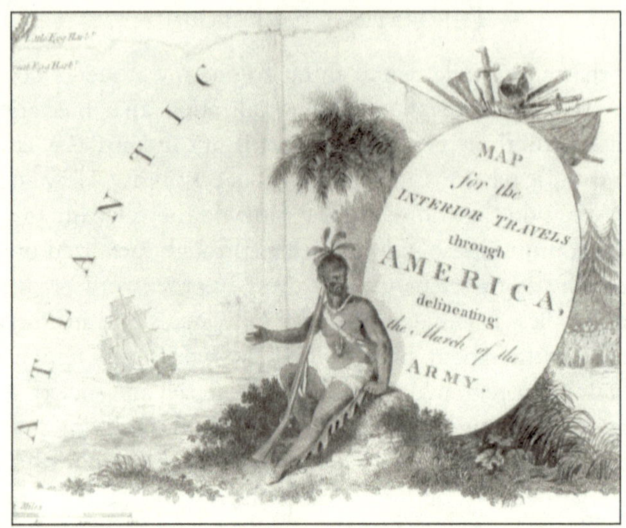

Figure 1a.

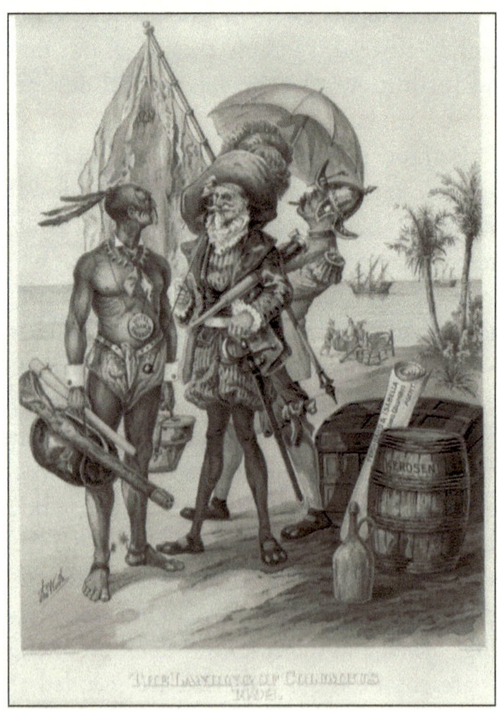

Figure 1b.

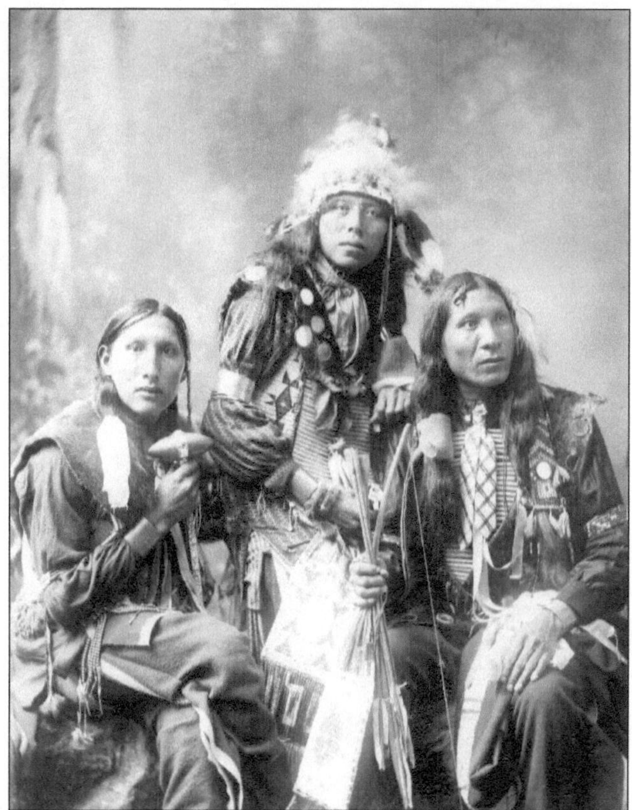

Figure 1c.

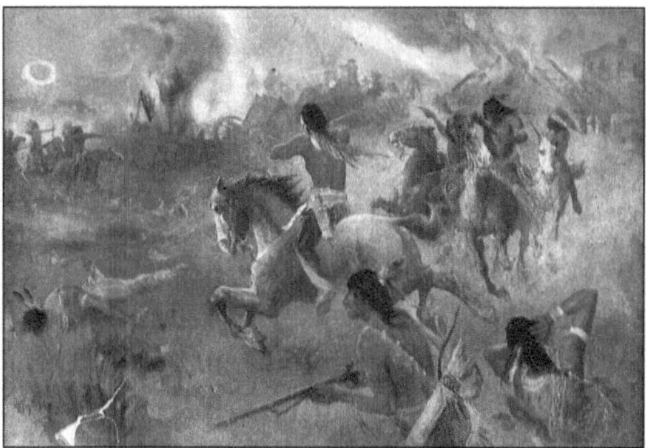

Figure 1d.

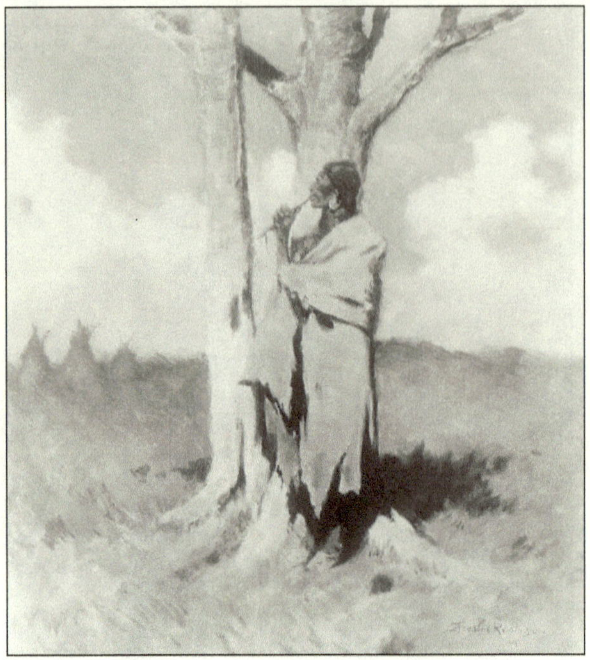

Figure 1e.

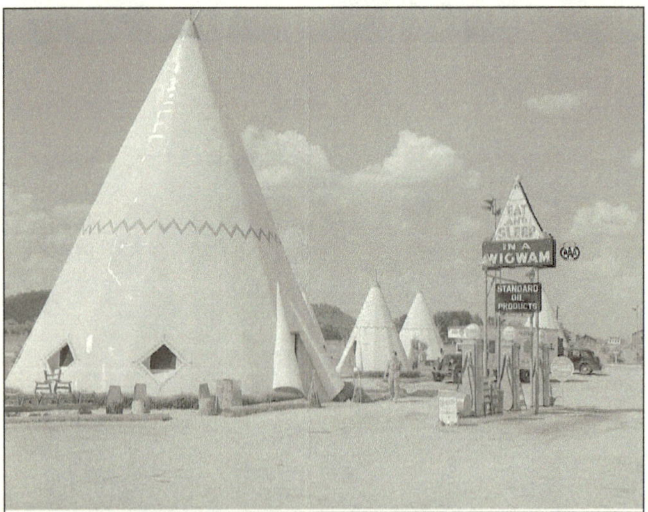

Figure 1f.

Figure 1. A range of approaches to representing Native Americans. Images of racial groups are saturated with historical meaning and can be powerful shapers of viewers and culture. (a) A warrior on the cartouche for *Map for the Interior Travels through America, Delineating the March of the Army*. T. Conder. 1789; (b) *The landing of Columbus*. Artist unknown. 1893; (c) left to right: Poor Elk, Shout For, Eagle Shirt. Artist unknown. 1899; (d) *The Siege of New Ulm, Minnesota*. Henry August Schwabe. 1902; (e) *The Love Call*. Frederick Remington. 1909; (f) *Cabins imitating the Indian teepee for tourists along the highway south of Bardstown, Kentucky*. Marion Post Wolcott. 1940. (All images used by permission of the Library of Congress Prints and Photographs Division, Washington, D.C.)

In thinking about racial images and/as visual rhetoric, I like to walk students through three types of signifying practices to clarify the ways in which individuals and institutions make arguments with symbols. Stereotyping is an obvious starting point. For ease, I often use white supremacist cartoons. These black-and-white line drawings render foundational arguments in simple and pure terms. For instance, I commonly use an image from *White Aryan Resistance* that depicts a white male with an overly large mosquito that has a human head (with stereotypically Jewish features) sucking his blood. The image reveals how many white supremacists and nationalists think about and distinguish between whiteness and Jewishness. Although easy to dismiss as extremist, it exposes a worldview that asserts that Jews are not white and, more, that they wish to injure, if not destroy, racially pure, non-Jewish, Aryan whites. In this context, the image makes clear claims about the character of Jews (parasites who take from whites) and whites (victimized and bled dry) and, by extension, the world order. After establishing this foundation, I like to move beyond stereotypes and extremist discourse and examine the way that my home institution markets itself. The images on its pamphlets and materials sent prospective students and on its Web pages conform to a pattern—typically three people: one white, one female, one person of color. In contrast to life as lived on campus, the university is saying not only is our school diverse, but we embrace each other's differences. Importantly, racial difference is being marshaled to make an argument about us, not them. Finally, as the rest of the chapter explores, it is crucial that students not only grasp conventional, overt racism and stereotyping and the sanitized racialization associated with color blindness and multiculturalism, but that they also appreciate how analogies, juxtapositions, borrowings, and substitutions—what I have here dubbed *racial metaphors*—work to make claims and advance arguments about race through visual representation.

Racial Metaphors Module

In this section, I outline a sequence of exercises that together encourage reflection on the use of racial metaphors with social justice movements and, in turn, critical thinking about the implications of this visual rhetoric. I have endeavored to construct a flexible framework, allowing teachers to incorporate those elements that fit best with their teaching goals and philosophies. Although I have envisioned this as a two-week segment of my social justice course, it is conceivable that the module could be condensed to one week or even a single class period and that it could be refocused for use in a number of Native American studies classes, as well as courses concerned with social movements and the rhetoric of race. Before detailing the individual components of the module, I briefly flesh out the objectives and context of the module.

The Class

This module was designed for a senior level, writing-intensive course that attracts a large number of non-majors fulfilling a capstone requirement. The students write a series of brief position papers on social justice and American culture and undertake a term project in which they *do* social justice (for example, organize a teach-in on the prison industrial complex or stage a protest against sweatshops). The course accepts that injustice is paradoxically central to the American experience and that injustice is almost invariably linked with difference; moreover, it forces students not simply to lament or to critique systems of inequity, but rather to promote efforts to question, counter, and eradicate them. The course seeks, moreover, to illuminate the cultural dimension of (in)justice by emphasizing multiple axes of oppression, competing forms of resistance, and signifying practices. Readings, discussions, and activities are meant not to champion any one approach to social justice; rather, they seek to facilitate critical reflection on the advantages, implications, limitations, and dilemmas of these approaches. The racial metaphors module falls in the latter half of the semester. It follows initial discussions of the key elements of power, injustice, and stratification—namely oppression, domination, and privilege, as outlined by Iris Marion Young, and consideration of a series of strategies for achieving social justice: resistance, empowerment, redress, reconciliation, abolition, and redistribution (Brooks, Charlton).

Background Knowledge

Familiarity with a number of substantive areas will enhance a teacher's capacity to facilitate critical inquiry into the place of racial metaphors in the visual rhetoric of contemporary social justice movements. These areas include (a) an awareness of the histories of indigenous peoples in North America and their resulting marginalization and invisibility (Allen, Nagel), (b) debates over the uniqueness of the *Shoah,* compared with other genocides, and the controversies over the Holocaust industry (Finkelstein, Flanzbaum), (c) an appreciation of the changing socio-political landscape in the United States, especially new social movements and the importance of media and spectacle (Giroux, Kellner), (d) the uses of race in popular culture and political discourse (Bonilla-Silva, McPhail, Santa Ana), and (e) the ongoing struggles over Native American mascots (Churchill, King and Springwood, Spindel).

Preliminary Activities

Before launching into the visual rhetoric of racialization, teachers may wish to have students learn more about the controversy over Native American mascots and/or process the ideas they carry around with them about mascots, American Indians, and race. Show Jay Rosenstein's *In Whose Honor?;* or have them read an introduction to the subject (Churchill; King and Springwood; Spindel). Even more productive, ask students to write down every word, image, or sentiment that comes to mind when thinking about Native American mascots, such as the Cleveland Indians' Chief Wahoo, Chief Illiniwek of the University of Illinois, or the Washington Redskins. Then, whether or not you incorporate other material, identify and interpret, as a class, those themes and patterns emerging from the exercise.

Exercise 1: Racialization

To sharpen students' skills, before turning to the use of racial metaphors, you might encourage them to work through the rhetoric central to the creation and defense of anti-Indian imagery in athletics. This task can be accomplished through two distinct interpretive exercises.

First, teach students how to read a mascot. Either outside of class or in as part of a group discussion, have students view a number of distinct images of mascots, past and present. Identify what they have in common, what they say about Indians, what they might tell us about the myths of frontier, what stereotypes they draw upon (for instance, the defiant Plains warrior). Make connections by talking about Hollywood westerns, Outkast's performance at the 2005 Grammy Awards, comic books, the game of cowboys and Indians, and advertising. Then, perhaps, compare and contrast mascots that represent animals and ethnic groups. How is using names such as "Vikings" or "Fighting Irish" (un)like using names such as the "Redskins," "Savages," and "Fighting Illini"? What do these differences suggest about how Americans have understood race and ethnicity? What do they tell us about racial identity, privilege, and relations in the contemporary United States?

For a fully-rounded understanding of the use of racial metaphors, study the defense of anti-imagery in sports. *In Whose Honor?* surely is helpful here, but to stay visually focused, have students go to <http://www.honorthechief.org/history.html> or <http://www.aztecwarriorfoundation.org/index.php>. How have these booster sites used photographs of school mascots to evoke a sense of honor, respect, and dignity? Why have they done so?

Exercise 2: Name Calling

Having traced the context and the conventional visual rhetoric, now push students to grapple with racial metaphors. Begin with the simplest uses of juxtaposition—editorial cartoons. Thom Little Moon, for instance, in 1995 encouraged readers of *Indian Country Today* to reflect on the appropriateness of Chief Wahoo, mascot of the Cleveland Indians (<http://aistm.org/ cartoonwhichone.jpg>). Two children ponder the question, "Which one is the mascot?" as they look at four portraits: one of Chief Wahoo is labeled *Indians*; the second, dubbed *Blacks*, features the same smiling visage, darkened with a large Afro and pick comb in place of Wahoo's feather; the third, named *Jews*, renders a smiling Hasidic complete with yarmulke; and the final image, labeled *Chinese*, has slanted eyes and a goatee. What is Little Moon suggesting about race and racism? Why are there no Black mascots? Is it problematic for Little Moon to recycle derogatory images of other groups to help people understand what is wrong with mascots?

Exercise 3: Jim Crow and the Nazis

Clem Ironwing and Matthew Richter have fashioned a more elaborate and arguably more charged series of racial analogies (<http://www.iwchildren.org>). First, they juxtapose a photo of school children in blackface in 1941 with an image of elementary students dressed as Indians in 2000. Next, they present parade imagery, contrasting an image of children marching in a Nazi preschool primer and a photo of children marching in support of their primary school symbol, "the papooses." Next, referencing a billboard welcoming folks to Redskin country, Ironwing and Richter make an explicit comparison between Redskin Country and Hymie Country. Against this background, noting that both Jews and Indians were killed for practicing their religions, they present a pair of disturbing photos, one of Nazi soldiers, poised above a pit, methodically killing Jews, the other of a burial trench at Wounded Knee in which U.S. soldiers prepare to place Indian corpses. Finally, these authors probe the rich similarities between Native Americans and African-Americans, noting in word and image the lynching of African-Americans in the South and the equally arbitrary killing of Native Americans at Wounded Knee. The anonymous African-American youth lynched by a laughing crowd of southern men poignantly contrasts with the frozen body of Bigfoot after the massacre at Wounded Knee. Throughout, unsettling questions are posed: is the NAACP racist? Is there a difference between the legacies of African slaves imported to the Americas and the indigenous peoples? Have African-Americans forgotten the racist past?

What do Ironwing and Richter convey about the experiences of indigenous peoples, Jews, and African-Americans? How do they say it? Are these images compelling? Why? Must they use such harsh imagery? Why? Are the images effective?

I have found that students are troubled by the use of racial metaphors at this site. On the one hand, they are moved by images, many of which they have never seen. Disturbed by these intertwined and parallel histories, they have very visceral reactions to the photographs and the arguments they advance. On the other hand, they often resist the implications. They will not allow themselves to internalize the experience of Native Americans as comparable to the Holocaust. To be sure, some, perhaps many, will admit that what happened to indigenous peoples was horrific, tragic, but they do not want to think of these histories as cut from the same cloth. The shock of seeing and learning the world anew does not prompt them to embrace fully a history rewritten in light of itself.

Exercise 4: A Comparative Example

Animal rights activists have also found racial metaphors to be useful in their effort to educate the public about the effects of factory farming and meat consumption. At the start of this chapter, I described PETA's "Holocaust on a Plate" campaign. Marjorie Spiegel makes a similar rhetorical move, drawing parallels between the treatment of animals in industrial agriculture and that of blacks under slavery. She sprinkles her text with paired images meant to underscore the equivalence of the experience of animals and slaves: a photo of cattle branding juxtaposed with a painting of the branding of slaves; an advertisement for a shock collar for a dog counterposed with a sketch of a slave in an iron collar; a cutaway of a slave ship showing the crowded conditions aside a photo of a silo type egg factory; and so on. Like Ironwing and Richter's Web page, both PETA's campaign and Spiegel's tract draw parallels between the experiences and oppression of two distinct groups, but push beyond the bounds of speciesism. In fact, animal rights activists, in common with the PETA Web page, trade on the moral authority of recognized crimes against humanity. What is the difference between using racial metaphors to talk about another racial group and using them to talk about animals? When animal rights activists borrow from Jews and African-Americans, do they dilute the meaning of their historical experience, blur the contours of the identity, or undermine the significance of genocide as a legal and moral construct?

Exercise 5: An Unneeded Complication: Metaphors Used by White Supremacists

If teachers really want to challenge students and complicate their thinking about visual rhetoric and racial metaphors, they should include the ways in which white supremacists trade on the notions of holocaust and ethnic cleansing. Students can be sent to websites such as <http://www.whiteextinction.com>. After viewing the introductory montage at the former or viewing the artwork on the latter, they can reflect on what it means for anti-Semitic, overtly racist groups to assert that as members of the dominant racial group they face systematic elimination at the hands of the state. Push students, moreover, to contrast how it might be different for historically marginalized and oppressed peoples to use such racial analogies.

Interpretive Essay

I ask that students write a brief interpretive essay (three to five pages in length; it can be longer, of course) addressing the uses of racial analogy, comparison, and juxtaposition in contemporary social movements. Students should focus on what the metaphors argue about indigenous animal rights and how they assemble these arguments. Students should take a position on the effectiveness, limitations, and implications of such visual rhetoric. If appropriate, they should contrast animal rights, struggles against mascots, and/or white nationalism (see appendix).

Significance

What do I want my students to get out of this? First, I want them to understand the workings of visual rhetoric, the claims made and arguments advanced, and the big picture painted by the increasing use of racial metaphors.

Racial metaphors work (to the extent that they do) precisely because comparing Indianness (or animalness) with Blackness, Jewishness, and so on, borrows power, claims moral authority, and secures visibility from these already-marked categories of identity, experience, and oppression. They denaturalize accepted relations, categories, and sentiments. As such, this rhetorical strategy seeks to interrupt, forcing readers to pause and reflect for a moment, to see falsity, and ideally to find themselves compelled to change the world. It encourages the recognition of everyday forms of oppression.

Ironically, to establish injuries, rights, and visibility through juxtaposition, activists and their allies simultaneously reiterate stereotypes and (particularly in the case of the Holocaust) diminish the experiences of others. It is troubling that the critical strategies deployed to demonstrate the inappropriateness and hurtful effects of Native American mascots and factory farms pivot around ugly images and ideas about other marginalized groups and often recycle shallow images of past horrors in decontextualized ways.

Importantly, these struggles against racist iconography also say something important about racial politics. To problematize factory farming and anti-Indian imagery, and literally enunciate the issue and its implications, critics and activists rely on a visual language of injury and victimization. In the case of animal rights, advocates ironically seek to secure greater rights for animals by speaking for them in terms that accentuate their innocence, defenselessness, and arguable dependence. And although trauma (caused by others) may well describe the Native American experience, making trauma the central lens through which to see history anew eclipses, effaces, and literally negates indigenous survival, creativity, solidarity, and other key values. Casting Native Americans as victims traps them within a single condition, simplifying complex histories, diverse cultures, and human experience; it literally dehumanizes them like other stereotypical images (like the Indian alcoholic or the defiant warrior) do. Attentive instructors can counter these difficulties in three ways: (1) they can offer a fuller, more rounded rendering of Native America; (2) they can push students to question the implications of speaking for others; and (3) they can encourage students to discuss the implications of victimization for social movements and those on whose behalf they seek justice.

Moreover, all of the uses of racial metaphors explored through these exercises point to shifting cultural politics. The protests against mascots emerge from the resurgence of cultural sovereignty in Indian Country (Nagel); however, the reliance on racial analogies departs from standard idioms of indigenous rights, specifically treaties and tradition. Animal rights, in turn, pushes the language of rights and the notion of personhood beyond the human, unsettling accepted relations between culture and nature, humanity and wilderness. And white nationalist uses of racial analogy exposes the cynical, if not paranoid, reasoning of privilege under siege in the post-civil rights era.

The prevalence of racial analogy in arguments against Native American mascots and in support of animal rights and even white nationalism mirrors a pervasive crisis in critical thought (both vernacular and academic). In the absence of critical distance, the unifying metanarratives of modernity (such as progress, truth, civilization), or the assured rhetoric of the Civil Rights Movement, racial analogies pivot on hyperbole and superficial contrasts at worst, substituting allusions for analysis, image for introspection, style for substance.

Conclusion

I have outlined one way to work through the visual rhetoric of race and racialization in the classroom. I have advocated a critical pedagogy that is rooted in the traditions of cultural studies, poststructuralism, and semiotics and that can encourage learning about how racial claims are made and how teachers might begin to unmake them. Specifically, I have detailed a module of activities that afford teachers and students an opportunity not to unpack visual rhetoric, but to connect the cultural work of racial metaphors to a broader social context.

Practical applications of this essay include a fuller understanding of how individuals and institutions use images of race to claim rights, identity, and equality and the shape of a critical, antiracist pedagogy devoted to interrogating the significance of racialization in the contemporary United States.

I hope that exploring the ways in which individuals and institutions use racial metaphors, analogies, and juxtapositions will convince teachers interested in visual rhetoric of the necessity of antiracist pedagogy, and those dedicated to antiracist work of the importance of engaging visual rhetoric. An antiracist pedagogy seeks to expose the intersections of signification, power, and race. First, teaching against racism means teaching about the articulations of visuality and racialization, equipping students with the tools to recognize, engage, and challenge the centrality of visual regimes in the formulation of racial identities, ideologies, and hierarchies. Second, antiracist teaching must be rooted in a pedagogy that is about more than difference or even stereotypes, a pedagogy that directs its attention toward the disruption of white supremacy as a structured field of vision no less than system of economic, political, and social relations. Third, the approach must be comparative, stressing ways in which visual rhetoric differentially racializes human communities, social problems, identities, possibilities, pleasures, and privileges. Finally, antiracist pedagogy can be most effective when it teaches and passionately joins key conflicts of the day.

Appendix: Position Paper

We have addressed the use of racial analogy, comparison, and juxtaposition in contemporary social movements. We have, specifically, directed attention to the visual rhetoric used in struggles for indigenous sovereignty, animal rights, and white nationalism. For this assignment, you will offer an interpretation of the uses and implications of racial metaphors. At root, I want you to formulate an argument, grounded in the readings and class discussion, about visual rhetoric in the pursuit of justice and empowerment, synthesizing what you have learned in support of your position.

Select *one* of the following prompts.

1. Respond to the following statement, taking a position for or against it. "Racial metaphors are effective ways to call attention to social injustice, forcing individuals and institutions to pause, reflect, and change their beliefs and behaviors."

2. Respond to the following statement, taking a position for or against it. "Although racial metaphors seem to empower marginalized groups, granting them voice and visibility, in fact, the visual rhetoric employed by proponents of indigenous and animal rights disempower them, casting them as victims."

3. Respond to the following statement, taking a position for or against it. "The invocation of the Holocaust to advance animal rights or white nationalism is offensive, demeaning the memory of those who were murdered while silencing survivors."

4. None of the above. If none of these possibilities spark your imagination or another problem preoccupies you, feel free to pursue it. Students who choose this option should discuss their selection with me in advance.

Do not feel confined by these ideas; they are starting points. The key is to write clearly, logically, and creatively, and to support your claims effectively.

Papers must be three to five pages in length and should conform to standard stylistic constraints (typed, double spaced, legible, etc.). Moreover, papers should incorporate the readings, citing sources, and providing a bibliography. Papers will be evaluated for clarity, cohesiveness, logical development, creativity, argument, evidence, and adherence to these guidelines.

Works Cited

Allen, Chadwick. *Blood Narrative: Indigenous Identity in American Indian and Maori Literary and Activist Texts.* Durham: Duke UP, 2002.

Aztec Warrior Foundation. 31 Jan. 2005 <http://www.aztecwarriorfoundation.org/index.php>.

Bonilla-Silva, Eduardo. *Racism Without Racists: Color-Blind Racism and the Persistence of Racial Inequality in the United States.* Lanham: Rowman and Littlefield, 2003.

Brooks, Roy L., ed. *When Sorry Isn't Enough.* New York: New York UP, 1999.

Charlton, James I. *Nothing About Us Without Us: Disability, Oppression, and Empowerment.* Berkeley: U of California P, 1998.

Churchill, Ward. "Let's Spread the Fun Around." *Indians Are Us? Culture and Genocide in Native North America.* Monroe: Common Courage P., 1994. 65–72.

Finkelstein, Norman G. *The Holocaust Industry: Reflection on the Exploitation of Jewish Suffering.* New York: Verso, 2000.

Flanzbaum, Hilene, ed. *The Americanization of the Holocaust.* Baltimore: Johns Hopkins UP, 1999.

Giroux, Henry A. *Impure Acts: The Practical Politics of Cultural Studies.* New York: Routledge, 2000.

Hall, Stuart, ed. *Representation: Cultural Representations and Signifying Practices.* Thousand Oaks: Sage, 1997.

Honor the Chief. 31 Jan. 2005 <http://www.honorthechief.org>.

Ironwing, Clem and Matthew Ritcher. "American Holocaust." 31 Jan. 2005 <http://www.iwchildren.org>.

Kellner, Douglas. *Media Culture: Cultural Studies, Identity, and Politics Between the Modern and the Postmodern.* New York: Routledge, 1995.

King, C. Richard and Charles F. Springwood, eds. *Team Spirits: Essays on the History and Significance of Native American Mascots.* Lincoln: U of Nebraska P, 2001.

Little Moon, Thom. "Which One Is the Mascot?" Editorial Cartoon. *Indian Country Today.* 1995. 5 Feb. 2005 <http://aistm.org/cartoonwhichone.jpg>.

McPhail, Mark L. *The Rhetoric of Racism Revisited.* Lanham: Rowman and Littlefield, 2002.

Nagel, Joanne. *American Indian Ethnic Renewal: Red Power and the Resurgence of Identity and Culture.* Oxford: Oxford UP, 1997.

People for the Ethical Treatment of Animals. "Fur Is Dead. *NYPD Blue's* Charlotte Ross: 'Wearing Fur is a Serious Offense.'" 31 Jan. 2005 <http://www.furisdead.com/feat-ross.asp>.

People for the Ethical Treatment of Animals. "Meet Your Meat." 31 Jan. 2005 <http://www.masskilling.com>.

Rosenstein, Jay. *In Whose Honor? American Indian Mascots in Sports.* Hohokus NJ: New Day Films, 1996.

Santa Ana, Otto. *Brown Tide Rising: Metaphors of Latinos in Contemporary American Public Discourse.* Austin: U of Texas P, 2002.

Spiegel, Marjorie. *The Dreaded Comparison: Human and Animal Slavery,* 2nd ed. New York: Mirror Books, 1989

Spindel, Carol. *Dancing at Halftime: Sports and the Controversy over American Indian Mascots.* New York: New York UP, 2000.

White Extinction. 31 Jan. 2005 <http://www.whiteextinction.com>.

Young, Iris Marion. *Justice and the Politics of Difference.* Princeton: Princeton UP, 1990.

6 Seeing the Unspeakable: Emmett Till and American Terrorism

Jane Davis

"I think the picture in *Jet* magazine showing Emmett Till's mutilation was probably the greatest media product in the last forty or fifty years," Congressman Charles Diggs explains in *Eyes on the Prize* (Williams 49). The story and photographs of the murdered youth, which galvanized the slowly evolving Civil Rights Movement in the 1950s, remain in the consciousnesses of many who lived through the times. Likewise, images of terrorism, bigotry, racial stereotyping, deprivation of rights, trauma, and grief haunt the post-9/11 world. The media broadcast images of gruesome violence: planes slamming into the World Trade Center; people jumping from the Towers to certain death rather than be burned alive; beheadings, viewable on the Internet; Iraqi children burned severely and languishing in understaffed hospitals as a result of the U.S. government's "preemptive war"; faces of dead American soldiers, many having only begun adulthood, broadcast "in memoriam" on national news programs; Iraqi prisoners dehumanized by Americans who have joined a mission to bring democracy and safety to a country they know little about; corpses barely recognizable in streets most Americans have never seen, except on television. Did the *fin de siècle* usher in a global reign of terror? What remnants of the past can illuminate the cultural cycle of hatred and trauma and how to combat it?

Our guide to answer these questions is Emmett Till. His story provides an entryway to examine that particular form of American terrorism known as lynching; the nature and impact of racial stereotypes; the power of visuals as well as what may be termed *word pictures* to perpetuate or combat bigotry; and the need for educational institutions to open the window on the past so that we can learn from it in order to improve the present and the future.

This essay examines aspects of the historical, societal, theoretical, and pedagogical issues which are manifested in the murder of Emmett Till and its aftermath. Anne Moody recounts in *Coming of Age in Mississippi* how hearing of Emmett's murder introduced into her young life the fear and hatred of whites who could kill another teenager. Moody describes the dread that she and her peers, as well as other blacks, felt when acknowledging that they might become victims of such shocking violence. My own interest in the event was sparked when, as a child, I experienced the horror of seeing a reprint of the *Jet* photographs. While viewing *Eyes on the Prize* two decades later, I became convinced of the need for more people to know about this murder. I have shown the video and discussed the event in writing classes and have heard my students of various races use the video as a framework for reflecting honestly on past and present race relations. Visual media have had a tremendous impact on me as a person and educator, as well as on my students, and nowhere more so than in the retelling of Emmett's story and in the analysis of what that story has to say to us, today, about terror and compassion. His continued relevance is evident in the fact that in June 2007, after hearings that included the subcommittee on Crime, Terrorism and Homeland Security, the House of Representatives passed the Emmett Till Unsolved Civil Rights Crime Act by a vote of 422 to 2. Main provisions of the Act are that it

> [d]irects the Attorney General to designate a Deputy Chief in the Criminal Section of the Civil Rights Division of the Department of Justice, [m]akes the Deputy Chief responsible for investigating and prosecuting violations of criminal civil rights statues in which the alleged violation occurred before January 1, 1970 and resulted in death [. . . and] [a]uthorizes the Attorney General to award grants to state or local law enforcement agencies for the investigation and prosecution of such cases. (washingtonwatch.com)

You did not give your life for nothing, Emmett Till.

The Media as an Aid to Civil Rights

2007 marked the 200th anniversary of the end of the transatlantic slave trade. 2004 marked the fiftieth anniversary of the landmark Supreme

Court case on desegregation, Brown v. the Board of Education. 2005 marked an occasion less well known, but one that is part of the cultural memory of many African-Americans: The murder of fourteen-year-old Emmett Till, which occurred in August of 1955. James Baldwin once said that the Birmingham church bombing was segregationists' answer to the March on Washington. It may be said that the murder of Emmett Till was segregationists' answer to Brown v. the Board of Education. In light of the fact that Emmett was murdered for whistling at a white woman, it is important to note the sexualized hysteria that was a traditional part of segregationist thought. An Alabama state senator of the time, Walter C. Givhan, voiced this ideology succinctly, saying that the real purpose of the NAACP's fight for school desegregation in Brown v. the Board of Education was "to open the bedroom doors of our white women to Negro men" (Williams 38). And the event might have been largely ignored if not for the horrifying close-up of Emmett's face in his open casket, a picture that made visual the brutality of racism to many Americans. The event itself was violent and grotesque; but the picture summed up the hatred and dehumanization the Civil Rights Movement was combating and shed light on the consciousness that was capable of producing such violence. It has been widely accepted that pictures of the violence of segregationists—especially on television, but also those in magazines—greatly advanced the Civil Rights Movement by bringing a visual knowledge of Southern brutality into homes across America. Children arrested for protesting, people fire-hosed and chased by dogs, clubbed by police, and called racial epithets by whites all were brought into living rooms by the mass media.

David J. Garrow's Pulitzer Prize-winning biography of Martin Luther King, *Bearing the Cross,* recalls the power of the media to aid the Civil Rights Movement, in an episode describing how a white racist ironically spurred more support for the Montgomery Bus Boycott by denouncing it on television. Montgomery Police Commissioner Clyde Sellers went on local television to criticize the planned boycott. As a result, the television coverage reached more blacks than organizers and supporters had been able to. Consequently, "the organizers were overjoyed at the unwitting assistance the whites were giving them" (19–20). The Civil Rights Movement is proof that seeing injustice, rather than simply knowing of it, can mobilize resistance.

A contemporary development also makes evident the importance of gaining insights into the Civil Rights Movement through a visual medium. Montgomery, Alabama County Chief Deputy Derrick Cunningham recently found in a sheriff's department storage room a box containing mug shots, ranging in date from 1948 to 1965, of civil rights activists. Two of these photographs were of a youthful Martin Luther King and Rosa Parks, dated February 22, 1956, when they were arrested during the Montgomery Bus Boycott. As Kyle Wingfield of the Associated Press reported, "The mug shot of King depicts the intense determination he relied on to spearhead the civil rights movement" (10A). Dressed in suits and each showing a serene demeanor, King and Parks appear poised to stare down the barriers to civil rights, even at their own personal cost. Horace Huntley, Director of the Oral History Project at the Birmingham Civil Rights Institute stated, "I think this is a tremendous find. It gives us a window into the past that we absolutely would not see otherwise" (10A). The fact that the books containing the mug shots are labeled by race and gender (e.g., King is in a book labeled "Negro male") indicates a segregationist system that certainly must have made the tracking of the civil rights endeavors of black activists straightforward for white law enforcement (10A).

The existence of this "one of a kind time capsule" is important in several ways (10A). As Cunningham, a black man, says of the documents, they reflect the sacrifices made in the fight for equal rights. He states simply, "A lot of these people paved the way for us to ride around and be deputies. They stood up for the rights of people sitting on the bus. They stood up for the rights of people to get jobs" (10A). Poignantly, King's ultimate sacrifice is marked on the 1956 photograph, which someone pulled out of the files to scrawl sloppily across the top in large print, "DEAD," on the top left side, followed by "4-4-68" on the right (10A). (Exactly who did this and why would be an intriguing reflection on the times. Was it a racist ignorantly noting his feeling of triumph? Someone simply making note of an historical event?) In any case, such images join the case and the photographs of the murdered Emmett Till to teach us a lesson not only about race relations but also about the condition of human relations and human rights. These lessons are timeless reminders of our own better and worse natures.

The Story of Emmett Till

In the summer of 1955, Emmett Till's mother, Mamie, sent Emmett from their home in Chicago to spend part of the summer with his grandfather, Mose Wright, in Money, Mississippi. One day during this visit, Emmett was talking with other youngsters his age and showing them pictures of his classmates. He jokingly said that one of the white girls was his girlfriend. His cousin recalled that one of the other boys said that Emmett probably wouldn't have the nerve to speak to the white woman who was working in the grocery store they were playing near. Emmett took up the dare, and whistled and said "Bye, baby" to her. One can imagine the adolescent bravado of the Northern youngster playing at challenging one of the ultimate taboos of the South—flirting with a white woman—to show his bravery to his friends. In a rational world, this incident would have been forgotten. But "reckless eyeballing"—a black male's flirting with or showing any (even feigned) sexual interest in a white woman—was an action punishable by death in the Old South (Figure 1). It was, as the teenager would find out, grounds for lynching. The woman's husband, Roy Bryant, was out of town when Till whistled at her; three days after the event, Bryant and his brother-in-law, J.W. Milam, went to Mose Wright's house and demanded to take the boy with them, ignoring Wright's pleas that they not take Emmett away but punish him, if they insisted, at the house. They threatened to kill Wright if he tried to stop them (Williams 42). The situation was hopeless. Emmett was taken off into the night, beaten and pistol whipped for hours, and, finally, shot in the head and thrown into the river.

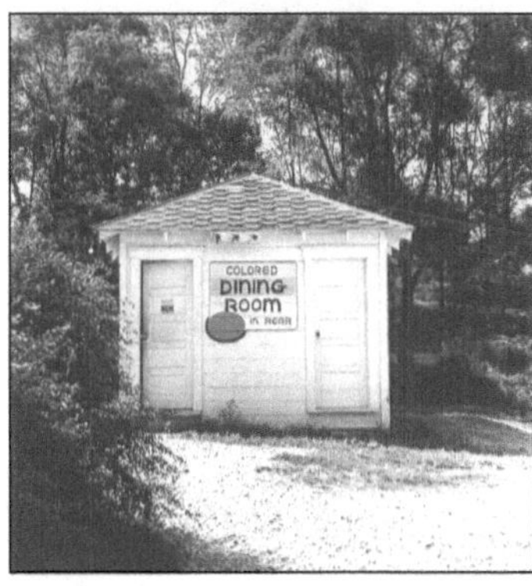

Figure 1a.

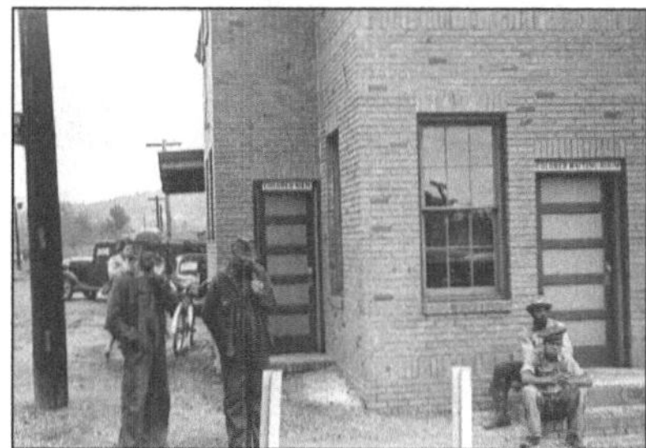

Figure 1b.

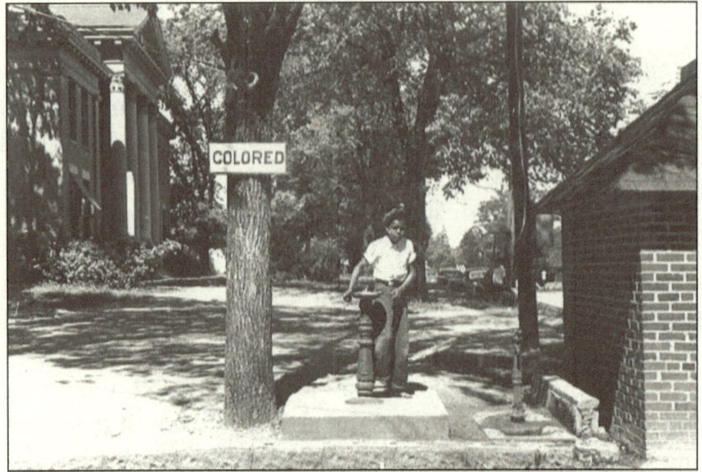

Figure 1c.

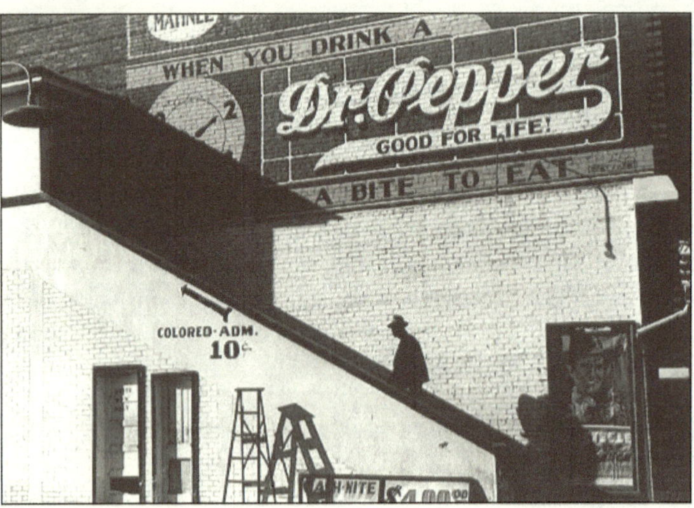

Figure 1d.

Figure 1. At the age of fourteen, on a visit to Mississippi from his hometown of Chicago, Emmett Till discovered the Old South. (a) *A rest stop for Greyhound bus passengers on the way from Louisville, Kentucky to Nashville, with separate accommodations for colored passengers*. Esther Bubley. 1943; (b) *A railroad station*. John Vachon. 1938; (c) *A drinking fountain on the county courthouse lawn*. John Vachon. 1938; (d) *Negro man enter-*

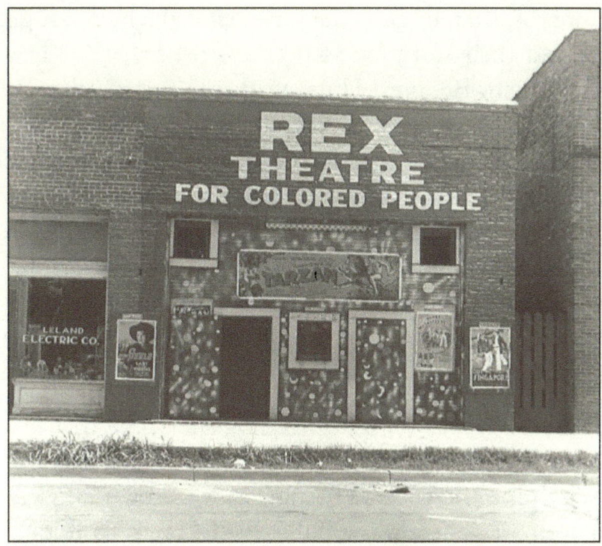

Figure 1e.

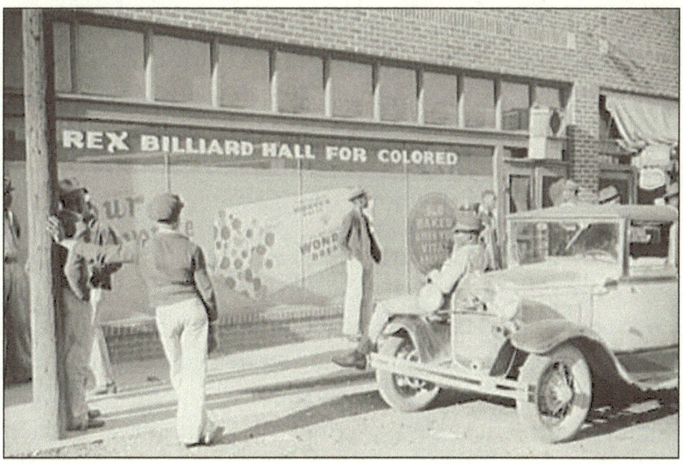

Figure 1f.

ing movie theater by "Colored" entrance. Marion Post Wolcott. 1939; (e) *The Rex Theater for colored people.* Dorothea Lange. 1937; *Beale Street, Memphis, Tennessee.* Marion Post Wolcott. 1939 (?). (All images used by permission of the Library of Congress Prints and Photographs Division, Washington, D.C.)

Two months after an all-white jury found the men not guilty, the murderers told their story for $4,000 to *Look* magazine in an interview with William Bradford Huie. Without remorse, they recounted murdering Emmett, allegedly because he said he would have sex with white women. (As Williams points out, it is highly doubtful that a beaten and frightened teenager, one with a mild stutter at that, would be so bold as to challenge the men after hours of beatings so brutal that some people heard his screams from a distance and afterwards saw blood in the men's car [38]). The inadequacy of even the most powerful words to describe what happened to Emmett Till is evident in the following account:

> Till's body was found three days later. The barbed-wire holding the cotton-gin fan around his neck [to weigh him down] had become snagged on a tangled river root. There was a bullet in the boy's skull, one eye was gouged out, and his forehead was crushed on one side. [. . .] The tortured, distended body pulled from the river became the focus of attention. It was so badly mangled that Mose Wright could identify the boy only by an initialed ring. The sheriff wanted to bury the decomposing body quickly. But [. . .] [Emmett's mother] demanded that the corpse be sent back to Chicago. The sheriff's office reluctantly agreed, but had the mortician sign an order that the casket not be opened. (Williams 43)

Southern law enforcement (pillars of racism in the Old South) knew that it was not in their best interest for Emmett's body to be seen. They were right. The sight helped to expose and thus to overturn the legalized inhumanity of the segregationist South.

Emmett's mother had the casket opened on its arrival at the train station in Chicago. At the sight of his disfigured body, she cried, "Lord, take my soul," and had to be taken from the station in a wheelchair (Williams 44). She later said poignantly to reporters: "Have you ever sent a loved son on vacation and had him returned to you in a pine box, so horribly battered and water-logged that someone needs to tell you that this sickening sight is your son—lynched?" (Williams 44). Thousands of people came to the public viewing of Emmett Till in his casket; many in the crowd fainted at the sight. Mamie Till Bradley's determination to let "the world see what they did to my boy" had an outcome far beyond what she could have expected; the sight of Emmett Till is iconic in capturing the manner and consequences of that method of American terrorism known as lynching and in inspiring greater interest in the fight for civil rights (Williams 44). As Williams points out, the black weekly magazine *Jet*'s decision to run the photographs of Emmett Till's horrifically disfigured face mobilized interest in civil rights in an extraordinary way. Though the NAACP had been struggling to pay its debts even after the Brown v. the Board of Education triumph, after publication of the picture, contributions poured into the NAACP fund dedicated to aiding victims of racist attacks (44). Furthermore, Congressman Charles Diggs of Michigan, who attended the trial of the murderers, stated that the pictures of Emmett Till in his coffin were of monumental importance because of the outrage they provoked and that both the photographs and the trial itself angered many people across the nation (Williams 49). Filmmaker Stanley Nelson, whose documentary *The Murder of Emmett Till* is an exhaustive examination of the case, best sums up the significance of the image of the dead teenager:

> Emmett Till's body, the condition of his body [. . .] horrified people. And I think because Mamie Till was in Chicago [and not in the South], she could get the word out. I mean, people had been lynched for 100 years, but in the Emmett Till case, people could actually see it with their own eyes. They could see the brutality that they had [. . .] just heard about. [. . .]
>
> And then, at his funeral, 50,000 people actually went by and saw his body, and then *Jet* magazine published the pictures, and those pictures went around the world. (Online Newshour 3)

David D. Perlmutter raises questions about whether photojournalism sometimes evokes "a form of ritual response ('I was shocked') that requires no commensurate action" (5). However, the image of Emmett Till's brutalized corpse is an example of how a photograph can evoke outrage that can impact societal attitudes and public policy (precisely because it makes real how unacceptable the suffering of others is. (Although the photographs of Emmett are widely available online, we were not granted rights to reprint them here.)

Emmett Till and the Lethal Nature of Racial Stereotypes

What did the racists *see* when they looked at Emmett Till, having come to murder him? Certainly, they did not see an adolescent who had just turned fourteen. They clearly saw Emmett as a lust-crazed black threat to "the purity of white womanhood," as the time-worn phrase goes, or to borrow a phrase from Fanon, as "a terrifying penis" (177). A useful definition of such racial stereotypes is that they are "cognitive distortions" intended to simplify racial data and thus leave one clinging to an illusion of control in a world of complex beings who have been reduced to predictable types (Pettigrew 7). Moreover, to paraphrase Barbara Christian on white stereotypes of Blacks, "Black people don't look like that. But if you look at them [the stereotypes] long enough, they [blacks] start to look like that" (Riggs). Christian means that people can internalize these twisted images of blacks which, as Marlon Riggs makes evident in his Emmy Award-winning documentary *Ethnic Notions,* were created to justify white supremacy and thus to deny racial equality. (For the purposes of understanding the usefulness of visual rhetoric in order to deconstruct racist thought, it is interesting to note that "[t]he term 'stereotype,' taken from printing, was introduced by Walter Lippmann. He thought of stereotypes as 'pictures in our heads' that were acquired culturally rather than through personal experience" [Pettigrew 7]). Such essentialist racial stereotyping provides a brutal and pathological logic to the murderers' aforementioned rationale for killing Emmett: as Lyle, the killer in Baldwin's play, *Blues for Mister Charlie* (which was inspired by the Emmett Till case), explains his murder of a black man: "I had to kill him. I'm a white man!" (157). Here, we have obviously moved from race as a biological fact to race as a psychological and sociological construct: at best, a neurotic one; at worst, a lethal one. When members of a dominant group have already internalized racist stereotypes and thus erased a people's identity and worth as human beings, this psychological act of murder (of the others' humanity) seems to be a prerequisite for the physical act of murder. Evidence of negative stereotypes of blacks to counter progress to racial equality is too plentiful to recount in full here. Most interesting, perhaps, is William Faulkner's stance against civil rights. Likening blacks to "unbridled horses" and "unassimilated dogs," Faulkner argued that integration would cause chaos in the South (209). By reducing blacks to animal status, he attempted to bolster his argument that "the Negro is not yet capable of, or refuses to accept, the responsibilities of equality" (210). Continuing his animal analogy, Faulkner further argued incoherently,

> I used the horse as a quick analogy to state a condition. What I meant by that was the horse that can be trained and maybe was trained. We'll assume that while that horse was a Slave, that he was a docile, well-behaved horse. But then the burden of slavery was lifted from him and he was suddenly free. That he is still capable of being a docile member of society, but the condition in which he was compelled to be a docile member is gone, and so we [Southern whites] will have to establish a new condition in which he is docile. (Gwynn and Blotner 213)

Cats, horses, docile horses who were human slaves: completely senseless but compelling word pictures that reflect blacks' images in his own (and other racists') mind while erasing blacks' humanity and canceling their membership in the human race.

Images of another sort help to illustrate bigotry that transforms racist ideas into violent actions. In understanding such distorted perceptions and the consequences of them, an indispensable educational tool is Donald Bogle's groundbreaking and comprehensive book on stereotypes of blacks, *Toms, Coons, Mulattoes, Mammies, and Bucks: An Interpretive History of Blacks in American Films.* Relevant to the Emmett Till murder and other lynchings is Bogle's analysis of D. W. Griffith's *The Birth of a Nation.* This film was a catalyst for the revival of the Ku Klux Klan. And one of the most incendiary devices in the film's expression of racism is its use of the stereotype of the black man with a diabolical desire for white women. Explaining the stereotype of "The Brutal Black Buck" (10–18), Bogle writes:

> [I]t was the pure black bucks that were Griffith's really archetypal figures. Bucks are always big, baadddd niggers, oversexed and savage. No greater sin hath any black man [. . .]. [This image] revealed the tie between sex and racism in America. Griffith played on the myth of the Negro's high-powered sexuality, then articulated the great white fear that every black man longs for a white woman. Underlying the fear

> was the assumption the white woman was the ultimate in female desirability, herself a symbol of white pride, power, and beauty [. . .] . [I]n uncovering the attraction of black to white [. . .] . Griffith attributed the attraction to an animalism innate in the Negro male. Thus the black bucks of the film are psychopaths, one always panting and salivating, the other forever stiffening his body as if the mere presence of a white woman in the same room could bring him to a sexual climax. Griffith played hard on the bestiality of his black villainous bucks and used it to arouse hatred. (13–14)

The scene in which a black man (played by a white actor in blackface) stalks and attacks Lillian Gish is the quintessence of the distorted image of black males that Griffith so successfully represented to the public (13–14).

But what is the connection between the image of the "huge, savage buck" and Emmett Till? How could the stereotype and the reality of a youngster barely in his teens have blended together into one entity in the mind of his murderers? Perhaps because the reduction of black males' identity to that of "a phobogenic object" (Fanon 157) was used boldly from slavery to the Civil Rights Movement as one means of justifying racial segregation and the denial of equal rights. J. W. Cash argues in *The Mind of the South* that protection of white womanhood from black males possessed by a lust demon for white flesh was merely a ruse by which white males wanted to maintain their position of power. But if it was a ruse, it was an illusion that white racists in the Old South treated as a lived reality, in several hundreds of lynchings (at the very least) and in such cases as that of the Scottsboro Boys. To the racist mind, as Christian pointed out, if you look at a distorted image long enough, the image is superimposed on the person, resulting in blacks' being given a pseudo-identity by whites; one from which, in the course of American history, many whites "defended" themselves by murder. (I use the term *defended* in the sense of Freudian defense mechanisms: counterproductive or destructive reactions aroused by perceived threats to the ego, in this case, white ideas of supremacy over blacks.) On these topics, Emmett Till's murder opens the door for people to understand perhaps the oldest form of terrorism in America: lynching.

In teaching, I have found that students have little understanding of lynching (perhaps because most American history courses are silent on it, I would venture to say). Education about this topic enables people to understand the depth of racial hostility in America's past and to understand it in America's present, as in the case of the 1998 racially motivated dragging death of James Byrd in Texas. Based on my teaching experiences in courses on African-American literature, on issues of race in American literature and culture, and in multicultural composition courses, violence in contemporary films has not dulled the psychological impact on students of visualizing these actual cases.

Ralph Ginzburg's *100 Years of Lynchings* is an invaluable source not only in contextualizing racial violence but also in painting word pictures that make a powerful imprint on the cognitive and affective parts of the mind. At the very least, students studying the role of race in American culture should read and discuss some of the accounts in this text as a means of understanding both race relations and the conscious and/or unconscious memories of racial violence which can still be a factor in blacks' perceptions of whites. In addition, one might try a variation on an exercise that is used to foster empathy (not mere sympathy) and to diminish fear when confronting difficult subjects.

When I once trained to work as a counselor at a suicide prevention center, training involved a meditative exercise in which potential counselors had to visualize themselves in a desperate situation. Likewise, teachers might ask students to engage in creative visualization before beginning to write on the topic of race relations (see appendix). In my teaching experience, I have found that when most students (of any race) meditate on vivid descriptions of lynching, their shock is superseded by the feeling that a central part of American culture has been hidden from them. They also come to understand the nature of racist terrorism, which is a part of blacks' cultural heritage. Moreover, they do not need to wonder why, for instance, Richard Wright is so concerned with white violence in such works as *Black Boy, Native Son,* and *The Long Dream;* they do not need to wonder why Bigger Thomas in *Native Son* is so hysterical with fear after he helps the drunken Mary Dalton to her bed and her blind mother enters that he inadvertently smothers Mary to keep her from making noises that would make her mother come closer to them and discover him. After all, it is mentioned briefly in a different part of the text that Bigger's father was killed in a riot in the South (one can deduce that he was killed by a white mob). Thus, although his family moved to Chicago after his father's death, Bigger is conditioned by the cultural memory that being discovered in close contact with a white woman, however innocent his actions, could lead to his own murder at the hands of whites.

Such stories of racial violence as the Emmett Till case and the lynchings recounted in Ginzburg's book not only help explain America's racist past but incidents in more recent history. Lethal dehumanization of others is evident not only in the aforementioned case of James Byrd, whose arms, head, and other body parts were torn off as his killers dragged him along the road but also such cases as occurred in the mid to late 1980s, not in the South but in New York. In one case, white hunters in upstate New York, frustrated by not killing a deer when they were out hunting, decided to kill a black man instead. In a case which rocked New York City in December 1986, a black man named Michael Griffiths was killed in Howard Beach, Queens, when an angry white teenaged mob chased him and two other black men after the car they were in broke down, and the men had left it to make a phone call. The bat wielding teens forced Griffiths to run onto a highway to escape, only to be fatally hit by a passing motorist. Such a hate crime in New York City was so shocking that Ed Koch, then mayor, called the incident "the worst crime in the recent history of the city" precisely because it was, he declared, a "modern lynching" (Mills 73). The sad case of sixteen-year-old Yusuf Hawkins, a black teenager murdered in a predominantly Italian section of the city, Bensonhurst, most closely parallels the Emmett Till case in its homicidal psychosexual hysteria. (Ironically, the murder took place on August 23, 1989, very near the thirty-fourth anniversary of Emmett Till's murder.) Hawkins went to Bensonhurst to look at a used car he was interested in buying. Unbeknownst to him, the stage was already set for a senseless tragedy. A young man named Joey Fama had heard a rumor that his former girlfriend had invited black men to a party that night. Starting in the afternoon, he made plans to round up several friends to wait outside the party with bats to attack any black males who might show up. The group grew to about thirty whites armed with bats and sticks (AIM Report). Fama brought a gun. On seeing Yusuf Hawkins, who could not have known that he had just entered the stage of a pathological racial soap opera, Fama fatally shot the black teenager, assuming he was there to party with white women. What was Yusuf Hawkins (or any black male) to his assailants? Certainly not a human being, but just another objectified black male reduced to hypersexual status; as with Emmett Till, he was just "a terrifying penis" to his killer. In each of these cases, first, black people's humanity was erased; as a result, so were their lives.

All people can benefit from the remembrance of such incidents and an understanding of their multiple causes if this nation is to actualize fully its espoused belief in our shared humanity. Studying and understanding the American racial terrorism of the past can possibly guide us towards a more humane future.

Theoretical and Pedagogical Issues

In *Cultural Creation in Modern Society*, Lucien Goldmann addresses the issue of persuasion, especially when it concerns bigotry. He states several ideas that can be applied to the case of Emmett Till—and to bigotry in general. One of Goldmann's key concerns is whether the psychic structure of many people's minds rejects information contrary to their beliefs. In this regard, Goldman's idea of "the limits of a social group's incomprehension of a certain type of message originating in another group" (39) is exemplified by racists' inability to process the demands for civil rights or even to recognize the humanity of people different from their group. Goldmann's concepts are also illustrated by the potentially deadly consequences of stereotypes not transformed by the stereotype's contact with reality (e.g., in the racial violence recounted above). Goldmann is concerned with the potential for change and growth in consciousness, stating that "if the considerably increased quantity of information in all domains which the mass media transmit is to be assimilated, it requires a particularly powerful synthesizing activity" (47).

In "The Psychology of Rhetorical Images" Charles A. Hill explores viewers' reactions to the persuasive power of both vivid images and word pictures. Psychologists agree that individual values are constructed over time, and with deeply held values a "three-way relationship is being brought to bear, between the image [. . .] the value [. . .] and the emotions that are schematically linked to that value" (35). Thus, an image can create emotions without the intermediary step of recalling the values, bypassing the viewer's cognitive schema. Narratives and images countering these values, even when they are strongly emotive, may not be successful. Although the reader may respond briefly, Jens E. Kjeldsen explains that "the persuasive power of vivid images is shortlived, and is not really effective for convincing someone to change his or her beliefs over the long term" (qtd. in Hill 36). Thus, objectives to erase prejudice are best approached using both visual and textual image-making delivered over time. The effects of both pictures and accompanying narratives of Emmett Till gave momentum to the Civil Rights Movement. A study of these and other strategies of countering prejudice make valuable classroom activity. Education stressing active learning, critical thinking, and analytical discussion can be a key agent enabling people to process the different meanings of the societal significance symbolized by the photographs of Emmett Till and of the stories of the Civil Rights Movement.

Conclusion

Such works as Judith Herman's *Trauma and Recovery* and J. Jeffrey Means's *Trauma and Evil* discuss the disempowering nature of surviving violence, whether terrorism or physical abuse. Issues of recovering a feeling of control over one's life and of maintaining and/or reviving connections to others are central topics. The reactions provoked by the stories and photographs of Emmett Till are examples of how fear, shock, alienation, and grief did not terminate the struggle for civil rights but, ironically, empowered it. In the age-old redundant definition, the purpose of terrorism is to induce terror—in the case of racial violence, terror that was meant to cause blacks to accept the erasure of their humanity and "place" on the margins of American society. That civil rights workers continued their struggle despite the trauma of violence is a testament to their remarkable courage.

Mamie Till Bradley, who lectured for many years after her son's death, said soon after his murder that she considered herself a "nobody" and her son "a little nobody who shook up the world" (Williams 57). She realized that before Emmett's death, the bigotry of the South seemed a distant fact with little relevance to her life in Chicago. Yet, she confessed, "Now I know how wrong I was. The murder of my son has shown me that what happens to any of us, anywhere in the world, had better be the business of us all" (57). No better words can convey the relevance of the story of Emmett Till to the violent world in which we live today.

Appendix: Potential Assignments

Both of these assignments are appropriate for courses on composition or visual rhetoric, or for any course with a segment on race or civil rights.

Assignment One: Understanding the Rhetoric and Psychology of Racism

Show students Stanley Nelson's documentary *The Murder of Emmett Till* (approximately one hour). Distribute a copy of William Bradford Huie's *Look* magazine interview with the murderers: "An Approved Murder in Mississippi." After showing the film, have students briefly discuss what struck them the most about it; this discussion is designed to gauge their immediate response to such a shocking situation. At the end of class, distribute the *Look* interview. Announce the following assignment as an analysis of the article: for the next class, turn in a two- to three-page analysis of the murderers' stated rationale for killing Emmett Till. Analyze the killers' tone and their argument that they were justified in their actions. Then hold a class discussion in which students share the ideas that are in their papers. Discussion should address whether students feel that the killers' justifications are the logical conclusion of a racist mentality and what students feel they have gained from knowing the story of Emmett Till. Also, given that, as Perlmutter writes, regarding "the long term reaction to an icon of outrage [e.g., the picture of Emmett Till in his casket], we should never underestimate the ability of the human mind to forget" (133), what do students feel contemporary society can gain from remembering the Emmett Till case?

Assignment Two: Visualizing the Experiences of Victims of Terror

Ask students to visualize themselves as witnessing the events described below. Have them write about and discuss their feelings and thoughts arising from the exercise.

Passage One

> Because he is alleged to have hugged and kissed a white girl, daughter of a farmer, Charles Fisher, a

> Negro youth, was recently badly mutilated by a mob near here [Marshall, Texas]. According to Sheriff Sanders and County Health Officer Taylor, the mob sheared off the youth's ears, slit his lips and mutilated him in other ways below the belt. (Ginzburg 90)

Passage Two

> An eye-witness to the lynching of Luther Holbert and his wife, Negroes, which took place in Doddsville [Mississippi] yesterday, today gave the *Evening Post* the following details: "When the two Negroes were captured, they were tied to trees and while the funeral pyres were being prepared they were forced to hold out their hands while one finger at a time was chopped off. The fingers were distributed as souvenirs. The ears of [the Holberts] were cut off. Holbert was beaten severely, his skull was fractured and one of his eyes, knocked out with a stick, hung by a shred from the socket. Some of the mob used a large corkscrew to bore into the flesh of the man and the woman. It was applied to their arms, legs, and body, then pulled out, the spirals tearing out big pieces of raw, quivering flesh every time it was withdrawn." (Ginzburg 63)

Works Cited

AIM Report: "Racism in Bensonhurst." Report 4. 2001. 11 Nov. 2004 <http://www.aim.org/publications/aim_report/2001/4>.

Baldwin, James. *Blues for Mister Charlie.* New York: Dell Publishing Company, Inc., 1964.

Barthes, Roland. *Camera Lucida: Reflections on Photography.* Trans. Richard Howard. New York: Hill and Wang, 1982.

Bogle, Donald. *Toms, Coons, Mulattoes, Mammies, and Bucks: An Interpretive History of Blacks in American Films, New Expanded Edition.* New York: Continuum, 1990.

Cash, J.W. *The Mind of the South.* New York: Random House, 1984.

Garrow, David J. *Bearing the Cross.* New York: HarperCollins, 1986.

Fanon, Franz. *Black Skin, White Masks.* Trans. Charles Lam Markham. New York: Grove, 1967.

Ginzburg, Ralph. *100 Years of Lynchings.* Baltimore: Black Classic, 1988.

Goldmann, Lucien. *Cultural Creation in Modern Society.* Trans. Bart Grahl. St. Louis: Telos, 1976.

Gwynn, Frederick L,. and Joseph J. Blotner, eds. *Faulkner in the University.* Charlottesville: U of Virginia P, 1959.

Herman, Judith. *Trauma and Recovery.* New York: BasicBooks, 1992.

Hill, Charles A. "The Psychology of Rhetorical Images." *Defining Visual Rhetorics.* Ed. Charles A. Hill and Marguerite Helmers. Mahwah, NJ: Lawrence Erlbaum Assoc. 25–40.

Huie, William Bradford. Interview. *Look* 24 Jan. 1956. Reprinted in *Reporting Civil Rights: American Journalism (1941-l963).*

Means, J. Jeffrey. *Trauma and Evil: Healing the Wounded Soul.* Minneapolis: Fortress, 2000.

Mills, Nicolaus. "Howard Beach: Anatomy of a Lunching." *In Search of New York.* Ed. Jim Sleeper. Edison, NJ: Transaction Publishers, 1988. 73-75.

Moody, Anne. *Coming of Age in Mississippi.* New York: Dell Publishing Company, Inc., 1968.

Online Newshour. "The Murder of Emmett Till." PBS. 11 Nov. 2004 <http://www.pbs.org/newshour/bb/jan-june03/till_1–20>.

Pettigrew, Thomas, et al. *Prejudice.* Cambridge: Harvard UP, 1982.

Perlmutter, David D. *Photojournalism and Foreign Policy: Icons of Outrage in International Crises.* Westport, CT: Praeger Publishers, 1998.

Riggs, Marlon, producer and director. *Ethnic Notions,* 1987.

Washingtonwatch.com. 20 June 2007. "H.R. 923, The Emmett Till Unsolved Civil Rights Crime Act." <http://www.washingtonwatch.com/bills/show/110 HR 923.html>.

Williams, Juan. *Eyes on the Prize: America's Civil Rights Years, 1954–1965.* New York: Penguin Books, 1987.

Wingfield, Kyle. "Civil Rights Treasures Found in Alabama Basement." *Des Moines Register.* 25 July 2004: 10A.

7 A Study of Photographs of Iran: Postcolonial Inquiry into the Limits of Visual Representation

Iraj Omidvar

President George W. Bush's 2002 State of the Union address plunged the Iranian-American community into a state of turmoil about the future of family and friends in Iran. The president categorized Iran as a member of an axis of evil and forcefully affirmed his commitment to the belief that the United States has the right to make pre-emptive attacks on militarily weak countries that he considers hostile. Shortly after the speech, I scrambled to prepare talks to college students and faculty in order to counter widespread stereotypes of Iranians, which had created a dangerous framework for the president's remarks. My presentations attempted to contextualize the concepts of *Iran* and of *Iranian* in the minds of my audience. I began with a great deal of historical and sociocultural information, but I gradually incorporated large numbers of photographs and other still visuals because of their power to capture and hold the audience's attention.

In time, however, I became less sanguine about the usefulness of images of Iran and Iranians for the purpose of countering stereotypes. E. H. Gombrich's insight that viewers bring their own interpretive schemes to images implies a warning against too light a handling of some types of visuals. The warning is as old as Plato, who, in one reading of his work, cautions us against forgetting the experiences and stories or underlying relations that have brought about the object that an image may be representing. This reading is especially pertinent when, for example, photographs are presented as representatives of stereotyped groups. With such images, the experiences and stories that Plato wants us not to forget become interpretations, ideologies, and value-systems that the images serve.

This chapter provides a theoretical background for writing teachers who wish to address stereotyping through still images. After discussing stereotypical images of Iran in contemporary U.S. media, the chapter examines Plato's injunctions against visual representations, as well as contemporary thought on stereotyping, and concludes with an assignment that may be of interest to teachers who want to help students think critically about images. By analyzing the culture that does the stereotyping, students can be introduced to cross-cultural and multicultural analysis in the composition classroom and can embark on the difficult task of understanding relationships between self and other.

Postcolonial Scholarship and Iran

Iran and Iranians are routinely stereotyped in the United States in part because Iran represents a lacuna in Western studies of the Third World and in particular of the Middle East. This absence is especially striking in postcolonial studies (see, for example, indexes of *Colonial Discourse and Post-Colonial Theory: A Reader,* editors: Patrick Williams and Laura Chrisman and of *Dangerous Liaisons: Gender, Nation, & Postcolonial Perspectives* by editors Anne McClintock, Aamir Mufti, and Ella Shohat) because postcolonial studies owes much to the Iranian revolution, which in 1978 was shaking the West out of its complacency about the Middle East and the Third World. That year happens to be the year of the first edition of Edward Said's *Orientalism,* which ushered in postcolonial studies by offering an extended study of the representation of non-Western Arabs and Muslims by Western scholars. Said's book is a rebuke to Western scholars for their systematic prejudices regarding the Orient. According to Said, the Orient "that appears in Orientalism [. . .] is a system of representations framed by a whole set of forces that brought the Orient into Western learning, Western consciousness, and later, Western empire" (142). The revolution in Iran—till then among the closest allies of the United States—and the ensuing hostage-taking of U.S. embassy diplomats and guards in Tehran that absorbed the attention of Western countries up till 1980 served as a compelling confirmation of Said's thesis. The issue of systematic mis-representation has continued to be a driving concern of postcolonial studies, for example, in the works of prominent postcolonial scholar Gayatry Spivak, who has taken seriously such possibilities as the intellectual's complicity "in the persistent constitution of the Other as the Self's shadow" (qtd. in Leitch, 2193).

But the Iranian revolution has been unhelpful to other salient interests of postcolonial studies. As Terry Eagleton writes in *After Theory*, postcolonial studies also participates in a broader move by the Western intellectual left, away from a concern with collective political action to one with culture. This move, Eagleton argues, tacitly acknowledges the futility of political action. Offering a sharp critique of this move, Anouar Majid's "The Failure of Postcolonial Theory after 9/11" notes that despite important successes with theories of hybridity, displacement, and exile, postcolonial theory has failed to "attenuate the agony of uprootedness suffered by Muslims and other people in the last half century" (7).[1] It is in the context of this move away from a concern with collective political action that Iran's absence in postcolonial literature should be understood. Michel Foucault, who had visited Iran right before the fall of the shah, announced afterwards that in revolutionary Iran he had met "*an absolute collective will*" (215, emphasis added), which he had previously considered a "political myth." But the massive social movement that took place in Iran in 1979 and such testimonies as that by Foucault go against the main interests of postcolonial theory and are simply ignored by it. Thus, cultural and postcolonial scholars, let alone the public at large, know little about the country in which arguably the most important revolution of the second half of the twentieth century took place, a nationalist-religious revolution widely believed to have inaugurated the rise of fundamentalism in the Muslim world, a rise whose repercussions the world feels to this day. In the absence of any noticeable kind of critical engagement with Iran, what in the West we know of that country—its diverse peoples, its history, its lively intellectual communities, and its people's various lifestyles—has been mostly left to unreformed present-day Orientalists. And in popular culture, Iran and Iranians have been reduced to sound bites and stereotyped images.

The Original Presentation

My initial work on countering stereotypes of Iranians was not aimed at practice in the composition classroom. Like many other Iranian-Americans, I was concerned that the United States might invade Iran. And I was looking for ways to counter negative stereotypes that present Iranians as people who should be sacrificed for the greater good of humanity. An Iranian colleague and I, discussing Western representations of Iran, were struck by the distressing realization that we could not recall seeing a single image of Iran—in magazines, on television, or in the movies—that showed anything desirable from our native culture. After 9/11, several books came out arguing that Islam has had a particularly violent past.[2] In this context, connotations of the Shi'ite terms *mullah* and *ayatollah* (both associated with Iran) were acquiring truly dark implications at a time when the American public was being intensely propagandized for war. In drawings, photographs, and newspaper cartoons, *mullahs* and *ayatollahs* are regularly represented as autocratic figures although *ayatollah* goes beyond meaning merely autocratic to meaning bloodthirsty or criminally insane (Figure 1). Moreover, Iran is often mixed in with other countries and other cultures. For example, images of Iran in the media are overwhelmingly of deserts, and there has always been a fudging of lines between Arabs,

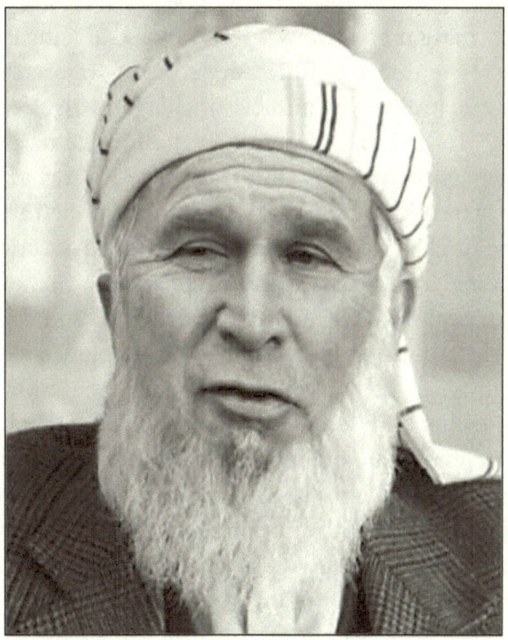

Figure 1. Satire and humor in general rely quite legitimately on stereotypes for their effects. This satirical image, distributed widely on the Internet in the months after 9/11, does its job of provoking because of the widespread background assumption in the West that mullahs are bloodthirsty and criminally insane. © Copyright 2001 Mister Hepburn.

Iranians, and Muslims even though (aside from the fact that there are Arabs who live in Iran and Iranians who live in Arab countries) calling Iranians Arabs mixes categories of as much importance and usefulness as those of Italians and British, or Catholics and Protestants. This absence of differentiation is also evident in the depictions of Iranian women, who—unlike women in some other Muslim countries—vote and drive, run for political office, travel alone, work as professionals in the private and public sectors, own businesses, and make up about 60% of the entering student body in national universities.

My work began when I accepted the suggestion by fellow anti-war activists in Iowa that I prepare a presentation on Iran for an American audience of churchgoers and other peace activists as well as high-school and college students and faculty in classrooms or at teach-ins.

To draw connections between the experiences of Iranians and the experiences of the audience, I planned to compare information about Iran, in terms of population, area, number of students, cell phones, etc., with information about Iowa. I also included a great many positive, basic facts—number of university students (more than 1.5 million), literacy rate (over 85%), number of villages with electricity (more than 40,000).[3] To give the audience a sense of the natural environment in which most Iranians find themselves, I included a discussion of Iran's two major mountain ranges and described and compared them with the Rockies in Colorado. I also included a section about the densely populated area twice the size of Taiwan on the southern coast of the Caspian Sea, which is heavily wooded and humid. To illustrate that most of the country is industrialized, I mentioned the number of workers employed in the automotive industry (about 500,000), who provide the livelihood for about a million and half others, the equivalent of half the population of Iowa. And I used the fact that Iran, with a population of about 70 million, is self-sufficient in wheat production to argue that such production levels cannot be achieved without extensive use of scientific and industrial techniques. In recounting the history of Iran, I focused on points of contact between Iran and the United States: the great respect afforded the American financial advisor W. Morgan Shuster about a hundred years ago for ordering the finances of the government of Iran before he was forced out of the country by foreign powers; the decision of the American teacher and missionary Howard Baskerville, a hero of the constitutional revolution of 1909 in Iran, to join in the defense of Tabriz against loyalist and

Russian forces; the American invasion and occupation of Iran during World War II; the American-financed and -organized coup d'état of 1953 against the democratically elected premier of Iran; the Iranian hostage-taking of the staff of the U.S. embassy in Tehran; and the U.S. government's support of Iraq during the bloody Iran-Iraq War, even after Iraq's use of chemical weapons against Kurdish civilians and Iranian soldiers, etc.

Concerns about the Presentation

Soon after beginning the project in earnest, I had to admit that because of my alarm about the war talk of the administration, I had in fact envisioned a presentation that conformed closely to an Aristotelian rhetorical framework. For Aristotle, rhetors have a vast advantage over the audience in terms of specialized knowledge, and the audience is considered incapable of following careful or lengthy lines of reasoning. Acquainting themselves with the audience's likes and dislikes, establishing their credibility, and using an abridged form of argument assisted with other techniques, for example, metaphors "to conjure before [. . .] [the] eyes an image" of what is being argued (Lawson-Tancred 238), Aristotelian rhetors can persuade in the unlikeliest circumstances. In the rhetorical situation that Aristotle envisions, however, rhetors do not aim to improve the ideas of participants (including those of the rhetors) through an *exchange* of views. Rather, rhetors already have the right ideas, and participants are there to be molded. The Aristotelian model has tremendous appeal to rhetors (a) who are completely sure of their causes (ideas or truths), (b) who believe the rhetorical situation does not permit a full exposition of the real reasons for supporting the ideas the rhetors advance, or (c) who consider their audience deficient in understanding or maturity. The Aristotelian model is the operating rhetorical framework in many professions, including marketing, advertising, public relations, and political propaganda. In the Western tradition, teaching and preaching remain paradigmatic Aristotelian rhetorical situations although strong currents in education and composition studies are moving away from the teacher-centered, top-down approach to education.

Use of the Photographs

In addition to my misgivings about the Aristotelian model of my presentation, I encountered another closely related difficulty due to the growing reliance of my presentation on photographs. The visual unit on stereotypes that I use in my composition courses, and which appears at the end of this chapter, originated in what I learned from exploring these difficulties. As I worked on the presentation, I became increasingly aware of the extraordinary power of the photographs as aids to discussions of complex topics. Passages without visuals and requiring extended discussions slowed down the presentation and demanded intense attention from the audience. In contrast, segments helped by visuals would be engaging, funny, or familiar. The visuals I had chosen purposely emphasized familiar sights and images, mostly from Tehran and larger Iranian cities: cars, expressways, parks, stores, houses and apartments, and children and parents. Other images were selected in order to give the audience something positive with which to associate Iran. These included photographs of stunning historical buildings and exquisite works of art (Figure 2). To give a sense of what the vast majority of Iranians see in their natural surroundings, I had included a large selection of beautiful photographs of mountain ranges, valleys, and summits. And to counter the idea that Iran is backward, I had included several photographs of manufacturing plants and other machinery.

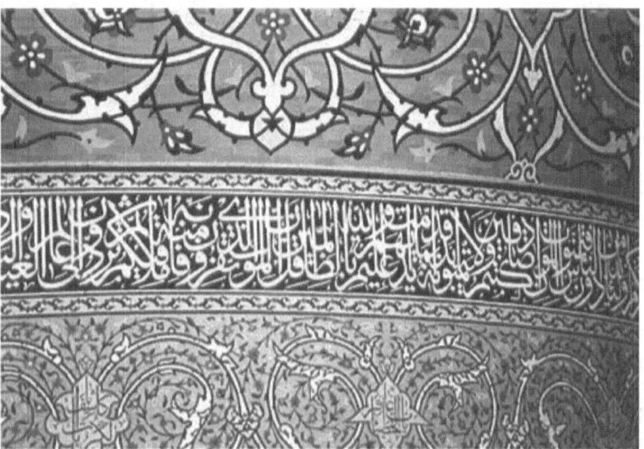

Figure 2. With a history that spans more than two thousand years, Iran is replete with artistic gems. (Photograph used by permission of www.sacredsites.com.)

I became aware of the difficulty with the photographs when I began using them to argue about topics such as the condition of women or the place of clerics in Iranian society. For example, I was using many photographs of Iranian women in positions of power and prestige (as physicians, dentists, vice presidents, faculty members, election campaigners, protesters, etc.) or engaged in activities such as driving, playing chess, riding horses, voting, debating, mountain climbing, skiing, sky diving, etc. But looking at the photographs, I knew that they were also grossly simplifying the condition of women in Iran. "Condition of women in Iran" is a phrase that may be understandable only through a serious study of an extremely complex set of historical, cultural, legal, religious, sociopolitical, economic, educational, and literary sources. There have been women's associations in Iran for at least 90 years. The positions of women as explained in religious texts are various and disputed. Accounts of Iranian women as passed down through national-religious myths compete with modern historiographic accounts. And modernization efforts of the Pahlavi kings resulted in two sharply differentiated groups of people in Iran: a small Western-educated middle-class and a vast traditional group of clerics, bazaaris, shanty dwellers, farmers, and artisans. Almost nothing in Iran, let alone the condition of women, can be understood without understanding the competing visions that these two groups continue to represent and the influences they have exerted on each other. The simplest fact about the condition of women also has to be understood in other dynamic contexts. For example, there are far more women than men entering colleges in Iran. But it is common knowledge among Iranians that men do not compete as hard for college slots, to a great extent because prospects for postgraduation positions are dim. But then there seems to be consensus across the cultural and political spectrum that the unprecedented presence of so many women in high schools and colleges is bound to transform Iran. Some interpret this transformation in strictly Western terms: a rejection of the theocratic underpinnings of the Islamic Republic and a return to secularism. Others note the traditional and conservative outlooks of many of the women entering colleges and argue that what will emerge from this infusion of educated women in society is unpredictable. Will the result of this transformation be emancipated Iranian women? And if so, in whose terms? (Figures 3 and 4)

Unfortunately, as modern studies in stereotyping show, even providing this type of complex information is woefully inadequate for countering stereotypes effectively since crucial features of stereotyping remain untouched. In *Stereotyping: The Politics of Representation,* Michael Pickering acknowledges the usefulness of the classical model

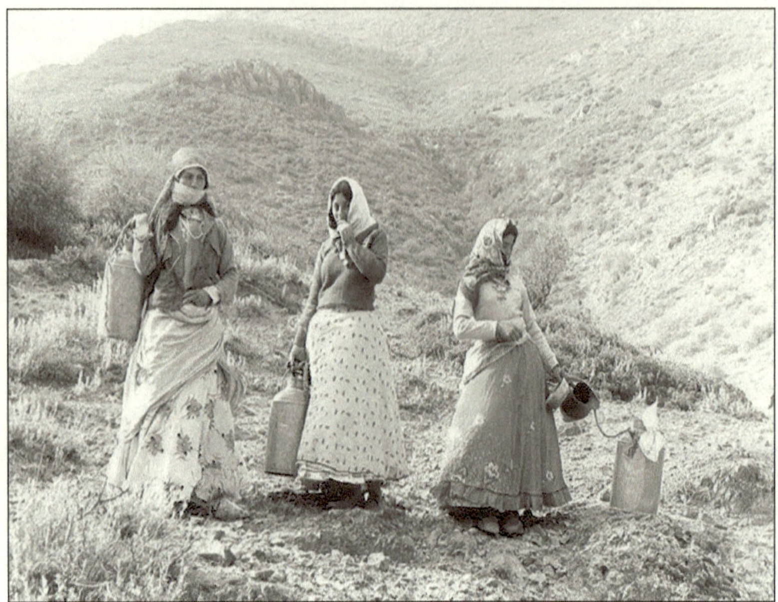

Figure 3a.

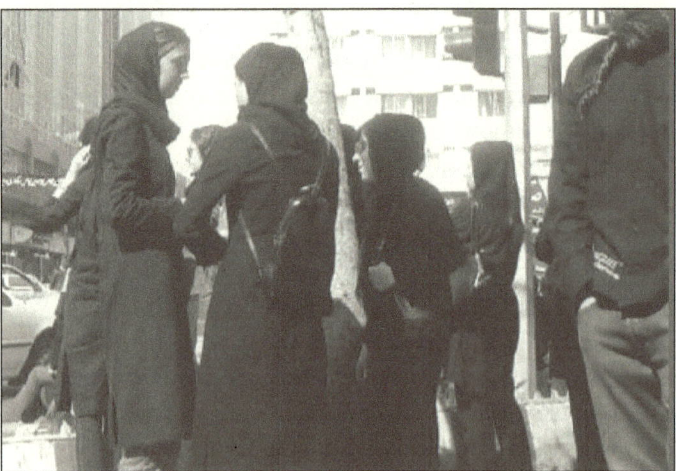

Figure 3b.

Figure 3. A photograph aiming to represent a type, such as the "Iranian woman," has the impossible responsibility of taking into account Iranian women's varied socio-economic statuses, alignments with traditional and Western cultural norms, education levels, urban versus rural backgrounds, ages, and many other factors. (a) Photograph used by permission of the Golshan Society. 2005; (b) Photograph used by permission of BIA. 2005. <bia2.com>.

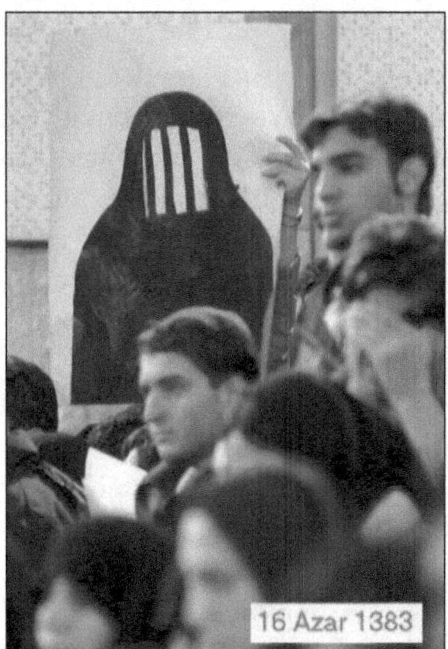

Figure 4a.

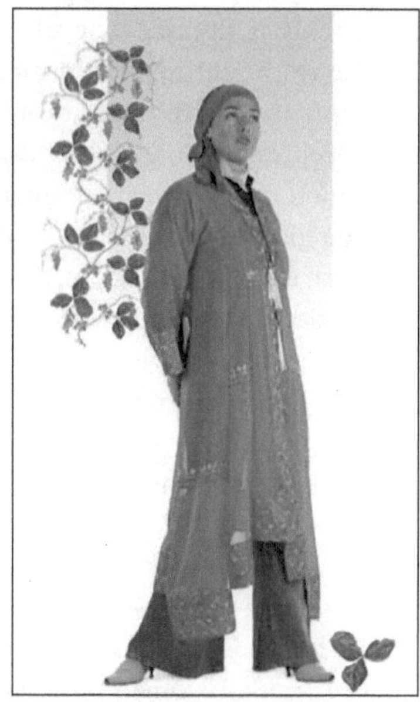

Figure 4b.

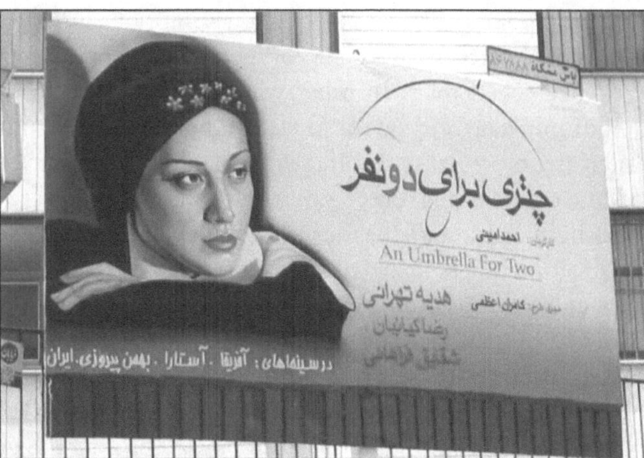

Figure 4c.

Figure 4. The condition of women in Iran also has to attend to the debates in the heterogeneous society that is Iran, debates that are taking place not only in obvious places such as the university, the media, and the government but also in fashion events, in streets, and on billboards. (a) Photograph used by permission of the Golshan Society. 2005; (b) Photograph used by permission of the Golshan Society. 2005;(c) Photograph by R. Dehdashti—http://www.iranpix.com. 2005.

of stereotyping—"stereotypes = 'distortions of truth'" (75)—and the remedy it implies, but advocates going beyond that model. According to the influential formulation of the classical model by Walter Lippmann, stereotypes result from "inadequate and manipulated media representations" (18). But Lippmann's model attributes two contradictory features to stereotypes. On the one hand, he considered stereotypes "inadequate and biased" and endorsing vested interests, obstructing "rational assessment," and resisting change in society. On the other hand, he considered stereotyping unavoidable for ordering the chaotic realities of modern, "highly differentiated societies." He thus identified stereotyping with "typifying," "representing," and indeed "thinking." According to Pickering, Lippmann's influential model has harmed subsequent efforts to study and remedy stereotypes in two ways: (1) The model has led to the belief that the remedy to stereotyping is *merely* provision of accurate information, and (2) the model sees stereotypes as a matter of oversimplification of complex facts. Thus, according to the classical model, the remedy for stereotypes of Iranian women or of gender roles in Iran is merely provision of further complex information.

But Pickering points out that objectivist assumptions lurk behind the link this model posits between stereotyped images and inaccurate representation of social roles. In other words, the classical view assumes an undisputed, agreed-on social reality about roles and cultural norms. And it assumes further that if the distorting clutter of prejudice is removed, the reality of the role of, say, women in Iranian society will be made manifest. But in fact the social reality of gender relations and norms is itself a function of ideological clashes and negotiations within and between cultures. Pickering argues that the concept of "the other," used extensively by feminist and postcolonial scholars, helps us see that characterizations of those who are othered say a great deal about those who do the othering. Moreover, the concept remains alert to historical, material, and cultural relations of power defining the terms of stereotyping (who can stereotype, what features will be stereotyped, how stereotyping changes).

Thus, any effort to counter stereotypes of Iranians has to be, at least in some respects, more attentive to the cultural norms and assumptions of Americans than perhaps it is to the complex conditions that obtain among Iranians. Stereotypes of Iranians by, for example, Americans say little of value about Iranians. But they do say a great deal about the interpretive framework of many Americans. And it is that ideological and interpretive framework that needs countering. My growing reliance on photographs in my presentation brought the issues that Pickering addresses into relief. For example, if the new cultural and educational developments in Iran are harbingers of a new emancipatory women's movement there, then who are the women at the forefront of this movement? Can a photograph capture this type of woman? To an American, the photograph of such an emancipated Iranian woman will likely not show her covered under the *hejab.* But then women strictly conforming to the *hejab* are entering clerical seminaries in the heart of shi'ite Islam. Some of the most powerful and outspoken feminist organizations in Iran can be described as conservative in just about every way except their commitment to greater legal, political, and economic rights for women.[4] It is easy to show in photographs, to an American audience, that Iranian women are not all literally chained to their houses. But can photographs say more? I believe they do say more, and much of what they say, in the absence of careful analyses of the complex historical, religious, economic, legal, and other contexts of Iran—and of the United States—can only be called "misrepresentation."

Standard Accounts of Plato's Injunctions Against the Visual

One of the earliest and most pertinent discussions of this misrepresentation remains Plato's injunctions against the visual. Unfortunately, standard accounts of his injunctions often miss the most important element of Plato's criticism because the accounts are usually placed in the context of a purportedly coherent Platonic doctrinal system. According to Moshe Barasch in *Theories of Art,* Plato cited optical illusions involving water and coloring to conclude that sense perception is "devoid of truth" (5), a view based on Plato's broader understanding of the hierarchy of knowledge. According to this hierarchy, behind the changing, day-to-day world of the senses exists an unchanging reality of Ideas or Forms, from which the world of the senses is copied (Huby 17–20). Plato considered true knowledge—what he called *epistêmê*—to consist of the knowledge of the world of Ideas. What could be known about the impermanent world—what he called *opinion*—he divided into *belief* and *conjecture*, belief being opinions about concrete empirical things and conjecture being beliefs in phantoms, reflections, and shadows (or what does not really exist even as part of ephemeral reality) (20–2; see also Marías, 50). Plato considered knowledge of the painter to be conjecture and explained painting in terms of the concept of imitation, or *mimesis* (Barasch): as the empirical world is a copy of the real world of forms, the pictorial image is merely an imitation of the material object. And because an image is always constructed from a certain angle or in a certain light, it can never be more than a "suggestion or evocation" (5). Thus painting is merely a copy of a copy (Barasch 5, see also *Republic* 596b-8c), an image of an image—a conjecture.

There are, of course, many problems with the concept of mimesis as it relates to paintings and other still images. For instance, Gombrich notes that art works do not always have to represent something. Moreover, he shows that the idea of the artist as an imitator of things in the phenomenal world (for example, more detailed imitation of human bodies in statues) was a historical development of art in Plato's time.[5]

But the standard accounts of Plato's injunctions often ignore at least three difficulties. First, not only is the use of images and of visual metaphors prevalent throughout the dialogues (e.g., metaphors of the chariot of the soul in *Phaedrus* and, in the *Republic,* of the cave, of the sun, and of the divided line), but visual metaphors are deeply embedded in the very concepts of Plato's philosophy (e.g., the word *idea* means image [Marías 46]). Second, stylistic studies of his writings suggest that Plato had a competent knowledge of the processes of painting (Barasch 8). For example, in *Republic,* Socrates explains that the ideal state must pass metaphorically through the three stages of painting: "the first consists in preparing a clean, probably white surface; the second is the outlining, the drawing of a contour.[. . .] The third step is 'shading and coloring'" (Barasch 9).[6] Third, Plato is not categorically critical of painters. He makes distinctions between illusionistic painters and poietic painters, approving of the latter as well as of Egyptian paintings, whose flat and rigid styles were supposedly closer to the permanent forms, or Ideas (Barasch 7; also Gombrich 126). In fact, according to an influential Platonism in medieval philosophy, artists—for example poietic painters (Barasch 7)—sometimes can see and represent the true forms (156). This idea is intimated in Plato's cosmological speculations in which a *demiurge*[7] sees the permanent forms and creates the phenomenal world as an inferior (Barasch writes "likely and analogous" 7) copy, or image.

Perplexities such as these have prompted some scholars to question and to abandon efforts to identify a coherent set of Platonic doctrines on the visual, the ideal forms, and a wide range of other topics examined by Plato. For example, Gerald Press, in *The Columbia History of Philosophy,* notes that Plato's Socrates frequently upholds *epistêmê* as the highest form of knowledge but just as frequently denies that he has any such knowledge. Plato goes out of his way to make discovery of his views difficult (note that in no dialogue is there a character by the name of "Plato"). What is more, the character of Socrates cannot be identified as the mouthpiece of Plato because Socrates is not present in all the dialogues and, in some, plays only a minor role. In various works, certain key ideas are strongly argued for, but in others just as strongly rejected. And finally, most dialogues end without settling the initiating issues.

Thus, according to Press, viewing the dialogues as a set of doctrines misses their most salient feature: their pedagogic function. Press argues that the dialogues enact the activity of philosophy embodied in the ideal philosopher (often Socrates) as a "gadfly" (37) to politicians and others, an inquirer "aware of persons, facts, details and as morally serious, intellectually seductive, a theorist in and of the practical world" (35). Instead of offering doctrinal answers, the ambiguous conclusions reached challenge participants in the conversation (and readers) "to work out better answers" (43). Press argues that Plato wanted to suggest or to guide a dialogue through dialectic, that is, through Socrates' oral method of questioning (*elenchos*), to teach students and other intellectuals to philosophize (34–35) or, in contemporary composition studies parlance, to think critically.

Press writes that the dialogues often begin with questions raised by Socrates "on matters of importance" (43), that is, on matters of value and ideology. The questions aim to draw out opinions and answers, many of which are systematically refuted (*elenchos*). This refutation will result in a crisis (*aporia*) "when insufficiency of answers is recognized." At this point in the dialogues, Socrates suggests a different intellectual perspective in order "to approach the problem (through play or myth)." After this suggestion, discussion returns to original difficulties, without coming "to final, specific, positive conclusions." Rather, the conversation partners, as well as readers of the dialogues, are left to "work out better answers for themselves" (43). The kind of knowledge found in the dialogues is not *epistêmê* or definitional knowledge, then, but *theoria*—vision (another important visual metaphor). Press writes,

> *Theoria* expresses how we encounter the Forms [. . .] and posits seeing with the eye of the soul as the kind of thinking characteristic of the philosopher. [. . .] Thus vision is a kind of knowledge that *can* be found in the dialogues, but it is not the dogmatic, propositional sort usually desiderated. It is the sort of thing about which it can truly be said, as Socrates does about the Parable of the Cave, "God knows whether it is true" (*Republic* 517b). (44)

This parable, Julián Marías argues, is meant to show that "what happens to the man in the cave is something that can be narrated, and it is, in its most profound dimension, the essence of philosophy . [. . .] more clearly arrived at in a narrative than in a definition. What happens to the philosopher, the drama of philosophy, is what makes clear the structure of reality" (50). Looking at Plato's dialogues as works in progress enacting the activities of an ideal philosopher moving between ignorance and wisdom (Marías 56–58) offers great insights into the pedagogical aims of philosophizing as (a) a set of historically, morally, and politically grounded problems and questions to which philosophers attempt to respond[8] (b) through a process of directed—but perhaps ultimately never-conclusive—conversational inquiry (Press 34–35). Freed, in this way, of the weight of various Platonisms, Plato's injunctions against the visual can be handled more flexibly and more usefully. Plato is not a foe of the visual, but rather, as Iris Murdoch argues, "a great artist attacking what he sees as bad and dangerous in art" (13).

And his injunctions against the visual express a powerful insight that remains pertinent in our time. In a classic statement of the injunction in *Republic,* Plato writes, "Only the horseman knows the forms of the reins; the leatherworker who manufactures them has only an 'opinion' or 'true belief'; the painter who represents them does not have even such an opinion; he is acquainted only with their appearance (X. 601)" (Barasch 6). In the context of Plato's broader views on *theoria* and philosophy, Plato seems to be saying that images may be fundamentally inappropriate for representing or understanding certain relations that obtain behind the visible. But how can a thinker, a student/intellectual, know about those relations? Plato seems to have answered us, not through the doctrinal content of his dialogues but through narrating (enacting) the activity of the ideal philosopher trying to understand various "important" issues.[9]

From this reading of Plato, the conceptualization of my presentation was fruitless if not dangerous if my goal was teaching (or comprehension in an audience). The visual elements in my presentation were being used the way the still visual of, say, a frowning person holding a product (or associating a product with something that evokes a negative feeling) may be used in order to counter the effects of an advertisement of a smiling person holding that product arguing that happiness can be had by using the product (or associating a product with something that evokes a positive feeling). The strategy would ultimately fail because although the effect of the original image in the ad may be muted or wiped out through the use of a counter image, the strategy concedes a much more important point: this use of image does not ask how we should go about trying to understand more pressing but ideologically fraught issues involved in a mundane matter like choosing a product, issues such as what makes us happy.

At some level, photographs are inappropriate for giving us knowledge of certain issues: a society's political system, the living conditions of its citizens, or its state of industrial development. They are especially inappropriate when used to give us knowledge of those issues about another culture when that culture has been subjected to persistent and deplorable forms of stereotyping.

Changes in the Presentation and Pedagogical Implications

But what is in fact an appropriate way of helping an American audience understand and learn about the socio-economic or cultural situation, the condition of women, history, heritage, etc., of a stereotyped society such as Iran? To begin with, the rhetorical situation has to be reconceptualized from an Aristotelian to a dialectic one. In the latter model, instead of an audience there are conversation partners. And knowledge is not conveyed but discovered through the exchange that takes place in a discussion, which is a quest or inquiry, or an activity that can be best described through narrative or drama with high and low points, moments of certainty and moments of confusion. The quest may result in resolution of some issues, but never completely and never beyond further need for inquiry. Most importantly, it focuses on the starting points for judgment, the principles, values, or ideologies that determine what topics are issues for discussion and what approaches are acceptable or promising.

There are close similarities between the (Socratic or) dialectic model and basic principles of critical pedagogy, just as there are close links between the Aristotelian rhetorical model and the banking model of education against which Paulo Freire warns. For Freire, teaching is really dialogue, which, as in the Socratic dialogue, is about ideological issues of concern to conversation partners (in critical pedagogy, as problems posed to students). As for Plato, for Freire the joint inquiry, or praxis, embodied in the dialogue is an activity that can best be described in a narrative.

For my presentation, I drastically revised my conversational posture. As Press explains, the drama of learning that Plato narrates in his Socratic dialogues has a pattern. A problem is posed or an issue raised; various solutions are examined and rejected through a process of *elenchos,* and an *aporia* is reached; standards of judgment or values, ideological issues are then explored; and conversation partners leave the conversation better informed although without having achieved unshakable certainties. Thus, instead of presenting my material to debunk misconceptions or merely to inform, I offered a narrative about why I became interested in preparing and making the presentation, my original conceptualization of the rhetorical situation and the types of information I presented, and the problems I encountered in terms of countering stereotypes and the use of photographs. Especially with my visual choices, I often paused to explain them and what they highlighted or concealed. For example, I usually present Mohammad Mosaddegh, the democratically elected premier who was deposed in the American-organized and -financed coup of 1953, with very positive photographs in which he meets people or is lifted by them. But of course there are other photographs of him in which he is, for example, kissing the hands of the shah or of the queen, as was expected of him during royal audiences. Or there are photographs, most likely taken by CIA propagandists, that show "Old Mossy," as *Newsweek* called Mossadegh, after his arrest—holding a prisoner's number plaque or looking childish sitting cross-legged on a bench and wearing an ill-fitting overcoat.

Of course I am far from hopeful about the ability of images to represent a complex condition such as that of Iranian women or the state of Iran's economic development. But by challenging stereotypes in their grossest manifestations—as simplified, contradiction-suppressing images—counter photographs may be able to result in Socratic *aporia* as one step, not in replacing stereotypes with knowledge, but in a wider effort to explore how stereotypes are formed as well as how a different approach to acquiring knowledge of other peoples can be envisioned. Thus, if the stereotyped image of an Iranian woman shows her to be home-bound, repressed, petty, idle, or subservient to men, I present photographs of women in a wide range of situations, some flattering, some not so flattering, but all serving at least to question and dislodge the deceptive simplicity and naturalness of the stereotype. My presentations also include a discussion of how the standards of judgment underwriting the stereotype are in urgent need of examination. For example, after presenting photographs of industrial plants and machinery, I ask why a society that does not have industrial implements is considered in some way backward. Where does that standard come from? How has it come to be adopted? Do we apply it consistently? Do we, for example, believe that Nazi Germany was a more advanced society than Sweden because of Germany's greater technological and industrial development?

Because stereotyping of Iranians continues to have potentially perilous consequences, I continue to make my revised presentation and to entertain reservations about it. But my experiences with the presentation have enriched my appreciation for the composition classroom as an especially suitable venue for a more dialectic approach to exploring and countering stereotypes through the use of photographs. A study of photographs that represent stereotypes can serve many purposes in the classroom, among them how stereotypes—at some level, just a set of ideas—are formed. Critically examining ideas and what goes into their formation is, of course, one goal of the college writing class. In my unit on stereotypes, I briefly introduce stereotypes and ask students to work collaboratively to bring to class photographs or other still images of stereotyped groups (immigrants, Arabs, Muslims, feminists, Jews, African-Americans, etc.). We discuss the photographs and explore the stereotypical elements. What is highlighted? What is considered positive, what negative? And how are negative and positive features indicated? In a subsequent class period, students bring photographs that directly contradict some or all of the stereotypical elements of the groups examined during the preceding class period. We discuss the ways in which the new photographs contradict the stereotypical elements. At this point in the unit, I introduce the idea that stereotyped images may say more about those who do the stereotyping than those who are stereotyped. This topic is introduced as part of a modified rhetorical analysis with which students should be familiar from previous units. In regular rhetorical analyses, students have worked on identifying the audience, context, and purpose of various texts and documents. The same will be done with these photos, but special emphasis is placed on the "photographer." I place photographer in scare quotes because stereotypes often function subconsciously. Students speculate about the subconscious attitudes and purposes of the photographer and try to see who the creator of the stereotype is (ethnicity, gender, class, nationality, etc.) by looking at what the creator sees in the stereotyped group. Students then gather information about the history of the relations between the stereotyped and the stereotyping groups. Students end the unit by writing a paper about class activities and the research they have done.

Appendix

In this unit, we will examine group stereotypes in photographs and single-panel cartoons as arguments about how certain groups should be viewed. The methods we use for this examination will be a modified form of rhetorical analysis. This unit will end with a researched rhetorical analysis paper.

Week 1

In the first class period of Week 1, I introduce the topic of stereotyping, including a discussion of the roots of the word *stereotype*. As a group, we will look at some stereotyped images from Iran and will come up with a preliminary definition. In subsequent periods of the week, you will bring to class photographs or one-panel cartoons of stereotyped groups (immigrants, native Americans, Arabs, women, Jews, African-Americans, etc.) for group and class discussions aimed at exploring the stereotypical elements of the images. What is highlighted? What is de-emphasized? What is considered positive, what negative? And how are negative and positive features indicated?

Week 2

For Week 2, bring to class additional photographs of the same stereotyped groups of people. But these photos should contain visual elements that directly contradict some or all of the stereotypical elements in the photographs of Week 1. We will discuss in groups and as a class the ways in which the new photographs contradict the stereotypical elements. This week, we will also turn the tables and discuss features of the stereotyping photographs (from the previous week) in order to discover what those features say about those who do the stereotyping. This discussion will be a special kind of rhetorical analysis. You already have worked on identifying the audience, context, and purpose of various texts and documents. You will do the same with these photos, but place special emphasis on the author/photographer. The goal will be to speculate about the subconscious attitudes and purposes of the creators of the photographs in order to discover who those creators of the stereotypes are (their ethnicity, gender, class, nationality, etc.) by looking at what the creators see in the stereotyped groups.

Week 3

For Week 3, bring to class the results of your collaborative research on the history of the relations between the stereotyped and the stereotyping groups. We will discuss your research results as we take another look at the photographs.

Week 4

This week will be spent on drafting and revising collaborative essays in which research results are presented.

Notes

1. Majid cites four Third-World novelists (Cheikh Hamidou Kane, Tayeb Salih, Marietou M'Baye, and Abdelrahman Munif) who have written about cultural dislocations, identity crises, effects of colonialism, and resistance to destructive Western values that nevertheless have been internalized gradually—in short, about the peoples, societies, and cultures slowly being incorporated in the leviathan of capitalist economic globalization, a process that is not designed to benefit those being digested.

2. For example, Morgon Norval's *The Fifteen Century War: Islam's Violent Past* and John F. Murphy, Jr.'s *Sword of Islam: Muslim Extremism from the*

Arab Conquest to the Attack on America depicted Islam as a virulent ideology relying on violence to spread itself.

3. These numbers are taken from the Statistical Center of Iran.

4. For a fascinating and rare glimpse into these contradictions of the Iranian society and the role of women, see Christiane Bird's excellent *Neither East Nor West: One Woman's Journey through the Islamic Republic of Iran.*

5. A competing and older conception of art saw the artist as creator, for the artist "has to know and construct a schema before he can adjust it to the needs of portrayal" (116). In other words, Gombrich argues, the work of the artist is much closer to that of the artisan (carpenter), at whom Plato looks so benignly.

6. Also, in *Statesman,* Plato uses a painting analogy to argue for further elaboration of the definition of statesman (277c page 1043).

7. A term used to describe artisans involved in manual labor.

8. For example, Hauser writes that Plato's comments on the visual were responses, in part, to the overvaluation of art as a result of the rise of the merchant class in Athens (90).

9. Again, freed of various Platonisms, the core insight of Plato remains significant and relevant. What Plato means by Form is more than what is usually thought of the term (i.e., some kind of a visual form). What is meant is something like relationships involved in use and production. Using a passage in *Republic* (484cd) in which Plato talks about the "good man gazing at the model (or form or image or idea) of spiritual truth (reality) in his soul" (11), Murdoch writes, "Both Plato and Kant use an image of referring to an ideal or original pattern, not as imitation either of the model itself or of some chosen instantiation (example) of it, but as an inspired interpretation into the realm of practical life of a deep and certain moral insight" (11).

Works Cited

Aristotle. *The Art of Rhetoric.* Trans. H. C. Lawson-Tancred. New York: Penguin Books, 1991.

Barasch, Moshe. *Theories of Art.* New York: SUNY P, 1985.

Bird, Christiane. *Neither East nor West: One Woman's Journey through the Islamic Republic of Iran.* New York: Atria Publishers, 2001.

Eagleton, Terry. *After Theory.* New York: Basic Books, 2003.

Foucault, Michel. "Iran: The Spirit of a World Without Spirit." *Politics, Philosophy, Culture: Interviews and Other Writings.* Trans. Alan Sheridan. New York: Routlege, 1984.

Freire, Paulo. *Pedagogy of the Oppressed.* New York: Continuum, 1993.

Gombrich, E. H. *Art and Illusion.* New York: Pantheon, 1965.

Hauser, Arnold *The Social History of Art, Vol. 1: From Prehistoric Times to the Middle Ages.* New York: Routledge, 1951.

Huby, Pamela. "Socrates and Plato." *A Critical History of Western Philosophy.* New York: The Free Press, 1964: 14–35.

Leitch, Vincent B. "Gayatri Chakravorty Spivak " *The Norton Anthology of Theory and Criticism.* Ed. Vincent B. Leitch. New York: W. W. Norton & Co., 2001: 2193–97.

Majid, Anouar. "The Failure of Postcolonial Theory After 9/11." *The Chronicle of Higher Education.* 30 Nov. 2002 <http://chronicle.com/weekly/v49/i10/10b01101.htm>.

Marías, Julián. *History of Philosophy.* New York: Dover, 1967.

McClintock, Anne, Mufti, Aamir, and Ella Shohat, eds. *Dangerous Liaisons: Gender, Nation, and Postcolonial Perspectives.* Minneapolis: U of Minnesota P, 2002.

Murdoch, Iris. *Metaphysics as a Guide to Morals.* New York: Penguin, 1993.

Murphy, John F. *Sword of Islam: Muslim Extremism from the Arab Conquests to the Attack on America.* Amherst, New York: Prometheus Books, 2002.

Norval, Morgan. *The Fifteen Century War: Islam's Violent Heritage.* Indian Wells, CA: McKenna Publishing Group, 2002.

Pickering, Michael. *Stereotyping: The Politics of Representation.* New York: Palgrave, 2001.

Plato. *Republic. Plato, The Collected Dialogues.* Trans. Paul Shorey. Ed. Edith Hamilton and Huntington Cairns. NJ: Princeton UP, 1996: 575–845.

—"Statesman." *Plato, the Collected Dialogues.* Trans. J. B. Skemp. Ed. Edith Hamilton and Huntington Cairns. NJ: Princeton UP, 1996: 1018–86.

Press, Gerald A."Plato." *The Columbia History of Western Philosophy.* New York: Columbia UP, 1999: 32–52.

Said, Edward. *Orientalism.* New York: Vintage, 1978.

Statistical Center of Iran. 20 Oct. 2004 < http://www.sci.org.ir>.

Williams, Patrick, and Laura Chrisman, eds. *Colonial Discourse and Post-Colonial Theory: A Reader.* New York: SUNY P, 1994.

8 Ethos on the Web: A Cross-Cultural Approach

Yong-Kang Wei

The World Wide Web is a medium—more dramatic, evidently, than print—that relies heavily on iconic, or visual, representations for its rhetorical effects. Richard Lanham notes that "[d]igital expression has resurrected the world of proverbial wisdom, but through vast databanks of icons rather than words" (37) and that the difference between the rhetorics of print and screen is that electronic media "are essentially dynamic rather than static" (16). An online text is rhetorical because it attempts to persuade the audience to take an action, for example, purchasing products, changing attitudes, or simply reading on. What is more, such texts reflect those elements, such as purpose, audience, and context, which are seen as shaping the production of conventional discourse.

Rhetoric as constructed by Aristotle consists of three appeals, the most effective of which is ethos, or character (Bizzell and Herzberg 154). According to Aristotle, "[p]ersuasion is achieved by the speaker's personal character when the speech is so spoken as to make us think him credible" (Bizzell and Herzberg 153). But perception and use of rhetorical ethos differs from culture to culture, just as rhetoric itself does (Oliver 358). I will describe in this chapter elements of design that differ between Western and Chinese cultures and trace the causes of these varied approaches by looking, specifically, at how ethos is constructed online from a cross-cultural perspective.

The chapter mainly serves to provide theoretical insights to teachers in both beginning composition classes and advanced professional writing classes who wish to include online texts as artifacts of analysis. Such sites can provide students with the opportunity to identify elements of appeal on websites aimed at local or global audiences and to speculate on the rhetorical success of hypertextual design. When initiating discussion on rhetorical strategies online or cultural implications of website design, for example, or simply when using websites as points of reference for analysis of the visual projection of ethos on the Web, teachers can also make practical use of the chapter by resorting to the key distinctions between rhetorical conventions that are discussed in this chapter. A sample assignment rounds out the chapter.

I will begin by discussing a theoretical framework for ethos and its place in visual arts and design.

Ethos: Western, Eastern

Although defining *ethos* as a rhetorical strategy involves the role of personal character, traditional Western rhetoric lacks a consensus regarding how to define that role. Two versions of ethos dominate in the history of Western rhetorical theory: one, the Platonic, recognizes ethos as an individual quality of the rhetor and independent of rhetorical manipulations; the other, artistic, treats ethos as something that can be created and manipulated through means of good sense, good will, and good use of language, as proposed by Aristotle in his *Rhetoric.* Obviously, the two versions are in conflict.

Strictly speaking, Plato himself never uses the word *ethos,* and his anti-rhetoric stance may well give the impression that he is also anti-ethos. His emphasis on "true rhetoric" and the truthfulness of human character presented through that rhetoric suggests, however, that he is just as concerned about identifying the self in speech/writing as his sophist rivals are. Thus, "by inference," writes Baumlin, one might still devise "a Platonic definition" of ethos (xiii). But Platonic, or transcendent, truth has to be brought into play. Plato insists that this truth has nothing to do with the worldly (rhetoric included) and that humans were somehow in contact with this truth before birth, "when [their] souls were with the Divine" (Bizzell and Herzberg 55). But how can humans possibly seek truth, existing, as they do, in the flesh? Plato offers by way of solution his dialectic, "the whole process of rational analysis by which the soul [is] led into the knowledge of Ideas" (Hunt 64). The notion of character is thus invoked, for one must be truthful to oneself in order to discover or express truth, an assertion made frequently by Plato in both the *Gorgias* and the *Phaedrus.* In Plato's eyes, only the philosopher, and not the rhetorician, possesses the necessary rectitude.

Plato's conception of ethos, or the truthful human character, is an embodiment of soul knowledge. As Baumlin points out, since dialectic "seeks to discover and express the truth of the soul, then ethos describes the inner harmony among language, character, and truth—in Platonic fashion, ethos defines the space where language and truth meet or are made incarnate within the individual" (xiii). Thus, Platonic ethos is essentially incarnationist in the sense that it projects truth by relating to what is deepest within the individual: the soul.

Clearly, Aristotle departs to a great extent from his mentor in defining ethos. Though he includes the aspect of moral character in the definition, his pragmatism gives rhetoric a much more significant role in connecting human character to the epistemic function of language. Aristotle argues that persuasion through ethos ought to be achieved by "what the speaker says, not by what people think of his character before he begins to speak" (Bizzell and Hertzberg 153). That is, the orator must construct his material (artistic proofs) to "make his own character look right" so as to "inspire trust in his audience" (Bizzell and Hertzberg 160–61). In contrast to Plato, who insists that the speaker's character must be upright for its own sake, Aristotle seems to say that it is sufficient to win an audience simply by making "ourselves thought to be sensible and morally good" (Bizzell and Hertzberg 161). Put bluntly, Aristotelian ethos can be faked.

In sum, the Western tradition of rhetoric has been marked by a tension between the Platonic and the Aristotelian in terms of how to identify ethos. Platonic ethos assumes the moral character of a speaker to be something innate and outside the confines of language and society whereas Aristotelian ethos reflects a rather pragmatic approach in discourse, stressing the need for a rhetorical reconstruction of human character.

By contrast, in Chinese rhetoric, especially in classical Chinese rhetoric (CCR), there is no such concern for the relation between human character and discourse. This difference does not suggest that ethos has no bearing on Chinese rhetoric but, rather, that ethos in CCR has taken on a different focus, with the sources of credibility shifted from self to nonself, or from the individual to the collective, communal, and cultural. It seems that Western ethos is anything but universal when perceived from an Eastern perspective, especially in light of the following three aspects of CCR: rhetorical function, epistemology, and "bamboo hypertext."

Rhetorical Function

Instead of alluding to the welfare of individuals, as characteristically occurs in Western rhetoric, CCR tends to emphasize the need for maintaining social harmony (Scollan and Scollan 142), with its discourse production essentially depersonalized. It is hard to imagine an ancient Chinese rhetor (*sui-ke*) standing above the crowd engaging in some kind of public speech or debate—not because the notion of democracy failed to prevail, but because such practice was out of character with the cultural themes of humility, collectivism, and adherence to social rituals.

Harmonic rhetoric should not be interpreted simplistically as avoiding conflicts or submitting to authority; rather, it speaks to positioning oneself fitly in the world (society and nature) through the medium of language. To achieve harmony is ultimately to seek unity between man and the Dao, a cosmic moral order of being in ancient Chinese ideology. Rhetorically, this appeal to unity would mean foregoing any individual appeal on the part of the rhetor, who, for the purpose of establishing ethos, would have to appeal to culturally and historically established authority, such as ancestral lineage and sage-kings such as Yao, Shun, and Yü. Ancestral lineage would give the rhetor a legitimate position in the social hierarchy; the sage-kings were thought to "maintain a divine afflatus" (Schwartz 26) and therefore to have the power to perceive the Dao. The appeal to such authority is essentially an appeal to the Dao, through which the rhetor builds up persuasive power.

Epistemology

Unlike Western rhetoric, CCR never embraced the ideal of language as "an enterprise to represent or depict or describe an external reality independent of man and society" (Lenk 6). Rather than attempting to express a transcendent truth as advocated by Plato and other Western thinkers, the primary epistemological function of CCR is to illuminate the nature of the world as an ontological Yin-Yang duality. For a Westerner, language and reality can be separable; for a Chinese, language and reality are one in the sense that we have to use language to make distinctions between Yin and Yang, good and bad, right and wrong, etc. Confucius is obsessed with the rectification of names (*zheng ming*) because he knows very well that the process can lead to the rectification of moral behavior. Within the Confucian system of ideology, and the Daoist as well, discourse constitutes social reality.

Thus, the epistemology underlying CCR turns Platonic ethos upside down. Because it never concerns itself with "an object-marking account of the way words relate to the world" (Hansen 71), CCR makes no issue of truth: the individual self seen as a potential embodiment of truth in the Platonic definition carries little weight in establishing ethos. Put another way, Chinese ethos requires no connection between the truthfulness of discourse and the truthfulness of human character, actual or made up.

We can also see that traditional Chinese epistemology implies a denial of human agency as presupposed in a Platonic definition of ethos. For Plato, the objective discovery and representation of truth must be done by (or incarnated within) an individual; but because truth is a nonissue in ancient Chinese thought, there is no need for human agency in the exercise of such objectivity. Indeed, discourse production in ancient China is agentless in the sense that the speech-act itself has never been assumed to be something individual—not only because discourse is essentially depersonalized for the sake of maintaining social harmony, as mentioned earlier, but also because there has been a widespread recognition of language's structuring impact on man's behavior. For Lao Zi, the "name" (i.e., language) is "the mother of ten thousand things" (1); for Confucius and followers like Xun Zi, morality comes out of naming, not the other way round. All this poses further challenges to the Western definition of ethos: If discourse practice is agentless, then where do we locate a rhetor's ethos?

Bamboo Hypertext

Classical Chinese rhetoric can be metaphorically described as bamboo hypertext in that it shares many textual features normally associated with modern electronic hypertext, which, according to Jay David Bolter, is "the interactive interconnection of a set of symbolic elements" (27). I choose the metaphor of "bamboo hypertext" furthermore because it conforms to the physical features of classical Chinese texts, as all were written (or occasionally carved) on strings of bamboo strips.

Like hypertext, CCR is nonlinear, open ended, collective, multi-accentual, interactive, and networked.

Almost all the Chinese classics we have access to today, including Lao Zi's *Dao De Jing* and Confucius' *Analects,* were created as a collection of short essays, paragraphs, or sentences written and rewritten by the disciples, or disciples of the disciples, of Lao Zi and Confucius over a span of decades or even centuries. As a token of respect, the text bore the name of Lao Zi or Confucius as its official author, but, as Mark Lewis suggests (53), the master may never have contributed a single written word to the collection (though of course it is popularly believed that those quotations by Lao Zi or Confucius bore the master's imprint one way or another).

Consequently, after passing through numerous hands, the texts would invariably become inconsistent or self-contradictory in both meaning and purpose due to the absence of individual authorship (control). In addition, many disciples would use the master as a source of authority to create their own texts (or *agendas,* in today's political terminology), with degrees of deviation and variance from the predecessors, depending on the then-current ideological climate and scholarly trends. Readers also took an active role in interacting with the texts and very often even were part of an ongoing process of textual transformation. It is not surprising, then, that a classic Chinese work credited to a historic figure could have numerous "adulterated" versions. The problem, of course, comes from a collective authorship responsible for the production of bamboo hypertext.

What is significant about bamboo hypertext is that its authorship seems to break away from all the "self-structure" (Alcorn 3) associated with Western ethos: character, personality, person(a), voice, image, and, above all, self, none of which matters much in CCR. Because of a collective authorship that transcends time and space, CCR texts typically are defined by motion rather than by "momentary location" (Moulthrop 303). That is to say, such texts aim to dissolve themselves and simultaneously the kind of stableness, however relative, that a self-structure requires to establish ethos (Alcorn 3 ff.).

Marshall Alcorn writes that "[a] theory of ethos needs to be grounded in a relatively clear, but also a relatively complex, understanding of the self" (4), but it is doubtful that this is true of CCR, whose tradition of collective authorship projects self-effacement rather than self-enhancement. A CCR text, however, like its Western counterpart, must establish credibility and trust to effect persuasion. Indeed, Confucius' *xiu ci li qi chen,* which is translated as "rhetoric oriented towards trust," may point out how important ethos is in Chinese rhetoric. But whereas ethos in the Western rhetorical tradition is created to gain the audience's trust in the rhetor as an individual, ethos in CCR has a broader purpose of telling or, to use Lewis' words, "writing the masters" (53) instead of one's self.

Ethos in Visual Arts and Design

Philip Rawson and Laszlo Legeza have argued that Westerners "tend to think, diagrammatically, of a world of separate things—some of them alive—arranged in an independent space" (9), a point that may explain, philosophically, why mainstream Western thought tends to focus on the self instead of the community or the social/natural environment, of which the individual is a part. To Western visual artists and designers, this individualistic view of the world may have two implications with regard to ethos: one is that ethos consists of an individual appeal, equal to self-representation; the other, also related to the first, is that the art of design is an isolated undertaking, its efforts focusing on creating character or ethos, with little limited reference to the surrounding environment. In defining the ethos of design, Richard Buchanan writes that "[p]roducts have character because in some way they reflect their makers,"

> and part of the art of design is the control of such character in order to persuade users that a product has credibility in their lives. In essence, the problem is the way designers choose to represent themselves in products, not as they are, but as they wish to appear. Designers fashion objects to speak in particular voices, imbuing them with personal qualities they think will give confidence to users [. . .]. (101)

While Buchanan may be echoing Aristotle's vision of ethos—projecting the self through artistic manipulation (of design, to be specific), he is also saying that the character (i.e., ethos) of design points to designers, and that credibility or confidence evoked through such design has much to do with how designers "choose to represent themselves in products."

But, as I have argued, ethos in the sense of self-representation is problematic from a classical Chinese perspective, not just because the individual appeal is out of the picture, but also because sources of ethos are considered nonindividual, located in ancestral lineage, culturally and historically established authority, etc., and, ultimately, the Dao. Thus, instead of representing one's self, the Chinese artist/designer may well choose, for the purpose of establishing ethos, to draw on the appeals of ancestry, sage-kings, or entities the Dao is believed to work through (nature, heaven, etc.).

From the perspective of CCR, another problematic aspect of Western ethos as self-representation is that it separates the design of an individual work from its environment, as if an object of design can stand by itself. We can see this clearly from Buchanan's emphasis on presenting "qualities of character" in design—to ensure that objects can "assert their own existence and, through that existence, the attitudes that are an integral part of an object's present being" (101; 107). Whether to assert the existence of one's individual work or to show "attitudes" as a means of that assertion, the Western ethos of visual design is clearly seen as something from within, to be built on the merits of "an object's present being." Thus, to a Western visual artist/designer, a golden temple is a golden temple: The beauty and craftsmanship declare themselves.

The Chinese counterpart would approach a golden temple differently. Rather than focus on the design itself, he or she would first ask where the golden temple was to be built and then decide how to match the design with the place, so that the beauty and craftsmanship of the building might reflect the unity of the natural environment. Thus, instead of asserting its own existence, a Chinese golden temple would derive its appeal from fitting into a natural scheme that transcends the physical limits of the temple. That is to say, the ethos of the temple would not stand by itself.

When visiting a traditional Chinese garden, a Westerner might be struck by its "irregular design, broken edges, meandering streams, and patches of plants" (Martin), elements that might seem not to assert either character or attitude by the Westerner's standards. But, as David Martin points out, such elements actually have been designed in line with the Daoist theme of expressing nature and harmony, a theme that by definition contrasts sharply with the Western ideal of expressing one's own individual character and passions. Unlike the

Western designer who deliberately incorporates manufactured objects, for example, setting sculpture or displaying ornaments in the garden, the Chinese designer would seek to transfer the garden into a natural setting—where twisted and eroded rocks and stone of natural shapes would greet a visitor's eye—to attain, as Martin has put it, "spiritual communion" with the Dao.

In Chinese visual arts, such as garden design, sculpture painting, and seal engraving, to express nature or, in the words of the fourth-century Chinese artist Gu Kai-Zi, to "portray the Dao through natural images" (*yi-xin-mei-dao*) (qtd. in Zhang Guang-Fuo 187), demands the ability to hide one's skill and craftsmanship or to erase traces of human effort in design. The Chinese considered skill or craftsmanship an indication of artificiality and not necessarily in keeping with the naturalness of the Dao. Therefore, great artists/designers often try to inject a "primitive" quality into their works, as if they are created by "awkward" hands.

Western ethos in visual arts and design is questionable from a Chinese perspective because it has been treated as a kind of individual property, with what many Chinese would consider a narrow focus on self-representation. Since the traditional Chinese artist/designer prefers a holistic approach (i.e., taking into consideration the relation of design product to the environment), efforts to deliberately boost the beauty or craftsmanship (i.e., ethos) of an individual work without due regard to context would be considered inappropriate.

I would describe the Western approach to design that emphasizes the individual work itself as "micro," as opposed to the Chinese "macro" approach, which generally values how pieces of design should relate to each other and to the surrounding world. A study by Qiuye Wang, comparing graphics from Chinese and American science magazines and manuals, seems to support my argument on the micro versus macro distinction, as the author found that the Chinese visuals were more context-oriented (i.e., providing more contextual information) than the American visuals, which were more "focused and direct" (553–60). Although Wang's study does not address visual ethos, it does reflect the fact that Chinese designers pay more attention to the question of how to relate design to context than American designers do.

Wang may echo Edward Hall, who describes Chinese and many other non-Western cultures as "high-context" (39) in the sense that communication relies on the context to deliver messages, which are generally less explicit and less elaborated than those of "low-context" cultures in the West (39). Hall's "high-context system" (105) does not speak directly about Chinese ethos, but it does point to the linkage between context and communication and, by extension, visual design. Since Chinese visual arts and design pay great attention to the environment that surrounds an individual work, we might say that the ethos created is one of high context.

In addition to the above-mentioned micro/macro distinction, we see yet another key difference between Western and Chinese design: the former tends to be more visually expressive, exhibiting what I would call a preference for definitiveness whereas the latter tends to exhibit a preference for simplicity. Like Western rhetoric, Western visual arts and design are, in general, more elaborate, more explicit, more colorful, and, of course, more fully expressed in comparison with their Chinese counterparts, which often value more open-ended expressions.

What underlies the Western preference is still the perception of ethos: i.e., how to regard the role an individual plays in his or her work. In the West, because ethos is associated with self-projection or self-representation, as discussed earlier, full and explicit expression is considered necessary to render ethos. Thus, unlike traditional Chinese artists, who would deliberately leave large chunks of space unpainted in order to suggest, say, natural beauty, Western artists might feel the urge to do the opposite—to paint every corner of a canvas—for fear of not expressing themselves fully. But because ethos is not necessarily linked with one's individual character and because design is valued for being integrated with nature and environment and, metaphysically, with the cosmic order of the Dao, explicit expression for the purpose of self-representation would seem out of the question in Chinese culture. Instead, we might encounter a different mind-set, one that prefers a more implicit treatment, for the whole is not seen as needing much from any individual, and design does not have to declare itself in full.

The implicit approach characterizing traditional Chinese visual arts and design might be better understood in terms of *wu-wei* (translated, literally, as "doing-nothing"), the Daoist ideal of cultivating virtue by abstaining from striving consciously in everyday life. In the philosophical sense, doing nothing is essentially allowing the Dao to prevail. But since the Dao takes care of everything under heaven, doing nothing is indeed doing something—and everything. That is why Lao Zi insists, "If nothing is done, then all will be well" (3). So doing less in design—with less artistic elaboration or fewer personal touches—could also mean doing more if perceived from the point of view of *wu-wei.*

This difference between Western and Chinese attitudes towards expression marks an important distinction between Chinese and Western Web design. Chinese websites are generally more plain-looking than Western websites, which tend to be comparatively elaborate and aggressive. Western ethos is individualistic, hence the need to strive to create personal attractions to deliver individual appeal. But because Chinese ethos is nonindividualistic and draws on appeals from outside the self, not striving for distinction would be more becoming, for it could both limit personal showing-off and allow the harmony of the Dao to unveil itself.

Ethos on the Web: Key Issues

Notwithstanding these cultural differences, students might find it difficult to draw distinctions when comparing Chinese and Western ethos on the Web. For one thing, digital expression has been shared across all cultures: whether one is Chinese or American, when it comes to designing an online text, more likely than not designers will resort to the same digital technique or to the same databanks of icons to create visual messages. (Microsoft has dominated the Chinese market.) For another, electronic technology has brought East and West closer together, even in the rhetorical sense. I have used the term *bamboo hypertext* to describe classical Chinese rhetoric in that it shares many textual features, such as fluidity and collective authorship, commonly identified in modern electronic hypertext. But I could also put it the other way round: that is, Western hypertext resembles classical Chinese rhetoric, especially in light of the issue of ethos. The collective authorship involved in online text production raises questions about the traditional Western way of identifying ethos in terms of personal character, individuality, etc. Can we still treat ethos online as some kind of self-projection? If we take a closer look at organizational, governmental, and corporate websites in the United States, we may see that ethos presented on these sites is more of a collective than of an individual type.

On the other hand, we can reasonably assume that even though the Internet has altered the perception of ethos, the way designers present their ethos may still be shaped by what I would call "cultural programming." That is, we might assume that the ethos presented online can still be categorized as collective or individualistic, depending on how the projection of ethos is perceived in the cultural tradition of the designer. For instance, a Western designer may believe that an online design is a source of ethos and therefore choose to use elaborate graphics to make the design stand out; in this case, the ethos presented would be considered individualistic because it points to a cultural tradition that separates design from its context or environment. Needless to say, if a Chinese designer decides to do the opposite, in order for the design to achieve moderation in terms of visual appeal, then the ethos generated can be categorized as nonindividualistic or collective, for it points to a cultural tradition that integrates design with contexts or environment. Likely, a designer will not be aware of the difference, but because culture shapes communicative behavior, we can expect that it also leaves its imprint on how designers present their ethos on the Web, wittingly or unwittingly.

Self-Representation or Self-Effacement?

Whereas the traditional Western definition of ethos in the strict sense of self-representation may not apply well online, Western Web designers may still find themselves unknowingly influenced by this tradition. For example, they may apply digital devices to deliberately enhance the visual glamour of Web design so as to assert, in Buchanan's words, its "existence" or "attitudes." Such a strategy would suggest that the designers deliberately ignore relations between design and context and environment.

We might be able to identify with relative ease the self-representation tendency on Western sites where the heavy application of graphics seems the norm. Generally, using graphics in design is seen as attempting to "maximize the impact of communication through the combined or disjointed means of the written message, the sign, or the image" (Moles 122). Because of its potential to make design objects visually appealing, graphic design may be considered an effective means of maximizing the impact of visual ethos (which is part of a communication after all). This potential seems true of design objects on many Western sites where the creation of ethos depends heavily on the visual appeals of graphics (Figure 1).

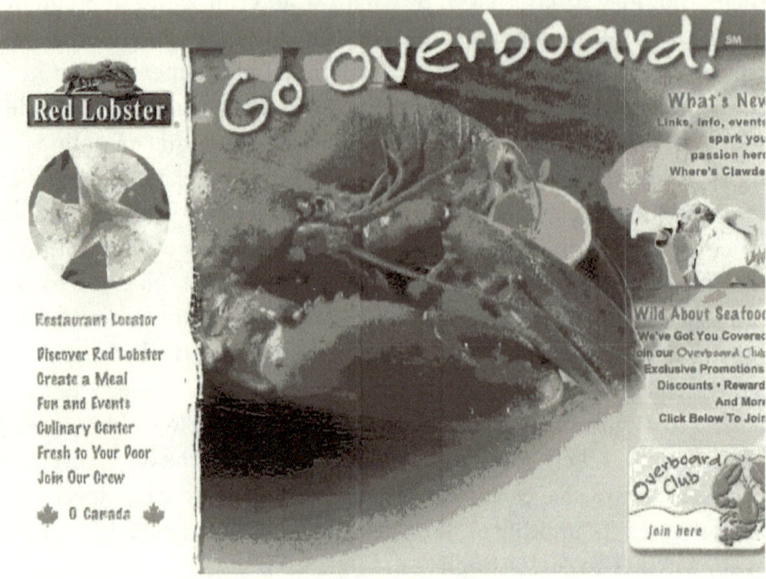

Figure 1. Red Lobster's homepage has used graphic design to achieve a powerful Web presence, or ethos. (Used by permission of Media & Communication, Darden Restaurants.)

Often a Chinese Web page looks dull by Western standards because of the limited use of graphics. The homepage of the Chinese Language Teachers Association, as shown in Figure 2, has reflected a conventional, rather symbolic design short of graphic detail even though it includes an image of bamboo. The phrase "self-effacement" describes this site, and much of Chinese Web design, in the sense that its low-profile approach (i.e., fewer graphics and less glamour) does not assert its own identity strongly. Bamboo does have its charm, but the charm of either the Red Lobster or the Misty Slims lady (Figure 3) is much more evident visually.

The attempt to use visually overwhelming pictures or images can be seen as indicative of a focused or high-profile design approach, but it may also point to an individualistic sentiment associated with the design ideology of the West, that is, to the desire to deliver distinction to individual design items. One such example would be the Misty Slims lady. We may even sense a deliberate play of ethos in the design, which centers on a female smoker who incarnates elegance, charm, beauty, and seemingly high social status. But, as we can see, this ethos

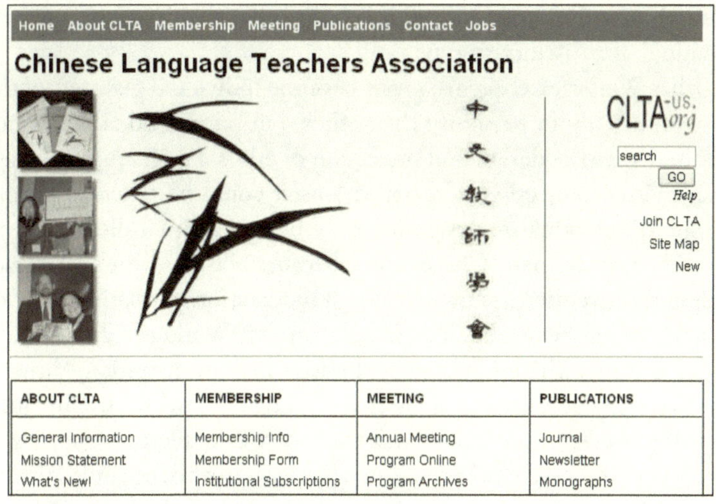

Figure 2. The homepage of the Chinese Language Teachers' Association has reflected a self-effacing ethos by Western standards. (Used by permission of Chinese Language Teachers Association.)

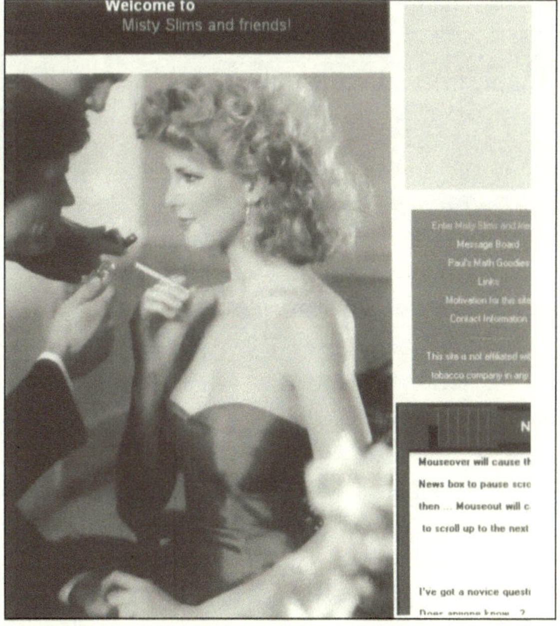

Figure 3. The visually seductive Misty Slims lady has been designed to kindle the viewer's admiration and desire. (Used by permission of Paul McCarthy.)

is also of an individual kind, as it is built upon the image of a female individual of a distinctive type.

Other Western websites may not have the individual glamour of the Misty Slims lady to personify their ethos, but an individualistic sentiment underlies the design and projection of ethos. For example, the aggressive visual projection of a boiled lobster could be taken to signify an urge to individualize design items by bringing visual distinction to them. In contrast, many Chinese sites, because of the culture's self-effacing design conventions, show a degree of moderation in treating individual items, as has been seen, for example, on the "World of Chinese Culture" (Figure 4), which is hosted by the Taiwan administration. Visually speaking, the whole site was unassertive if judged by Western standards. But perhaps even more telling was the moon-cake picture, which was treated as part of the whole since an aggressive treatment could disrupt its visual harmony or coordination with the rest of the page. We can imagine what a Western designer might do with the image: enlarge its size and use various visual "tricks" to dramatize the moon-cakes.

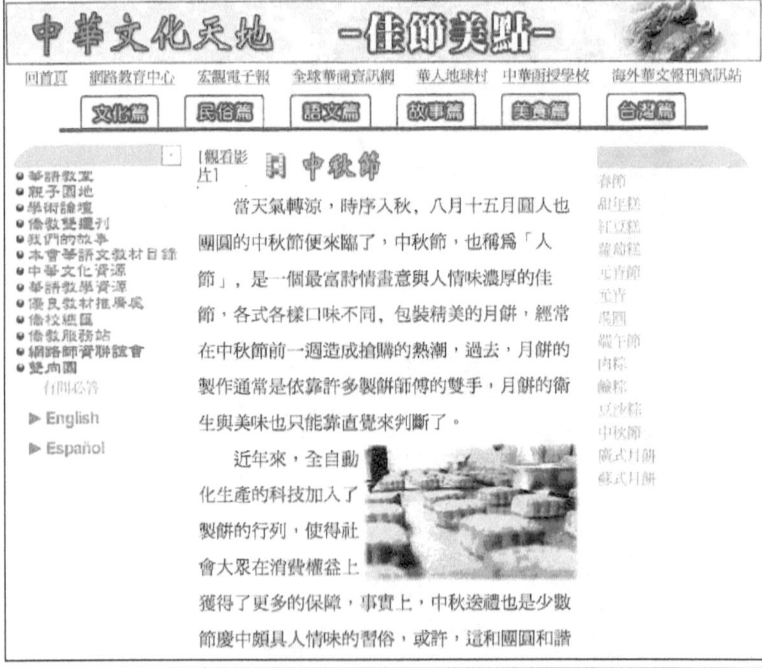

Figure 4. Taiwan's "World of Chinese Culture" site, visually unassertive site by Western standards, subtly incorporated an advertisement for moon-cakes. (Used by permission of Overseas Chinese Affairs Commission, Taiwan).

Students may witness the Western invasion of Chinese design on some of the Chinese sites because of the evident bent on using heavy graphics, color, and other sorts of digital expressions. However, I would not say that these Western-influenced sites are totally out of tune with the self-effacing design tradition in Chinese culture. For example, on a Chinese Coca-Cola site, the Coca-Cola bottle and sign were given much visual attention but did not appear so aloof as to give the impression that they stood as isolated design elements This is because they have been woven into a collage of icons featuring themes extraneous to Coca-Cola. Moreover, the Public Information column on the right side of the page offered a visual balance for the site so that the Coca-Cola bottle and sign did not rivet the spotlight. This balance might be dismissed by a Westerner as lack of focus in design, but I would argue that the design choices probably had more to do with the idea of contextualization in Chinese design.

Micro or Macro?

The Western Web samples, as discussed earlier, may well be labeled "micro" because of the underlying tendency in individualizing design items, but I also use the term to mean, specifically, the kind of design that does not connect design items to their contexts, or to something that does not appear directly related to design thematically (e.g., content or purpose).

Generally speaking, Western websites are more content-specific, with technical details well coordinated around the subject of design. That is, there is a close integration between design and content "to show the logical relationships among all elements that appear on the page" (Farkas and Farkas 241). For example, on an American Coca-Cola site, every design item, from the use of color (the Coca-Cola red) to the display of polar bear cubs, cohered logically with the "joy" theme of Coca-Cola. The integration of design and content suggested that designers' decisions had been directed towards design mainly at the micro level, such as concern over how to correspond to the theme(s) of a design project. As a result, Red Lobster's website was all about Red Lobster, and Coca-Cola's website was all about Coca-Cola or things that carried a Coca-Cola theme.

Because of design decisions being leveled at micro details, however, Western websites tend to exhibit a disconnection from the cultural context. For example, Budweiser's U.K. site once featured the

American lingo "Whassup?" The message was incorporated well with the theme of the site, as it was meant to lure curious Web surfers to click into the cyber world of Bud. However, this was also where we could sense a cultural disconnect: Would the British, who usually relish wry humor and polished usage of language, buy into the Americanism "Whassup"? The fine print at the bottom of the screen, which stated, "U.S. residents under 21 years old should not enter the site," might have exposed as well a lack of connection with the host country, whose residents are mostly non-Americans and are allowed to drink at age 16.

The "macro" disjunction, as seen on Budweiser's U.K. Web page, will certainly be less of an issue on Chinese websites, where designers tend to demonstrate more concern for how to incorporate their design items into the context of the host culture or society. However, such a broad approach could result in a disjunction in design, causing a website to be thematically digressive or, to use Wang's words, "loose and inaccurate" (557) in terms of correspondence between design and its subject. For example, the Chinese Coca-Cola website, mentioned earlier, was overlaid with links in the Public Information column that had virtually no bearing on Coca-Cola. Apparently, the goal of helping "express the theme of the website," as proposed by Farkas and Farkas for American Web designers (241), was never to be accomplished. But the design still could be credited with a degree of meaningfulness if critics appreciated the emphasis laid on contextualization in the tradition of Chinese design, which approaches design macrocosmically, through integration with cultural context.

The Public Info column seemed to tell what was currently in vogue in (mainland) China, especially with the younger generation, in activities such as sex (Dangerous Lovers), studying abroad (Overseas Campuses), and travel (Highlights of Exotic Lands). Despite the fact that it might have proved thematically irrelevant to the Coca-Cola Company and its products, the column played a role in connecting the website with the "in" trends in today's Chinese society. We might also sense an attempt on the part of designers to turn Coca-Cola, a drinking product, into one of those "ins," for Coke was presented as something to be associated with modern technologies (as seen on the Web page), which Chinese leadership, who have ambitions of industrializing the country in the new millennium, has been more than enthusiastic in embracing.

A moon-cake ad that once appeared on the Hong Kong "Yahoo! Finance" page also illustrated the notion of contextualization in traditional Chinese design. While the ad might not have integrated well in content or theme with the host page, which is dedicated to money and investment, it did demonstrate a sense of connection with Hong Kong's cultural environment, in which the Confucian tradition of filial piety is still being observed among the Chinese as the norm of family life. The ad might have been declared a design failure because there was no guarantee that those interested in buying stocks would be equally interested in buying moon-cakes. (It certainly would make more sense to place the ad on a website covering food items.) But one could argue that the design failed only at the micro level, for not corresponding with the finance theme of the host site; on the macro level, it fared quite well by linking ordinary moon-cakes to the possible fulfillment of one's filial duty and by creating an extraordinary cultural appeal in the host society. One could argue further that there was equally no guarantee that those who felt their filial piety inspired, whether stock junkies or Web surfers, would decide against ordering moon-cakes for their parents.

Whether the moon-cake ad was effective in targeting its audience I leave to the readers. My point is that it incorporated a design tradition (perhaps unwittingly on the part of designers) that is macroscopically attuned to the host site's cultural context, as opposed to a tradition that is driven microscopically by the design's inner coherence (e.g., close integration between host sites and ads published on them, as seen on the American "Yahoo! Finance" site). Again, we can imagine what a Western Web designer might do with the moon-cake ad. Because of the micro concern in design, he or she might well end up focusing exclusively on the graphic details of the moon-cakes so as to induce a "mouthwatering" effect on online consumers. Such an ad might have its own charm or ethos. However, ethos of this sort would be a "micro" ethos, based on devotion to details of a design. And, as we may recall, Chinese ethos is created at the macro level, with allusions made to sources of inspirations from outside a design, as seen in the example of an online moon-cake ad in Hong Kong that drew on Confucius's filial piety, a culturally popular theme in the host society, to build appeal.

Explicit or Implicit?

Earlier, I discussed two different design mentalities and pointed out that Western visual designers, because of the drive to express themselves in full, tend to express themselves more elaborately with design objects than do their Chinese counterparts, who are more concerned about letting nature, environment, and the ultimate Dao unveil themselves and therefore tend to express themselves in a more open-ended or implicit manner. At the center of such differentiation lies the perception of ethos: Western ethos is equated with self-projection or self-representation, the need to assert design features and, through them, the self; Chinese ethos, on the other hand, downplays personal excellence, emphasizing instead the necessity to abstain from "man-made" elaboration in design.

In online design, the "explicit" preference could result in, for example, complex combinations of content types (i.e., text, graphics, animation, video, and audio), heavy use of color, and frequent display of sleek icons and images, as we have witnessed on a number of Western, especially U.S., websites. Needless to say, the "implicit" preference would lead to simple combinations of content types, light use of color, and infrequent display of icons and images.

Graphic design can maximize the impact of a message, but this means that additional design efforts have to be made. For instance, the reason Western designers are likely to use a range of digital expressions to enhance the glamour of their design may well be that they like to assert the existence or attitudes of their works, as implied in the Western approach to ethos as some sort of self-representation. Further, such an approach may also relate to the individualistic understanding of the self in Western culture, in contrast to Eastern culture, where individualism and the self have been downplayed traditionally, and where, consequently, the projection of ethos is characterized by skills of (Web) design that reflect on the relationships of design items to objects or beings that are usually present on a larger scale (e.g., context and authority).

I don't wish to give the impression that Eastern online design is culturally oriented while Western is not. Postmodern critics, like Roland Barthes, would argue that a text (including those online), no matter where it is created, must "procee[d] from several cultures" (54), and that authorship is at best "a historical construct" (Tuman 64). This would mean that all of the Western samples selected for discussion in this chapter are, like their Eastern counterparts, "macro" in essence, culturally defined and even culturally designed. Indeed, we can clearly identify traces of cultural or macro design in some of those Western samples. In Figure 3 (a Misty Slims' homepage), for example, American pop-culture had left its unambiguous marks of celebrity-worship and sex-obsession, which was illustrated through the charm and elegance of a female beauty. When we look at the U.S. Coca-Cola website, we can feel the imprints of American consumerism on a Web design in a rather subtle manner: A consumer product (Coke) was being projected as an equivalent to the joy of life. If celebrity, sex, or consumerism has anything to do with cultural appeals, these (Western) Web pages clearly exhibit an approach to ethos that must be interpreted in a language beyond individualistic terms.

With an understanding of the elements and ideologies of Chinese and Western design, students might look for these or other distinguishing features used in global designs. Following is an assignment I give my students to sensitize them to cultural differences and preferences in visual design.

Assignment: Cross-Cultural Ethos

In Western rhetoric, ethos is defined as a strategy of using your status, moral character, credibility, image, etc., to persuade an audience. Sometimes, your voice and tone, your persona, your concern for beauty, and your professionalism in writing can all contribute to an effective projection of ethos. In Chinese and other Eastern cultures that traditionally value collectivism, ethos may have less to do with personal appeals, for it is often projected by invoking cultural forces such as tradition, authoritative figures, etc., with which the speaker or writer can effectively identify him-/herself.

In short, Western ethos can be created by making the speaker or writer look good whereas the Chinese ethos emphasizes the need to connect with good (sources) outside of oneself.

Since a Web page is a rhetorical text, the notion of ethos also applies online (e.g., the designer may want to make his/her website look attractive.) For this assignment (600–800 words), please select two websites, one from a Chinese (or another Eastern) organization and one from an American (or another Western) organization, and write an analysis examining how they present ethos differently by using one or all of the three categories we have just discussed: self-representation versus self-effacement, micro versus macro, and definitiveness versus ambiguity. As always, be specific and use details to back up your point(s).

The following questions may be helpful if you find it difficult to narrow your focus in analysis: (1) What makes the sites appear credible, or not credible, given the target audience and culture? Through what means, design, expression, etc.? Can you clearly identify the ethos of these websites? (2) What are the major differences between the two sites? Which appeals more to you? Why? (3) Is there any cultural reason behind the design of each site? Do any of the three distinctions apply well to the Web designs you're analyzing? Why or why not? Is there anything else you feel that would add to the understanding of online ethos from a cross-cultural point of view?

You will have two class sessions to complete the analysis. But first you will need to do some online research and brainstorm with your group members. Be sure to include the URLs in your analysis paper.

Works Cited

Alcorn, Marshall, Jr. "Self-Structure as a Rhetorical Device: Modern Ethos and the Divisiveness of the Self." Baumlin and Baumlin, 3–35.

Barthes, Roland. *The Rustle of Language.* Trans. R. Howard. New York: Hill & Wang, 1986.

Baumlin, James. "Introduction: Position Ethos in Historical and Contemporary Theory." Baumlin and Baumlin, xi–xxvii.

Baumlin, James, and Tita Baumlin, eds. *Ethos: New Essays in Rhetorical and Critical Theory.* Dallas: Southern Methodist UP, 1994.

Bizzell, Patricia, and Bruce Herzberg, eds. *The Rhetorical Tradition: Readings from Classical Times to the Present.* Boston, MA: Bedford Books of St. Martin's Press, 1990.

Bolter, Jay David. *Writing Space: The Computer, Hypertext, and the History of Writing.* Hillsdale, NJ: Lawrence Erlbaum Associates, 1991.

Buchanan, Richard. "Declaration by Design: Rhetoric, Argument, and Demonstration in Design Practice." *Design Discourse: History/Theory/Criticism.* Ed. Victor Margolin. Chicago: The U of Chicago P, 1989.

Budweiser UK. Homepage. 25 Mar. 2001 <http://www.budweiser.co.uk/home.htm>.

Chinese Language Teachers Association. Homepage. 2 Oct. 2004 <http://clta.deall.ohio-state.edu/>.

Coca-Cola China. Homepage. 23 Mar. 2001.< http://www.coca-cola.com.cn/index2.jsp.>.

Coca-Cola USA. Homepage. 23 Mar. 2001. <http://www.cocacola.com/alternate.html>.

Farkas, David, and Jean Farkas. *Principles of Web Design.* New York: Longman, 2002.

Hall, Edward T. *Beyond Culture.* Garden City, NY: Doubleday, 1976.

Hansen, Chad. *Language and Logic in Ancient China.* Ann Arbor: U of Michigan P, 1983.

Lanham, Richard A. *The Electronic Word: Democracy, Technology, and the Arts.* Chicago: The U of Chicago P, 1993.

Lenk, Hans. *Epistemological Issues in Classical Chinese Philosophy.* NY: SUNY P, 1993.

Lewis, Mark. *Writing and Authority in Early China.* Albany, NY: SUNY P, 1999.

Martin, David. "Asian Gardens." *BOTA 250: Cultural Botany.* 31 May 2001 <http://www.centralia.ctc.edu/~dmartin/Bot250/readings/u4-i.html>.

McCarthy, Paul. Homepage. 25 Mar. 2001 <http://misty120s.com/Misty120s/index.shtml>.

Moles, Abraham. "The Legibility of the World: A Project of Graphic Design." *Design Discourse: History/Theory/Criticism.* Ed. Victor Margolin. Chicago: The U of Chicago P, 1989.

Moulthrop, Stuart. "Rhizome and Resistance: Hypertext and the Dreams of a New Culture." *Hyper/Text/Theory.* Ed. George P. Landow. Baltimore: The Johns Hopkins UP, 1994. 299–321.

Oliver, Robert. "Culture and Rhetoric." *Rhetoric: Concepts, Definitions, Boundaries.* Ed. William Covino and David Jolliffe. Boston: Allyn & Bacon, 1995.

Overseas Chinese Affairs Commission. "Mid-Autulmn Festival." The World of Chinese Culture. 2 Oct. 2004 <http://edu.ocac.gov.tw/culturechinese/vod14html/vod_12.htm>.

Rawson, Philip, and Laszlo Legeza. *Tao: The Chinese Philosophy of Time and Change.* London: Thames & Hudson Ltd., 1973.

Schwartz, Benjamin Isadore. *The World of Thought in Ancient China.* Cambridge, MA: Harvard UP, 1989.

Scollon, Ron, and Suzanne Wong Scollon. *Intercultural Communication: A Discourse Approach.* Cambridge, MA: Blackwell, 1995.

Tuman, Myron. *Word Perfect: Literacy in the Computer Age.* Pittsburgh: U of Pittsburgh P, 1992.

Wang, Qiuye. "A Cross-Cultural Comparison of the Use of Graphics in Scientific and Technical Communication." *Technical Communication* 47.4 (2000): 555–60.

Yahoo! Finance Hong Kong. Homepage. 20 Sept. 2001 <hk.finance.yahoo.com>.

Zhang, Guang-Fuo. *History of Chinese Fine Arts.* Beijing, China: The *Zhi-Shi* Press, 1982.

9 Visualizing Discovery: Christopher Columbus's Maps

Jean Darcy

In our learning unit on discovery narratives, my students and I consider the ways explorers describe their conceptions of the unknown. Our task is to understand the kind of critical thinking that emerges from the visual and textual representations of "empty spaces" in the mind's maps. Specifically, we attempt to understand how, in Columbus's journals, his own critical thinking has shaped history, through representation. As the unit becomes an exploration into how we as learners also approach the unknown, we gain insight into our own styles of knowing and learning and become aware of how visual images can engender discovery and critical thinking. We begin by considering the visuals Columbus used when he entered those "empty spaces" where his maps contained uncertain references. We are interested in how praise and blame are distributed: using Mary Louise Pratt's formulation of art in "contact zones," we read texts in terms of the way that different cultures meet in social spaces [. . .] "often in contexts of highly asymmetrical relations of power [. . .]" (252). We also make use of Philip Fischer's metaphors regarding how cultures can bump into one another, become absorbed by one another, bounce off yet reflect one another, or develop parallel paths (vii).

My students, most of whom are recent immigrants or first generation U.S. citizens, have a personal stake in this topic: they, like Columbus, experienced the unknown and carried images in their imaginations throughout their journeys to America. Queensborough Community College, CUNY, is a commuter college within a half-hour drive to Manhattan. The student population is very diverse and interested in dislocation and cultural encounter. Our American literature course, described below, is an upper-level course required of education majors who are interested in the learning process. In my introductory level classes I use assignments that rely on visual evidence, but they are shorter one- to two-page essays (see Appendix 2). From a discussion of their own experiences, students move into a consideration of the cultural context of the readings. The literature class reads two journals by Christopher Columbus that have been edited heavily by Fray Bartolemé de Las Casas and are included in his *Historia de las Indias* (*History of the West Indies*). Portions of the journals are summarized by de Las Casas, and other parts are quoted directly. We are guided by Myra Jehlen's "Papers of Empire." While Jehlen does not claim that "reality is the product of its telling," she does claim that authors have achieved material power in the shaping of history (13). Indeed, the 1507 Johannes Ruysch Map of America represents the West Coast, which had not yet been explored by Europeans, as an unfurling scroll—as if the continent has yet to be written. In observing that only 30 years separate the first printing of the Gutenberg Bible from Columbus's departure for the Canary Islands, Jehlen speculates about the newly emerging connection between writing, representation, and political intention in the process of discovery (19).

Theoretical Overview

In using visual texts in relation to literary texts, students are encouraged to recognize in the two forms of representation two very different ways of knowing. We use W. J. T. Mitchell's way of characterizing the relation between a visual text and a literary text as one of "indiscipline." Playing on our understanding of the term *interdisciplinary*, the "indiscipline" between a visual and a literary text produces a rupture in our ability to form an illustrative relation between the two kinds of texts. The visual texts supply knowledge that is unavailable in the literary texts, and the relation between the two kinds of knowledge opens up into an inquiry path (540–44). In guiding students along it, the teacher encourages students to do research in selecting facts, connecting evidence, and constructing thesis statements in relation to primary documents. Within the construction of our tentative theses, we are aware of the alternative paths taken by other students. Although the focus is on the individual path taken by each student for the purposes of his/her paper, the class is aware of the extent of the wider exploration and the alternative branches in the study created by the class as a whole. This approach enables us to do more authentic assessment because we are approaching the text from the terms in which it is constructed. Thesis statements are concerned with examining the nature of the construction, and students become interested in various aspects of the work. Because each student pursues his/her own inquiry path, it is during class discussion that we begin to get a sense of a rich cultural description. In the process, we learn about the concept of the author, the way authority is represented, and the need for authenticity in the task of writing. While we are focusing on a close reading of text, we struggle to use what we have learned to make our own learning process visible to ourselves. How are we constructing ourselves as authors in our task?

Very much a product of his time, Columbus relied on precursor texts both visual and literary in navigating through space. Moving between conceptions of himself as *auctor,* a medieval writer who follows the authority of cultural precedents, and of himself as author, a writer who relies on his own experience to arrive at or to invent personal conclusions, Columbus creates in his journal an inquiry path of the third voyage by which he selects the texts that will influence his experience of place (Pease, 105–7). When confronted with evidence of a great river, the Orinoco, Columbus concludes that either he is near the Garden of Eden, which is at the top of a high mountain and is the source of all the great rivers of earth, or a vast continent exists to the south, never accounted for in the history of explorers. He opts for the latter explanation. How does Columbus navigate through the empty spaces in his imagination by filling in those empty spaces with visual images he carries in his memory? How does he come to understand this concrete evidence of a great river?

To understand how Columbus sees this new space, we supplement our reading of the journals with the kinds of visual references relied on, circulating in, or emerging within Columbus's culture: a celestial map, a thirteenth–century Psalter map, the 1490 "Columbus Chart," and the Piri Re'is map (1513), which is a *portolano,* or seaman's map. By exploring the visuals that approximate the kinds of maps of knowledge that were familiar to Columbus, students can better understand the problems Columbus faced in transferring visual knowledge to narrative description in his letter to Isabella. How does Columbus use representations to make his journey visible to Isabella, the one who makes his discovery possible?

Description and Discussion of the Assignment

Steps in the Process

Solitary Reading. Students are asked to look for places in the text where Columbus seems to have some visual in mind as he constructs a description of the new landscape. Previous images influence his description of the new land. Students are encouraged to read texts twice. The first reading is quick, so that they get the sense of the text as a whole; the second is slower, so that they can select the most relevant details in responding to the prompt.

Low-Stakes Writing. Class begins with a low-stakes writing in which students respond to the prompt that guided the reading: "Select three descriptive details from the text that seem to be inspired by an image from a visual. Is Columbus using his previous knowledge to understand a new encounter?" Students are encouraged to speculate on how the details are connected to one another. This writing is kept, to allow comparison with the writing done after group work is complete.

Small Groups. After the low-stakes writing, we divide into four small "navigation" groups. Each group is given a different map: a celestial map, a thirteenth-century Psalter, a *portolano,* or The Columbus Chart (a *mappi mundi*). We use the digital forms of these maps in class but also provide each group with a printed copy for individual examination. In a "slow seeing" exercise, students are asked to rely on their own instincts and observational skills.

Each student sees the visual alone, keeping a "captain's log." Next, each student lists all the details in the map, forming a tentative conclusion about the way whole and parts relate. Members of the group pool their information to create a group report. In the next step, the group is given a checklist of approaches to visual analysis that an expert might use (Anderson 9). This checklist takes them through a series of questions: What kind of orientation does the map have? How was it made? When? For what purpose? What is its actual size? Where is it located now? Do we know what materials are used in its construction? Is color used to represent geography? Do symbols take the place of the unknown? Is there writing on the map, and if so how does it function? Are edges blurred to indicate a lack of knowledge? Noting which skills they rely on intuitively and which skills they can add to their analytic approaches so as to take a more expert approach, they revise their report. They form one group description, keeping track of disagreements. Each group constructs a short report on the visual for the class presentation.

Jigsaw Groups. The next step asks students to think about how the different maps relate to one another in Columbus's thought process. Each student who dealt with a particular map now becomes part of a group that consists of students who each had a different map. The groups pool their information and produce a class report on the ways that Columbus seems to have valued the information in each kind of map.

Class Discussion: The Project Manager. To facilitate class discussion, a Project Manager is assigned who uses a grid on the board to keep track of group reports. As a class, we are interested in evaluating Columbus's process of critical thinking. How might the visuals influence his conclusions about spatial relations? In which parts of the argument does he use induction, and in which parts does he use deduction? He claims in his journal that previous cultural authorities use deduction and that he is in a position to use induction. How do the visuals influence the priorities he makes as he constructs an order and prioritizes his observations? The class lists Columbus's deductions and inductions in order of the importance he assigns. These questions help us determine importance: While he seems to be making an observation from experience, does he interpret that observation through reference to a visual that is part of cultural knowledge? How does he situate himself among other figures in the text who command authority over knowledge? Is he criticizing those who rely on textual knowledge while at the same time using visual images as a source of authority?

The Visuals

The British Library features Figure 1 on its website and provides an extensive and useful description. The map is so named because it accompanied the Book of Psalms, in which a description of the earth is found: "Thou hast fixed immovable and firm" (Psalm 93:1, addressing God). While small, the Psalter Map is full of symbols and depictions of Biblical events. Moses is crossing the Red Sea in the large red expanse at the top right. The world itself is a perfect circle, for God

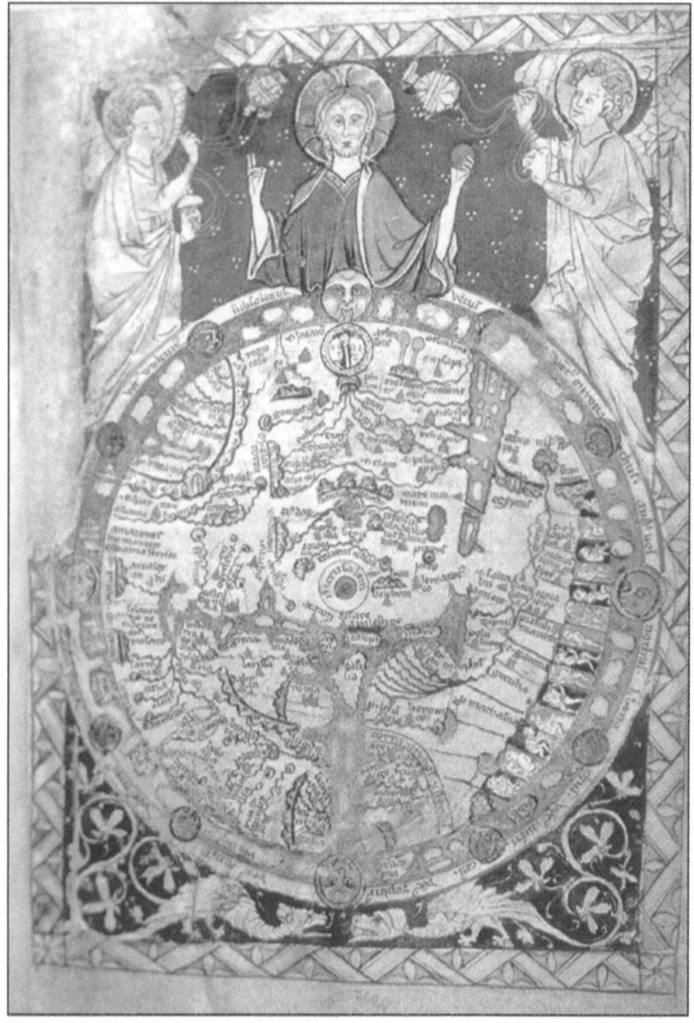

Figure 1. Psalter Map, c. 1250; 15cms X 10cms. <http://www.bl.uk/ whatson/ exhibitions/ mapmaker.html>. (Used by permission of the British Library.)

creates only what is perfect. The land is divided into a T-shape to represent the cross. In this early form of map-making, called the T-O map, the T is contained within the perfect circle. East is at the top because the sun rises in the east—the promise of Easter. Jerusalem is at the center, and Jesus, like a sunrise, is at the top holding a small T-O globe in his left hand. The Garden of Eden is seen just beneath the figure, with rivers flowing out from the earthly paradise. These rivers are the main rivers of the world, which flow underground until they come up again in their more familiar geographic locations. One of the four main rivers of the earth mentioned in Genesis 2:10–14 has not been identified by explorers. The river, Pishon, flows through the land of Havilah, where there is abundant gold. We note that according to Wilcomb Washburn, in his article "Exploration and Discovery before 1492," navigators frequently refer to "islands" in the Atlantic as the site of the Hesperides (producer of Golden Apples), the Fortunate Islands, the Terrestrial Paradise, and other attractive locales (257). A snake is wrapped around the figures of Adam and Eve. At the edge of the map to the right, or south, people are represented in fantastic fabled images at the edge of the world. At the bottom of the map, monstrous creatures meet in symmetrical movement.

The second group obtains a celestial map from the Sky and Telescope website, where they can access an interactive sky chart allowing them to select a date, time, and location. Because the site begins only at 1600, our class can only approximate Columbus's location in time and space: July 13–22, 1498, at latitude 9^0 30' N and longitude 29^0 W. Samuel Eliot Morison, noted biographer of Christopher Columbus, posits that Columbus, a Mediterranean navigator with a geocentric conception of the world, had little knowledge of celestial navigation because ports in the Mediterranean are all in the same latitude. In the Atlantic, however, celestial navigation is more useful. An Atlantic navigator would have been more accurate than Columbus proves to be in his third voyage (Morison 140).

The Christopher Columbus Chart appearing in Figure 2 is named for its approximate year of publication, not because Columbus used it. This map is a combination of *mappa mundi* and *portolano*. A *mappa mundi* is a map that is philosophically and abstractly conceived, while the *portolano* is more like the maps we keep in our glove compartments, to get from place to place. As such, the latter is fragile; few survive. The main portion of the Christopher Columbus Chart is the *portolano.* Inserted in the neck of the narrow portion of the parchment is the very mathematically geometric *mappa mundi,* a small circular map of the spheres, yet within the *mappa mundi* is a detailed map of the coast of Africa. It may be that the spherical representation is to remind the navigator that the plane of the sailing chart is an illusion and that he is in a world circumscribed by the movement of the

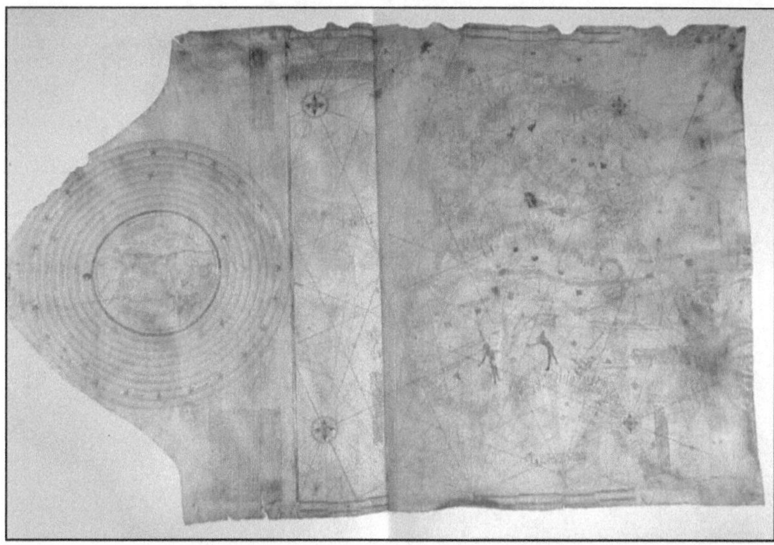

Figure 2. The Christopher Columbus Chart, c. 1490; 70 x 110 cm (28 x 44 inches). <http://www.henry-davis.com/MAPS/LMwebpages/257A.html>. (Used by permission of *La Bibliotheque Nationale de France.*)

heavenly bodies. Jehlen claims that Columbus was caught in the same contradiction as the map. On one side is the sailor's chart and on the other the geometrically perfect circle of a created world containing the seaman's chart. Jehlen argues that an allegory is created by this attempt to contain "human mobility and mutability" in "abiding cosmic relations" (13–25). In this attempt to create allegorical relations, the exception or unfamiliar detail can be disregarded or left unrecognized (Pease 107).

The fourth group is given the Piri Re'is map c. 1513, which appears in Figure 3. Some historians claim that this map was made from information gathered by Columbus and supplied to a Turkish sailor (Lepore 32). The map is a *portolano* because it relies on the direct experience of sailors who share information in conversational exchange. What is interesting about this chart is how much narrative is written in the visual to explain the spatial context. The edges of the spaces are finished by the written word, as if the world could no longer be described visually but required written explanation. While the inscriptions are in Arabic, the very useful website devoted to the map supplies a translation. The narrative contains a mixture of fact and fable.

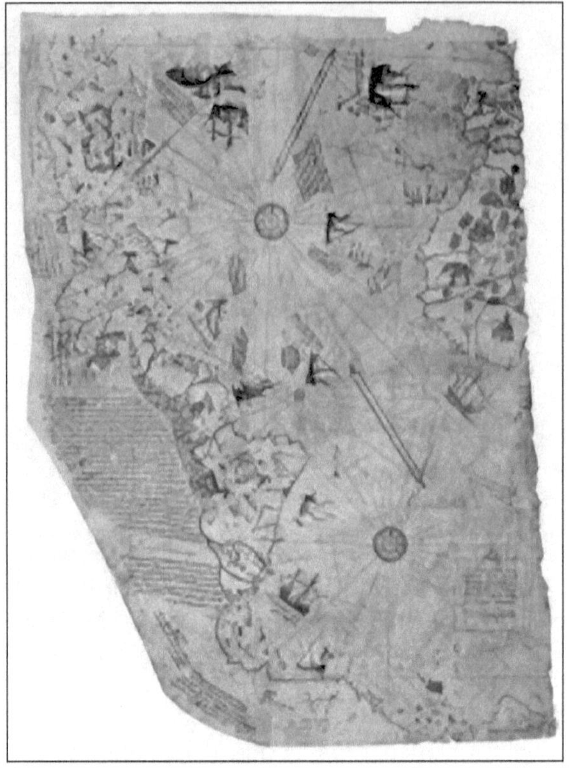

Figure 3. The *Portolano.* <http://www.sacred-texts.com/piri>. (Used by permission of The Internet Sacred Text Archive.)

Student Outcomes: Low-Stakes Writings and Mid-Term Papers

Student outcomes are determined by comparing the low-stakes writing done before and after the visual exploration. Both writings are produced through brainstorming. The first is usually a plot summary in general terms. In the second low-stakes writing after the group work with visuals, students gain confidence and add to class discussion and research by focusing on their own observations. This writing is rather like drafting a mid-term paper. Students begin a process building up to a thesis.

Many students pick up on some aspect of the literary text and its relation to a map. Their writings tend to address an aspect of class discussion that has been left unresolved. In addition, the notes from group work and individual work with the visuals provide evidence of the kinds of careful, slow seeing that students use when guided to make specific observations. Students from the Caribbean or who are taking classes in astronomy are intrigued by the ways they can bring previous knowledge into their readings of text and into their understanding of maps. Art students have unique perspectives to contribute and tend to build on their senses of art and design.

Mid-term papers are submitted after thorough revision. Although papers are only three pages long, they are usually structured around the questions that emerge as students find visual evidence affecting their interpretation of written text. Students tend to focus on using writing to establish a thesis that speculates about process and relation. By carefully stepping through the kinds of information gathered from a celestial map dependent on the laws of physical motion, a map made for the purposes of religious celebration, and a map whose information relies on direct conversation, students begin to recognize different kinds of knowledge and how each influences the others to create a way of communicating new information within cultural context.

One student developed a hypothesis that Columbus was much more comfortable speculating about the celestial chart and the differences that he observed in the heavens than he was when he was observing the differences among the peoples he encountered. Even his mistakes in celestial navigation were more interesting than his general descriptions of vegetation and animal life that relied on comparison. By comparing the landscape favorably to what he had seen in Spain, Columbus manages to evade description entirely. He tended to describe animals and vegetation in terms that were so general that Isabella would not fail to have associations with them. In addition, the student argued that Columbus subordinated his understanding of the differences among the people to his navigational imperatives. His comparisons also lacked a sense of relation within and among the native peoples. He related differences in skin color to the shape of the earth. He was able to formulate surprising speculations about the shape of the earth being like a pear or a woman's nipple, but he was not able to form equally surprising speculations about the identities of the people in relation to their lives. Other students compared the descriptions in the maps to the descriptions in texts. They noted that in exchanges with native people Columbus received information about cannibals, yet there never was any real evidence of their existence. In this manner, students infer why there are representations of people on the Piri Re'is map that seem to come from unsubstantiated reports.

Most students understood that Columbus was deeply influenced by Isabella's vision of the world and constructed his descriptions to accommodate her worldview, especially in the use of the Psalter map. Students speculate about Columbus's description of the mighty river in his journal. Is he implying that the river flows out of Eden? Does this mean he made a choice not to acknowledge the possibility of the vast continent that might be in a new, if less sacred world? What surprised students was that in his descriptions of the native people and his claim to have found the earthly paradise, Columbus does not seem to make any connection between the gentle, nonaggressive, gift giving characteristics of the people he meets, and the fact that these might have been what people were like in a place like Eden, an earthly paradise before civilized institutions. Instead, Columbus seemed impatient to get to China and to see its vast civilized centers.

Yet other students have also researched Marco Polo's accounts to uncover differences in descriptive writings by a trader and by an explorer. These students have researched the map of Polo's travels along the Silk Road and have gained experience with Arab maps and their more geometric conventions. Students note in their papers that Columbus seemed to be sailing "through" the lands while Polo's descriptions dwell on the uniqueness of the lands, which achieve a presence in the text.

After viewing the maps, students revisit their initial impressions, reported in many of the first low-stakes writings, that Columbus was becoming delusional. Instead, they see that his idea of an earthly paradise is the Khan's world of gold and trade. While using Mitchell's ideas about indiscipline to guide their exploration, they tend to look for the ways human relations are constructed but also modified by context. Although Columbus is the subject of the research and exploration, students keep foremost in their minds as they write that they are also constructing meanings in their own cultural contexts. They are aware of transforming information in their learning practices (Meyer 24–27). They become aware of the way they are making selections among details, focusing on a specific path of inquiry, evaluating evidence, and bringing information together to create a thesis. This process is possible because they see how different the end point of each path is.

Using Mitchell's approach to visual and textual knowledge has made it easier for me as a teacher to set up an active group-learning experience for students. Each learning unit is designed to encourage students to imagine how the author of a text is constructing a way of understanding information in order to solve a problem intrinsic to a cultural context or problem. As Mary Louise Pratt explains, by exploring visual and/or literary texts, students come to understand the pressure on authors to represent cultural encounter; and, in the text, visual and/or literary, the artist/writer is seeking to organize information through a basic conflict or boundary negotiation (Pratt 249 ff). Students observe how authors strive to achieve coherence or authority over the experience of encounter by negotiating visual and literary representations (Bizzell and Herzberg v–xi).

Appendix 1: The Assignment

Read the first and third journals of the voyages of Christopher Columbus. Keep a reading journal that notes the places in the text where Columbus seems to be using a visual you cannot see in order to describe what he is observing. Be prepared to write a low-stakes writing in class that describes your observations of the text.

During group work, make careful observations of the map you have chosen. Make a group report of the individual observations, keeping track of differences. After getting the checklist of observations an expert might use when looking at maps (based on Anderson), note which skills you use intuitively and which you might add to your skills base.

In the jigsaw groups, note how the different visuals influence one another and create relations that influence Columbus's thought.

In the final low-stakes writing, feel free to speculate according to an inquiry path that seems most interesting to you. Make sure you are referring to visual and textual evidence while you speculate.

The midterm paper is three-pages long. You may select any of the texts we studied in the first half of the semester. In this more formal paper, you may want to follow your inquiry path and produce an analysis of your observations. The paper will have a main idea that sums up in one paragraph the entire argument of your essay, including the forms of evidence you will cite and how you will go about establishing relationships. The body of the paper will be an analysis in which you carefully examine each part of the argument and relate it to both your main idea or main thesis and to the other parts of the analysis.

Appendix 2

I give the following assignment in conjunction with the reading of "The Discus Thrower," by Richard Selzer. Students are asked to consider how a work of art has influenced a writer; thus, they can infer what the visual and the written text each contribute to an indiscipline that details human character in the story. Other assignments using combinations of an author's visual and written texts may be chosen for the discovery of the indiscipline. For instance, teachers of technical writing might ask students to analyze how a visual has contributed to the writer's thought processes and conclusions. In the case of the sciences and engineering, the controlling metaphors will refer less to symbols or poetic allusions than to real dynamics contained within the project.

Freshman Composition

Perspective Essay #1
Dr. Darcy

Read "The Discus Thrower" by Richard Seltzer.

Select one of the characters for analysis: the doctor, the nurse (and aid), the patient.

Collaborate in your group about your character.

Jigsaw your groups so that now you can see your character in the context of all the characters.

Organize a group report on the way the characters are interacting with one another.

Discuss as a class the patient and his character. Consider how silent he is, how he speaks in a riddle. Why does Seltzer, who is a surgeon, create such a character?

Report to the class the final evaluation of your group in a group report.

Research: On the Web find a visual of Myron's "The Discus Thrower," or "Discobolus." Go to Google and do an image search. Look carefully at this digital image of the statue. How would you describe the way that the mind, body, and spirit of this athlete come together in this pose? It must be noted that the artists of the day hoped to capture individuals in the moment when each is able to achieve excellence. Poets, sculptors, historians hoped to preserve in memory the visual representation of that fleeting moment when the mind, body, and spirit of the individual were in complete harmony. Think about moments of transition or liminal spaces. Is the patient in a moment of transition, in a liminal space? Go to <http://www.wsu.edu:8080/~dee/GLOSSARY/ ARETE.HTM> or <http://www.stanford.edu/dept/news/pr/2004/olimpics-84.html> and research the Greek idea of *aretê*. Think about the gesture of the patient. Why does he throw the plate the way he does? Why does he refuse the bowl of oatmeal? Why did Seltzer call his patient the discus thrower? How does that visual image connect the metaphors he creates for his patient: a bonsai, a sailor athwart a slanting deck, a snow-bound cottage? How does the visual change our understanding of the story?

Write a five-paragraph essay in which you "steal" writing techniques from Seltzer. Create a situation of your own in which there are three perspectives. Give your narrative a title that provides the reader with a strong visual image. Introduce yourself in the first paragraph in the way that the doctor introduces himself. He names his perspective in the essay. However, in the second paragraph he completely shifts his focus and concentrates on the patient. He provides rich metaphors that are unique to give the character a real presence. Again, he shifts his perspective in the next section and sees the patient from a very different perspective, through the nurse. Next, Seltzer allows the patient to speak for himself mainly in gesture, action. He creates a very slow careful description of action. In the end, he allows the reader to come to his/her own conclusions.

Works Cited

Anderson, Jeremy. *Teaching Map Skills: An Inductive Approach.* Macomb: National Council for Geographic Education, 1986.

Bass, Randall and Joy Young. *Beyond Borders: A Cultural Reader.* Boston: Houghton Mifflin, 2003: 249–60.

Bizzell, Patricia and Bruce Herzberg . *Negotiating Difference.* New York: Bedford Books, 1996

Columbus, Christopher. "The Journal of the Third Voyage." *The Heath Anthology of American Literature.* Ed. Paul Lauter. Boston: Houghton Mifflin, 1998. 125–28.

Fisher, Philip, ed. *New American Studies: Essays in Representation.* Berkeley: U of California P, 1991.

Jehlen, Myra. "Papers of Empire." *The Cambridge History of American Literature.* Ed. Sacvan Bercovitch. New York: Cambridge UP, 1994. 13–36.

Las Casas, Bartolomé de. *Historia de las Indias.* Ed. J. Pérez de Tudela Bueso. Biblioteca de Autores Españoles, 95–96, Madrid, 1957–1961.

Lepore, Jill. *Encounters in the New World: A History in Documents.* New York: Oxford UP, 2000.

Meyer, Katrina A. *Quality in Distance Education: Focus on On-Line Learning.* Hoboken: Jossey-Bass, 2002.

Mitchell, W. J. T. "Interdisciplinarity and Visual Culture." *Art Bulletin* 70.4 (1995): 540–44.

Morison, Samuel Eliot. *Christopher Columbus, Mariner.* Boston: Little, Brown & Company, 1952.

Pease, Donald. "Author." *Critical Terms for Literary Study.* Ed. Frank Lentricchia and Thomas McLaughlin. Chicago: U of Chicago P, 1995. 105–07.

Pratt, Mary Louise. "Arts of the Contact Zone." *Beyond Borders.* Ed. Randall Bass. New York: Houghton Mifflin, 2003. 249–62.

Selzer, Richard. "The Discus Thrower." *Harper's Magazine,* November 1977: 22–23.

Washburn, Wilcomb. "Exploration and Discovery before 1492." *The Christopher Columbus Encyclopedia,* 1992.

10 Drawn to Multiple Sides: Making Arguments Visible with Political Cartoons

Alyssa O'Brien

Several years ago, as I was teaching a class on the rhetoric of the news, my attention shifted sharply to the importance of visual rhetoric. I had asked groups of students to choose a topic from among those addressed by the chapters of our textbook and to read the articles included in that chapter to prepare for writing their position papers. As I moved from group to group, I observed one set of students involved in a heated debate. But it wasn't an article that had engaged these students; rather, it was the political cartoon prefacing the chapter. I remarked in an offhand way to the class that this image functioned as an argument. Suddenly, other group members turned their attentions to the images prefacing their own chapters. A photograph of a black youth holding a gun initiated the section on juvenile crime, a series of ad icons set up the section on intellectual property, and a blurred still shot of a boy in front of a computer screen introduced articles on video game violence. The conversation around the room intensified as students began analyzing the arguments of these images and the appropriateness of their selection to frame the issues. The students did not see these images as decorative or illustrative; they read them as rhetorical stance, as editorial pronouncement, and as a key text in the collection of "articles." Then and there, I realized that visual texts provide excellent material for analysis in the writing classroom and constitute complex hybrid forms of argument and cultural production.

It was a subtle shift in some ways. I had always included film, photography, painting, cartoons, and trips to the museum in my teaching.

I used cartoons on assignment sheets and as decorative images in my syllabus. But, in my courses, visual texts had always functioned as illustrative mimesis or cultural context materials rather than as argumentative texts in their own right. As I made what W. J. T. Mitchell terms "the pictorial turn" with my students, I came to center my writing courses around visual cultural materials that they selected: those images from the news and popular media that were persuading us to view our world in a particular light.

Out of that early encounter, I developed for the first-year writing classroom a visual rhetoric pedagogy that takes the form of the "Feature Article Multiple Sides" (FAMS) Project, a complex student production entailing selecting, composing, and designing visual-verbal texts around a specific issue. The students construct their own collections of articles about a topic of importance to them. In the process, they move from looking at visual texts to constructing them as visual rhetoricians; they compose visual-verbal arguments of importance to share with a broad audience. Drawn to this project over and over for its pedagogical benefits, I am reassured by course evaluations that identify it as the students' "favorite assignment," "most valuable writing work," and "the turning point" in understanding visual rhetoric. My purpose in this essay is to delineate the ways in which the project can make arguments visible through the persuasive power of visual rhetoric.

Looking Forward in our Teaching Practices: Opening Frames of Reference

In his article "Image, Word, and Future Text: Visual and Verbal Thinking in Writing Instruction," Ronald Fortune identifies two urgent issues confronting teachers and institutions: first, that we need to incorporate "attention to the interaction between word and image into a writing course," and second, that writing teachers "do not already possess and therefore must develop the knowledge about visual communication and its relationship to verbal communication" (102). His recent words echo the 1996 assertion by David Birdsell and Leo Groarke that "our contributions to understandings of the visual will come from our ability to flesh out theories of visual argumentation as rich and as rigorous as those we have developed for verbal argumentation" (1).

In writing this article, I hope to help meet this need. Specifically, I seek to build on what we might already do with visual rhetoric—such as writing in response to advertisements, photographs, film, and cartoons—by proposing interactive and transformative ways of teaching the power of visual persuasion "as writing." As we challenge ourselves to move beyond textual analysis paradigms and to extend the writing process across multiple genres and modes of knowledge production, we need to interrogate the old cliché our students love to quote, "a picture is worth a thousand words," and explore the ways in which *visual rhetoric* signifies a choice about arrangement of both visual and verbal elements. We then need to ask, as part of our pedagogy, what kinds of influence or power such images have on their viewers. How do visual texts communicate ideas and convince readers to see the world through particular frames? How do images function as arguments that can teach students about the writing process? Through such questions, we can sharpen students' visual literacy and, simultaneously, turn to visual rhetoric as a site of production.

Fittingly, our students are leading the way in this regard, producing multilayered argument projects that provide diverse perspectives on visual images, innovative approaches to the visual layout and content arrangement, and hypertextual versions of traditional writing assignments that now use visual rhetoric as a strategy of argument. By celebrating this work and constructing feasible means of teaching it, we can transform our pedagogical and curricular methodologies to accommodate the increasing importance of visual texts in our schools and in our culture. In this way, as teachers developing pedagogies of visual rhetoric, we can explore how "what it means to write" has changed in an era marked by the pictorial turn, to include the visual not as "mere" decoration but rather as a text to study on its own terms through analysis, argumentation, and innovative graphic production. That is, knowing our audience—the students—and how they turn to the visual, we can also use visual texts to teach rhetoric and composition in first-year courses; we can turn to visual rhetoric to meet the more traditional pedagogical goals of teaching argument, thesis, claim, evidence, and the rhetorical terms *audience, persona, modes of argument.*

The FAMS Project offers a site of dynamic intersection between the visual and the verbal; it can help us theorize how visual rhetoric works and how the visual operates in relation to the verbal as a form of argument. The remainder of this article delineates the parameters of the FAMS Project—a practical pedagogy of visual rhetoric that leads students from analysis, through argumentation, to production.

Assessing the Angle in Political Cartoons: Developing Visual Literacy

The preliminary step in a pedagogy of visual rhetoric is analysis, and as so many teachers do, I often begin with a look at current political cartoons available in national, international, and campus newspapers as well as through online cartoon banks. I then move to challenge students to participate in the production of visual-verbal texts by modifying part of the cartoon's argument in a way I'll describe shortly. In these ways, we use political cartoons in class to develop visual literacy and to begin to grasp the diverse meanings conveyed through these texts.

Such work sometimes meets with initial resistance. Often, political cartoons do not seem serious enough to merit more than a brief chuckle as we glance at the morning paper, and they certainly do not seem rigorous enough for inclusion in the university curriculum. Yet the practical function of political cartoons as visual rhetoric texts is not new. As Lisa Melandri argues in "Drawing the Line," "the power and efficacy of political cartoons has long been recognized; because of their readability and visual immediacy, they appeal to and are understood by a wide audience" (par. 2). From the densely symbolic eighteenth-century plates of William Hogarth, to the biting social satire of *Punch*'s illustrators, to the edgy work of political cartoonists such as Ann Telnaes and Mike Luckovich in this century, the political cartoon has provided a sharp, compact form of argument on contemporary issues. Today, cartoonists continue both to reflect and to shape public opinion, and the plethora of printed collections, online cartoon banks, and historical cartoon websites makes this form of visual rhetoric a rich one for analysis, research, and use in the FAMS Project. Increasingly, we are looking at such texts to find out how they make contemporary arguments visible in graphic form and also how they contribute to the public sphere through their own arguments on current issues.

As cultural critic Matthew Diamond asserts in his defense of political cartoons as important visual rhetoric texts, "political cartoons are an important mode of communication. [They] provide alternative perspectives at a glance because they are visual and vivid and often seem to communicate a clear or obvious message" (270). Diamond examines how political cartoonists depict the situation in the Middle East after September 11 through what he calls, following Janis Edwards, "a kind of rhetorical 'tool kit' for constructing meaning" (253). Diamond's emphasis on a rhetorical reading of illustrative texts opens the door for new approaches to visual media such as cartoons, one that employs rhetoric as a lens and a disciplinary methodology. Thus, there is another reason for zooming in on the political cartoon rather than the ad, the photograph, the film, or the poster: political cartoons are drawn visual-verbal texts that often appear with an author's signature and a specific place of publication. They are perfect texts for initiating a rhetorical approach to visual media, one that necessarily includes discussion of audience, persona, text, context, and the persuasive appeals of pathos, logos, and ethos. In other words, while visual culture theorists over the past 20 years have constructed a rich apparatus through which to read political cartoons, including the categories of caricature, intertextuality, visual analogy, and cultural memory (Werner, par. 3; 9), some of the most useful ways of developing visual literacy in our students is through a return to rhetorical terms. Deploying a rhetorical tool kit in this first step, analysis, makes possible rigorous work in visual literacy and facilitates a productive discussion about the argument of the image that extends beyond individual interpretation.

To assess the angle of political cartoons, I begin with several, such as those I will discuss below, in order to initiate analysis and to introduce the concept of diverse interpretations as a part of visual literacy. In past classes, for instance, we have examined the political cartoon by Ann Telnaes from March 12, 2003, parodying U.S. Congressional representatives who renamed French Fries in House restaurants as *freedom fries* (Figure 1). At first, students laughed at the sharp contrast of image and idea: the notion that renaming *French fries* to be *freedom fries,* and *French toast* to be *freedom toast* signifies a sort of nationalist rebuttal to France's anti-Iraq-war stance. The sharp, clear lines of each element of the image convey its ostensible intellectual simplicity: the fries, the toast, and the circus figure all seem reminiscent of a child's cartoon book.[1]

What is important to emphasize, however, is that in Telnaes' cartoon, the visual functions as persuasive rhetoric calling into question America's growing cultural discrimination against France's decision to refuse participation in the Iraq war. The ostensible simplicity of line

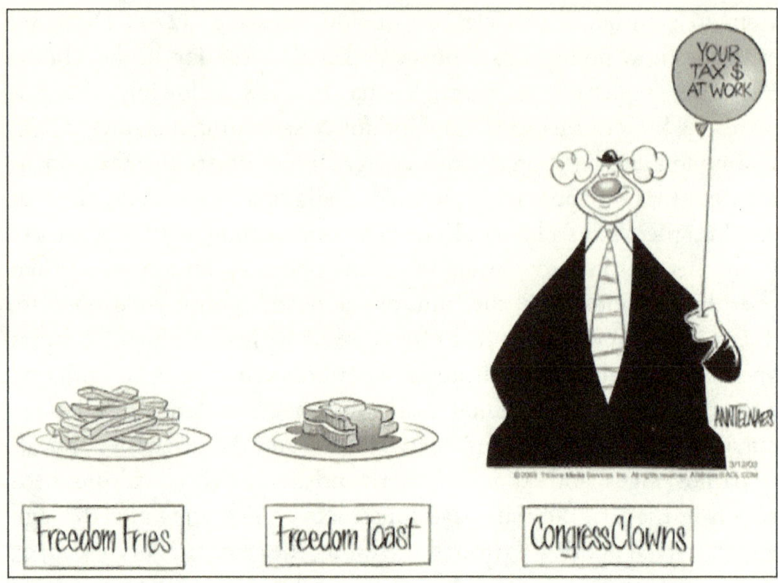

Figure 1. *Freedom Fries*, Ann Telnaes, Tribune Media Services, March 12, 2003. Accessed 15 Oct. 2004. (Used by permission of Ann Telnaes, TMS Reprints, *Los Angeles Times*. http://www.anntelnaes.com/thumbnail%20images.1/images /031203FreedomFries.jpg>.)

and figure provides clear-cut elements for rhetorical analysis and an argument constructed through obvious parallelism. The subtle sophistication of design, layout, color, and composition in fact offers a compelling arrangement to be analyzed both rhetorically and politically.

If we examine such texts in our classrooms, we can open dialogue on an entire host of important questions, including the question of why politicians conflate national identity with political stance. How does food serve as a signifier for cultural identity? What purpose does political caricature serve in national agendas? What is the argument of this image? Where do individual readers break the chain of associations in this cartoon—do some agree with all connections implied by the sequence of elements? What role do such visual rhetoric texts play in shaping the consciousness of readers in a specific country?

Similarly, another cartoon by Ann Telnaes raises key questions—along with potential FAMS Project subjects and research topics for further study—concerning nationalism, gender, politics, and visual markings. The cartoon, which appeared on September 25, 2001 (when the bombing of Afghanistan had begun and the attention of the United States was focused on the plight of women under the Taliban regime), depicted an Afghani man painting over the familiar representation of Rosie the Riveter. Assessing the visual text, we embark on the first step in an assignment sequence that moves from analysis to production. First, we analyze rhetorically the way in which the erasure of the woman's strong body into a black scratch with eyes is a powerful appeal to pathos. Then we argue that such deliberate drawing reflects a historical moment from 2001 when political cartoons offered a Geiger counter for nationalist agendas and popular responses. We conclude that, from whichever way we consider the representation of this woman, political ideologies are literally written on her body. Finally, we extrapolate how the visual rhetoric text appeals to an American audience's values.

As this analysis of visual rhetoric reveals, we can in fact look to seemingly simple visual rhetoric texts to initiate a wide range of intellectual discussions or to accomplish a significant number of pedagogical goals, whether those include teaching composition, argument, visual design, cultural studies, or political controversies. Building on the work of Scott McCloud, Matthew Diamond, Walt Werner, and Lawrence Pollard, among others, we have come to see such images as powerful persuasive texts. We rely upon political cartoons—rather than other visual media—because as Pulitzer Prize-winning cartoonist Doug Marlette asserts, "the objective of political cartooning 'is not to soothe and tend sensitive psyches, but to jab and poke in an attempt to get at deeper truths, popular or otherwise'" (qtd. in Moore).[2] That is, political cartoons often use visual rhetoric to begin a dialogue about specific national or international issues. If we explore these texts in national newspapers, Internet galleries of political cartoons, and year-end collections of the Best Editorial Cartoons, we find a rich repository of material for consideration.[3] Assessed analytically as a dynamic social text that offers many possible arguments about a contemporary political issue, the political cartoon becomes a text at once both influential and complex.

While class analysis of this image brings to light diverse perspectives and opens the way for a true enactment of the public sphere, I next ask students to participate in meaning making not only through completing interpretative acts through rhetorical analysis, but also by collaborating as authors in the production of a political cartoon. To do so, I take a published cartoon and remove the words shaping the meaning of the image, either by photocopying the cartoon or scanning and modifying it on the computer. The task before my students then becomes to brainstorm words or a caption to complete the meaning of the visual argument. They can write on the photocopy or even suggest verbally how changing the hybrid elements of the cartoon changes its argument in significant ways. In such collaborative re-creations of the cartoon, analysis and production intersect to advance visual literacy to the realm of writing with visual rhetoric. Recognizing these differences in responding to and collaborating with visual texts, we then discuss the importance of audience in the rhetorical triangle. In this way, I can raise the prospect of multiple viewpoints and set the pedagogical foundation for the main project.

Making Arguments Visual: Producing the Multiple Sides Project

In working with political cartoons in the classroom, I find that it is important not only to analyze both visual and verbal aspects but, even more significantly, to allow students to move from being readers to being writers of visual rhetoric texts. Therefore, building on the work of rhetorical analysis, which includes both visual literacy and collaborative verbal-visual writing on a given text, we turn next to composing arguments through the FAMS Project, as a means of empowering students to write powerful thesis-driven texts that use both verbal and visual strategies of persuasion. The project demands attention to thesis statements, voice, structure, and the use of visual texts as evidence in written argument. At the same time, it offers excellent preparation for research-based inquiry by challenging students to understand the complexity of a topic through exploring multiple sides—or diverse points of view—on a chosen issue. Finally, students implement the rhetorical concepts of persona, rhetorical stance, and rhetorical canon in order to craft powerful, persuasive arguments about the world, using both written and visual texts.

As I'll explain shortly in more detail, the FAMS Project meets numerous learning goals. It allows students to explore the possible arguments, counterarguments, or side-arguments on an issue. In addition, the project helps students understand—through implementation—the dynamic relations between visual and verbal rhetoric, and it gives them practice using both modes. Moreover, the assignment asks students to experiment with various voices, stances, and variations in tone, organization, perspective, persona, audience, purpose, and rhetorical appeals. Finally, the assignment can work as part of an assignment sequence leading up to a major research paper by helping students narrow their proposed area of research inquiry and preparing them both intellectually and rhetorically for a major research project. The logistical parameters, or assignment guidelines for the FAMS, illustrate how such goals can be achieved.

Students find the assignment both challenging and rewarding, and I usually devote three weeks to completing the work from concept generation to final delivery. To facilitate their progress in drafting, writing, and revising the project, I lead students through the following steps, spacing the project process over multiple class meetings:

Step 1: Commit to an issue and bring in potential images to use in the project.

Step 2: Draft the FAMS Project articles, experiment with layout and placement of images, craft introductory and conclusion frame.

Step 3: Peer review drafts in small groups.

Step 4: Revise the FAMS Project; print or post online to share with the class.

Step 5: Deliver it as a presentation to the class. Explain the feature article format decisions and visual rhetoric elements, introduce the issue and personas in the project, explain the stances and the visual arguments, and raise questions for the class to consider.

Pedagogical Benefits: Meeting Multiple Learning Outcomes

The benefits of this project are many and can be mapped against conventional learning objectives in first-year writing, argument, and research courses. First, as students learn to work with written arguments or approach a potential research project, they need to break free from the "pro-con" model of argumentation. When students look at multiple sides of an issue, they begin to understand how alternative arguments offer new insights and broaden a topic for deeper understanding.

Second, in constructing the FAMS Project, students have an opportunity to construct multiple perspectives by writing short articles from the rhetorical stances of different personas, and thus they learn the importance of selecting effective evidence, modifying tone, and varying their use of appeals. Each persona might rely on a different image to make a visual argument that proves a specific point of view. Alternatively, each persona might posit a unique interpretation of a single image and argue accordingly. In this way, students learn to compose a distinct rhetorical stance—a position on an issue that is deliberately stated for the purposes of persuading an audience. To develop this stance, students need to work through the following questions: Who is writing the argument? What position does the writer hold? What is the purpose of this communication? These questions might be part of the brainstorming process students complete at the draft stage. Through this process, they develop skills of argumentation by generating convincing perspectives on visual texts.

Third, in addition to its focus on stance, each FAMS Project necessitates development of specific strategies of design, layout, and presentation. Such attention to format occurs not only because the project is constructed as a set of feature articles, but also because arrangement is a rhetorical strategy, a crucial one that writers use to persuade readers. As the second canon of rhetoric, arrangement governs the order of elements in a text. For each "side" of the project, the way in which students present material on the page, including images, will shape a reader's response. Where students position an image and when they refer to it also are important strategies of arrangement. When students format their work to imitate the look of a particular newspaper, they learn to analyze the visual rhetoric of that example and to apply what they have learned in the production of their own text. Often, the "sides" in the project will take the form of a popular article, such as the kind found in *Newsweek* or *Time,* or students will emulate an Internet journal such as *Wired.*

Finally, just as arrangement is imperative in constructing an argument and as a strategy of persuasion, so, too, are matters of style crucial in articulating a rhetorical stance successfully. As the third canon of rhetoric, style concerns expression and diction, or how an argument is made. Because students often translate "style" as "voice" to indicate a writer's unique persona and rhetorical stance as it is manifested in word choice, syntax, pacing, and tone, it is beneficial to ask students to experiment with different voices. As they develop their writing skills by working on visual and verbal arguments, they should pick the best voice to meet the needs of the rhetorical situation. They can use the rhetorical appeals of pathos, logos, and ethos as instruments of style. They can align each side in the FAMS Project with a particular rhetorical appeal in order to learn the power of such writing. If students will present their projects to the class as a whole, then they can embody these voices and explain the visual arguments in a multimedia delivery of their arguments. The benefits of working with visual rhetoric expand the more that students are encouraged to be creative in producing persuasive visual-verbal texts.

Showcase of Examples: Learning by Looking at FAMS

Perhaps one of the best ways of grasping the complexity of the FAMS Project is through a pedagogy of models, or by looking at examples of student projects. Indeed, most of my students struggle with the project guidelines until they consult previous models and then try the project out for themselves. We look, for instance, at how one student designed his project around a powerful political cartoon concerning the tensions between India and Pakistan. By composing diverse views embodying stances that support different interpretations of the meaning of this cartoon, he explored the power of political cartoons to disseminate cultural and political messages. He emphasized the difference that audience makes through voicing first an Indian perspective and then a Pakistani reaction to the cartoon. Another student focused her project around a political cartoon concerning cyberterrorism: she composed multiple perspectives revealing the powerful diverse arguments made by a single political cartoon, and she formatted the project effectively in the style of *Newsweek.* In a third project, a student offered arguments around the issue of stem cell research, by using three different political cartoons for her multiple sides and formatting the project in the style of *Time.* Each cartoon presented a powerful and unique perspective on the dangers and benefits of stem cell research.

A final student example merits a closer look since the writer, Julie Tung, explored diverse angles of public reaction to death penalty legislation and policies through a FAMS Project in which she not only used visual rhetoric as a strategy of argument but also included a convincing rhetorical analysis of each political cartoon as part of her written strategy of persuasion. In selecting three political cartoons, Julie made certain that her visual texts would serve as more than visual decoration for her arguments; they determined the argumentative stance and scope of the project. Her careful placement of each one throughout the FAMS, as well as her convincing verbal interpretations of each, enabled her to produce an innovative project.[4]

For her layout, Julie decided to replicate the format of her campus newspaper, *The Stanford Daily.* The newspaper design is perhaps one of the most feasible ways of completing the FAMS Project; students can format pages using a basic word processing program, and they can even manually cut and paste images on pages if they do not have access to sophisticated computers or printing facilities. Julie used Microsoft Word to reproduce the font and design of the masthead, the title, the date, and the feature article, thus taking a deliberate look at how visual rhetoric might shape our understanding of the debate. She then strategically inserted her cartoons on the opening page as a visual Table of Contents. Moreover, she decided to compose the introduction using the fictional persona of herself as editor. This choice gave her critical distance from the topic and allowed her to experiment with style and voice even while she established the topic, situated it, and delineated the credentials and rhetorical stances of the three personas to follow.

The first side featured the fictional persona of James Donovan, "the brother of a young woman who met a tragic end at the hands of a serial killer," as Julie's introduction explains; Donovan "tells of their family's ensuing grief, intertwined with their direct dealings with the death penalty, the justice system and all their nuances" (A1). As her language here reveals, Julie uses verbal argument, and primarily the appeal to *logos*, to echo the visual argument of the political cartoon, placed strategically in the center of the debate over capital punishment's legal process. In her article, the cartoon is ostensibly drawn by the persona, and a mass of entangled roads signifies the way in which "the capital punishment process has become so cumbersome and lengthy that it verges on the ridiculous." Donovan continues, "there is never any guarantee that the road will end somewhere—the roads interlace and intertwine until it is impossible to tell where the road begins, ends, or even if it ever ends" (A2). The stylistic visual metaphors of the writing make explicit the argument of the image, which Julie has appropriated as her persona's own. In this way, she learns how both the visual and the verbal offer persuasive rhetoric for diverse readers.

In the next section of her FAMS, Julie turns to pathos as the main appeal. She introduces the fictional Matthew Knowles, "a man actually exonerated from years of imprisonment on death row [who recounts] the horror story told by every lobbyist against capital punishment." For this argument, the cartoon is placed at the top right, rather than interwoven strategically in the middle, as fitting for the last article. Knowles provides his own interpretation of the cartoon as a near-victim of what he calls "a system already notorious for its mistakes," by leading the reader through a careful visual analysis of the cartoonist's humor, choice of word, line, caricature, irony, and message. Here, Julie provides a metalesson in visual rhetoric, using a cartoon to teach us how to read a visual in various ways.

Her third article experiments with ethos and, building off the powerful political cartoon at the top center of the page, looks at how "the blindfold on Lady Justice implies that those in the judicial system do not see, nor do they care, about the difficulties that exist within the system of capital punishment" (A4). This article, however, is composed by fictional persona Cathy Roberts, a district attorney who for 19 years has struggled with the necessity of making life-and-death decisions.

Julie's project ends with a conclusion written again in the voice of the newspaper's editorial staff. On this closing page, Julie offers a sharp assessment of both the verbal and the visual arguments deployed by each position in the FAMS Project. The analysis of the efficacy of visual rhetoric as a tool of argument signifies a crucial step in students' developing visual literacy—they must learn not only to locate powerful visual rhetoric, but also to assess it for persuasiveness and argumentative depth. Julie's conclusion includes a visual echo of a campus newspaper's additional visual modes: a box of statistics for the quick-reading, *logos*-seeking viewer; a closing title to indicate a balanced perspective; a glance ahead to future questions. Having mastered the production of the newspaper genre, Julie has accomplished much more: she has created compelling visual rhetoric in a practical format and explored the potentials of visual argument that she might in turn pursue in a lengthy research project.

From Julie's example, students can imagine the FAMS Project constructed with other kinds of visual texts, such as photographs, advertisements, propaganda posters, and even multimedia animations. Past students have chosen a variety of texts, including film posters, propaganda posters, civil rights photography, contemporary advertising, and even economic charts. In terms of layout, students have created realistic newspaper formats complete with tear lines, simulated scrapbook pages with photos taped onto the paper, and reproductions of popular magazine pages. Additionally, in writing arguments using these texts as persuasive evidence, students have shown creativity and innovation in both arrangement and style. One student wrote a letter as a historian, another crafted an interoffice memo from a marketing manager, another created a transcribed interview, and, increasingly, I find visual reproductions of email or IM correspondence as a mode of written argument for one of the perspectives of the FAMS Project. This, in turn, reflects shifting writing conventions that we need to include in our pedagogy and suggests how the FAMS Project can bring to light such new hybrid genres of discourse. I invite interested readers to explore additional projects on different topics and diverse media—not only political cartoons, but also advertisements, photographs, propaganda posters, and film stills—accessible as examples online.[5]

Closing Frame: The Pedagogical Value of Teaching Visual Rhetoric

In each of the projects I have seen in my classes, the simulated discourse about and through the image makes clear what Ron Fortune calls "the interaction between word and image." By discussing this assignment in class, we are able not only to begin to theorize the parallels between visual and verbal argumentation, but also to understand how the pictorial functions as argumentation in its own right. In this way, the FAMS Project helps both teachers and students arrive at new understandings of the power of images *as evidence for arguments* and *as arguments themselves.* As we can see, the benefits of this kind of work are many, and in addition the project seems to be more enjoyable for students to complete than standard written arguments.

Theory meets practice in the FAMS Project in three ways. First, by transforming visual rhetoric analysis into the production of argument and visual design of a feature article publication of their choice, students sharpen their creative, argumentative, and rhetorical skills; in the process of designing format and establishing three fictional personas, students develop strengths in style and voice. Second, students learn to break the mold of pro-con logic by exploring alternative visions while traveling into the constructed worlds of their personas. By complicating an issue through exploring it from diverse vantage points, students prepare themselves for rigorous and sophisticated research exploration of their topics. Third, and perhaps most important, they come to know first-hand that visual rhetoric is a powerful mode of persuasion. Having to combine image and written text—having to forge an argument out of a careful reading of an image and make explicit references to it by deploying the visual as evidence—shows students how to interpret, position, manipulate, and generate visual argumentation as rich and powerful as verbal argumentation. As students understand and harness visual rhetoric as a tool, the words they write need to explain the meaning of the image, or reveal it for writer and reader, and—as we know from educational theory—it is in the process of teaching others that the students themselves learn best.

For teachers interested in incorporating visual rhetoric into the writing classroom, political cartoons are an ideal medium for this project since, as Josh Greenberg argues, "Political cartoons not only grasp the way in which visual discourse conveys social experience, but cartoons also help constitute the subjectivities and identities of social subjects, their relations, and the field in which they exist" (par. 9). One way to show students how this process happens in visual texts that are indeed a powerful mode of public writing is through the FAMS Project. As we continue to construct new curricula, we need to develop more such creative classroom practices that emerge in collaboration with our students' interests and contribute in turn to new theorizations of visual rhetoric in our culture. As we continue to make space for visual rhetoric in our curriculum, we make visible the work of culture and the power of images to shape our world.

Appendix: Feature Article Multiple Sides Project

Description

Now that you have completed your rhetorical analysis of a visual text in the form of a compelling argument, it's time to build upon that work by exploring other views (multiple perspectives) of the issue at hand. The Feature Article Multiple Sides (FAMS) assignment is a five- to ten-page argumentative project exploring a topic in depth, as well as the importance of context and diverse viewpoints. You will compose this project in a creative manner by constructing a feature article that includes the following elements:

- An introduction to the issue you wish to explore and an identification of the personas, titles, and stances of the three articles in the project;
- Three articles that you compose as visual-verbal argumentative position papers (each one will be written by a different, fictional persona and each will use visual arguments);
- A conclusion that provides a critical evaluation of the rhetorical strategies of all three articles and assesses the effectiveness or persuasiveness of each side in the project; and
- A complete works cited list of all images, articles, and resources consulted.

Process

Each part of the FAMS Project should take the form of an article for a specific journal, written by a specific persona (you will fabricate the persona—this is an exercise in diverse arguments). You should experiment with multiple arguments that support positions that are not compatible with one another (and may not be perspectives that you hold) in order to expand your exploration of your topic. Think outside the box; avoid creating stereotypical perspectives. Each response also should include visual images as part of the argument and refer to the details of the visual explicitly as part of the written prose. You might present multiple perspectives on one image or present multiple perspectives each with its own image. Alternatively, you might write the different components of your project addressing different audiences by situating your texts in different publications, or you might make them all part of one publication. Compose both an introduction for the three articles and a conclusion that provides a critical evaluation of the rhetorical strategies and addresses the effectiveness of each article. Format the piece using the best rhetorical layout for your project. Allow yourself to experiment with appropriate forms and voices.

Visual Layout and Design

Consult different magazines, journals, and websites for examples of your potential layouts for this assignment. Then, select or design the most appropriate visual design. You might present it as a newspaper issue with letters to the editor or as a special journal issue; insert images right into your document (cut and paste images either manually or by downloading files through Microsoft Word); use the columns feature to present material in a way that entices the audience, privileges certain perspectives, or leads the audience through a series of interpretations. Make it clear and compelling, and be creative. Think strategically about the visual rhetoric of your project.

Notes

1. Telnaes's work often relies on such a hybrid discourse of text and image, as a search through her online gallery available at <http://www.anntelnaes.com/> makes evident.

2. In a separate interview with Jim Lehrer, Marlette explained that "the best [cartoonists] are giving their vision or their way of seeing things [and] simply holding it up and letting the world look through their eyes" (qtd in Lehrer, "Illustrated Men"). It is primarily through Marlette's notion of "seeing things through someone's eyes" that the FAMS Project moves students from skepticism about the value of the visual, to visual awareness, to rhetorical empowerment.

3. Perhaps one of the best online collections of political cartoons is Daryl Cagle's at <http://cagle.slate.msn.com/>.

4. See Julie Tung's project online at <http://www.stanford.edu/~aobrien/FAMS/julietung.doc>.

5. To see a wide range of student FAMS Projects, published online with student permission, visit <http://www.ablongman.com/envision>, and navigate to Student Resources for Chapter 3; then select Student Writing. My colleague and co-author, Christine Alfano, and I discuss variations on this project and provide peer review guidelines in our new book, *Envision: Persuasive Writing in a Visual World.*

Works Cited

Alfano, Christine L., and Alyssa J. O'Brien. *Envision: Persuasive Writing in a Visual World.* Companion Website. 9 Feb. 2005 <http://www.ablongman.com/envision/>.

Birdsell, David S., and Leo Groarke. "Toward a Theory of Visual Argument." *Argumentation and Advocacy* 33.1 (Summer 1996): 1–10.

Brooks, Charles. *The Best Editorial Cartoons of the Year 2002.* Gretna, LA: Pelican Publishing Company, 2002.

Cagle, Daryl. Professional Cartoonists Index. 9 Feb. 2005 <http://cagle.slate.msn.com/> .

Diamond, Matthew. "No Laughing Matter: Post–September 11 Political Cartoons in Arab/Muslim Newspapers." *Political Communication* 19.2 (2002): 251–72.

Fortune, Ronald. "Image, Word, and Future Text: Visual and Verbal Thinking in Writing Instruction," *Working with Words and Images: New Steps in an Old Dance.* Ed. Nancy Allen. Westport, CT: Greenwood Publishing, 2002. 97–119.

Greenberg, Josh. "Framing and Temporality in Political Cartoons: A Critical Analysis of Visual News Discourse." *The Canadian Review of Sociology and Anthropology* 39.2 (May 2002): 181–99.

Lehrer, Jim, "Illustrated Men." Online NewsHour Transcript. 31 Oct. 1996. 18 Mar. 2003 <http://www.pbs.org/newshour/bb/election/october96/cartoonists_10–31.html>.

Melandri, Lisa. "Drawing the Line." Philadelphia, PA. 4 Aug. 2000. 18 Mar. 2003 <http://thegalleriesatmoore.org/publications/cartoons/politicalcartoons.shtml>.

McCloud, Scott. *Understanding Comics.* New York: HarperPerennial, 1993.

Mitchell, W, J. T. "The Pictorial Turn." *ArtForumInternational* 30.7 (March 1992): 89–94, Rpt. in *Picture Theory:* Chicago: U of Chicago P, 1994. 11–34.

Pollard, Lawrence. "The Art of the Political Cartoonist." BBC News. 18 Aug. 2002. 3 Mar. 2003 <http://news.bbc.co.uk/2/hi/europe/2194967.stm>.

Telnaes, Ann. "Freedom Fries." Ann Telnaes, Tribune Media Services. 12 Mar. 2003. 15 Oct. 2004 <http://www.anntelnaes.com/>.

Tung, Julie. "In Focus: The Death Penalty." 17 Oct. 2002. 9 Feb. 2005 <http://www.stanford.edu/~aobrien/FAMS/julietung.doc>.

Werner, Walt. "On Political Cartoons and Social Studies Textbooks: Visual Analogies, Intertextuality, and Cultural Memory." *Canadian Social Studies* 38.2 (Winter 2004). Available: <http://www.quasar.ualberta.ca/css/Css_38_2/ARpolitical_cartoons_ss_textbooks.htm>.

11 Thirteen Ways of Looking at a Black-and-White Photograph

Ryan Jerving

I can't recall the first time that a student of mine turned in an essay that digitally had incorporated borrowed images directly within the text. I know I was duly impressed and I know I was interested first and foremost in finding out how the student did it and how I might do it, too. The images that in the early 1990s first began cropping up in student papers unexpectedly and furtively, fugitives from a signifying chain gang, spread like kudzu as the decade wore on, with all the biological assertiveness of a transplanted weed species. This was, to paraphrase W. J. T. Mitchell, a millennial phenomenon that had "legs" ("Surplus" 7). The potential rhetorical power of the digitally reproduced photograph—and it was and is still almost always a photograph: not a chart or a graph or a comic-strip panel or a work of original art—should be looked at as a concrete, perfectly mundane—and therefore perfectly instructive—manifestation of the "pictorial turn" that for Mitchell defines our current scene of cultural representation.[1]

To return to that scene now is to discover an instantiation of that classic crime story trifecta of motive, means, and opportunity. Motive was provided by those larger cultural and political "regimes of spectacle and surveillance" that Mitchell finds circumscribing our present-day intellectual life (*Picture Theory* 106), regimes lived at the subject level through what Susan Sontag once termed the "ethics of seeing," in which visual means come increasingly to supplement or to supplant textual or other means of expression and understanding (*On Photography* 3). The development and widespread campus dissemination of scanners, color printers, cross-integrated office software, and ever-more sophisticated browsing capabilities for an Internet increasingly stuffed with JPEGs, TIFFs, and GIFs meant that by the mid-1990s students had the means to trawl an ocean of digital images and to drag and drop the day's catch into their writing with no appreciable degradation of source quality. To the extent that we writing teachers have become comfortable ourselves with addressing visual rhetoric in the classroom—still very much a work in progress, I'll be the first to admit—our assignments have come to represent a welcome, organic opportunity through which students can demonstrate their image-using savvy, especially as our demands have innovated beyond the one-damn-essay-after-another model and into drag-and-drop-friendly forms such as PowerPoint presentations, course websites or blogs, poster sessions, and student writing conferences.

And yet, from the evidence to be gathered at this scene of digital re-presentation, it's clear that we haven't always been struck by the smoothest of criminals. Indeed, although students clearly regard the visual as a valued accomplice, images as actually put to use receive what can be quite shoddy treatment, reduced often to the same level of inscrutability as the fourth-generation photocopies I once stapled to the back of my own undergraduate essays: coarsely pixillated, monochromatically rendered, scotch-taped miniatures with all the impact of an IMAX film viewed over your cell phone. Decorative rather than integrated elements, photographs are sometimes dumped, uncaptioned and uncredited, somewhere in the middle of the page or partially cut off across the bottom, sometimes sent as afterthought attachments, sometimes printed out with the Corbis (or other) watermark still stretching diagonally across the borrowed image like a chalk outline at a murder scene. All told, the grading room floor is littered with the lifeless frames of photographs coldly dispatched like the disposable rhetorical henchmen they all too often are: used, but not acknowledged; attached, but not analyzed; referenced, but not critiqued; noted, but not contextualized—in short, their significance assumed as a transparent gift to the text and not as something itself constructed, contestable, or worth arguing about. This reductive, iconic approach bespeaks an ultimately iconoclastic disregard for the actual concrete, material manifestation of the image as anything other than a placeholder at which to jerk one's thumb. See this? This IS a pipe. Next!

Of all the work that has crossed my desk exemplifying this disregard for the material image, one instance stands out in particular. For a digital slide show on the development of the U.S. Civil Rights Movement, a group of students had pulled together many of the usual pictorial suspects. But within these dependably iconic images was embedded a more jarring one: Margaret Bourke-White's classic portrait of Mohandas Gandhi and his spinning wheel (*charkha*) taken in 1946 as part of a series on Indian leaders for *Life* (this is the Henry Luce magazine that debuted in 1936—with a Bourke-White photograph on the cover—and that, along with rival publication *Look,* was one of the first and foremost periodicals to exploit fully the aesthetic and commercial possibilities of feature photojournalism) (Bourke-White, "Gandhi").[2] If you're picturing Gandhi right now, and you're not seeing Ben Kingsley, then you've probably got this particular photograph in mind: Gandhi, unclothed from the waist up, seated cross-legged in the right upper-third of the image, looking down at his reading as though absorbed in his thoughts to the exclusion of even noticing the camera's presence (the photograph was taken on his weekly day of silence). The human figure is set against a woven rug and a silhouetted, flower-like spinning wheel that occupy the left and lower two-thirds of the frame, objects that metonymically place the anti-colonialist intellectual and activist within his politicized cultural context—the spinning wheel, which made possible and visible the boycott of imported British cloth, was, Bourke-White wrote, "the great symbol of India's fight for independence [. . .] positive, productive, nonviolent, and [something that] gave to each spinner a sense of personal participation in the struggle" (*Halfway,* 38–39).

The students' use of this image was jarring because they had (and without seeming to notice) elected to use, not Bourke-White's original photograph, but rather the image as lifted by computer manufacturer Apple for an ad campaign featuring Gandhi, Pablo Picasso, Martha Graham, and other twentieth-century artists and intellectuals all encouraging us to "Think Different" (Figure 1). The ad cropped Bourke-White's image to exclude most of the background and modified it so that the Apple logo and campaign slogan were pasted in the corner like a four-color wafer, in stark contrast to the studied asceticism of the original (Apple Computer, Inc. "Think Different"). I think I half-jokingly mumbled something at the time about the basic indignity of it all, the mahatma reduced to shilling for a corporation whose high-tech globalism couldn't exactly be characterized as "Gandhian" (Figure 2). And I kicked myself later for the teaching moment I'd missed. This re-imaged image represented a rare opportunity in its concrete

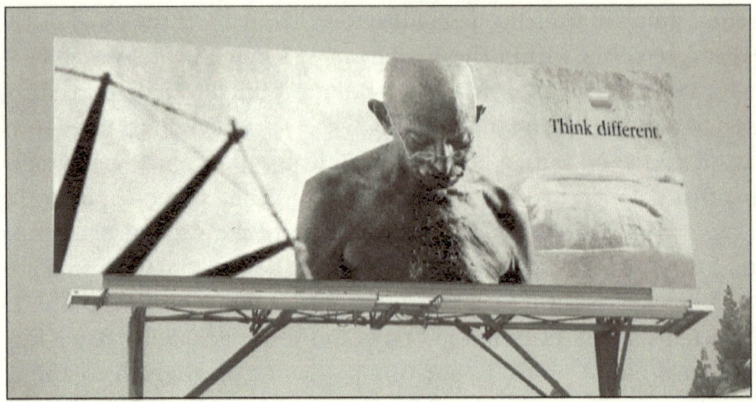

Figure 1. Margaret Bourke-White's portrait of Mohandas K. Gandhi, as put to use by Apple. The billboard image is organized horizontally while print ad versions of the same image are organized vertically; but both crop the original to center focus on Gandhi as an individual and not on his relation to his social context. (Used by permission of Apple Computer, Inc. "Think Different.")

crystallization of crucial theoretical questions of representation: of the commodification of dissent, of speech and subalterneity, of the technologization of the West and the traditions of the rest, of the othering of the other and the worlding of the world. Apple's colonization of the image (and, indeed, Bourke-White's before them) could provide the raw material for a fascinating case study of the text/image question, the juncture at which, as Mitchell argues, "political, institutional, and social antagonisms play themselves out" and the join at which "history might slip through the cracks" (*Picture* 9; 104).[3] But to have brought my students to these kinds of questions would have meant overcoming a certain ingrained (willed?) blindness to the material specificity of the image in practice as opposed simply to its iconic appearance as a name-checked reference. They'd have to taste the fruit of the tree of knowledge of object and representation. They'd have to learn to see the apple.

Thirteen Ways of Looking at an Apple

The handout I've included as the appendix to this essay is meant as something like my act of contrition for such missed teaching opportunities. My thesis is that these "Thirteen Ways of Looking at a Black-

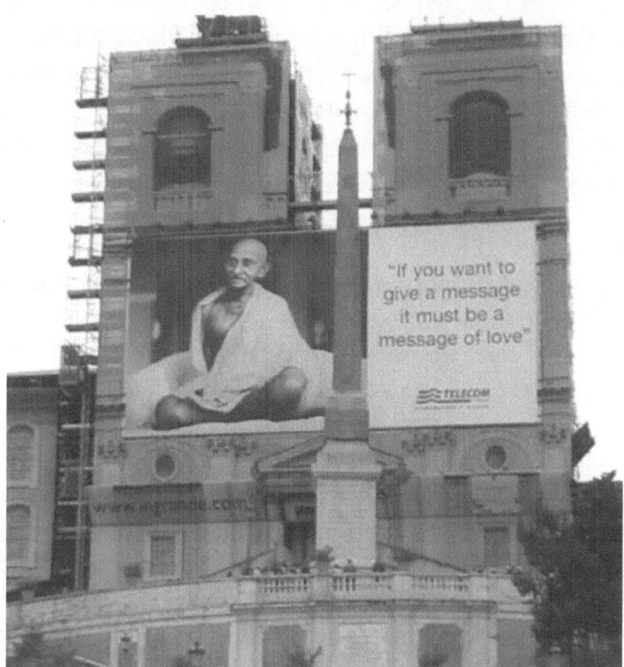

Figure 2. Apple is not alone in using the image of Gandhi—and again, notice, cropped to focus on the inspirational individual to the exclusion of any metonymic links to his political and social milieu—in efforts designed to humanize a multinational tech corporation. (Courtesy of Anne R. Richards.) See also Young and Rubicam, Milan's truly astounding television ad for Telcom Italia, directed by Spike Lee, featuring the mahatma broadcasting his 1947 "One World" speech via webcam to a giant LED screen in Times Square, to cell phones in use near the Coliseum in Rome, and to a nodding crowd gathered in Red Square.

and-White Photograph" can be used in the classroom to help unseat the iconic and to break apart that singleness of vision—our students' and our own—that encourages us to treat visual culture as a transparent or "merely decorative" window onto referentiality and not as something more interesting: acts of representation that are themselves potential objects of critique. The handout provides concrete tools and a shared vocabulary for doing so in the immediate context of news photography. But on a more fundamental level, it presents visual representation itself—the concrete means of production, appropriation, and abuse of images—as a problem.

This problem has been posed by a number of undergraduate writing texts that, in dealing with photography, photojournalism, and other forms of visual rhetoric, have begun to address the need to equip students in concrete ways for participating in our visual culture as critical consumers, producers, and writers. A literal supplement to *The Bedford Guide for College Writers,* Marcia F. Muth and Karla Saari Kitalong's *Getting the Picture: A Brief Guide to Understanding and Creating Visual Texts* (2004), is a thin but useful consideration of design as a factor in student writing, and it provides solid strategies (and a heaping helping of checklists) for identifying purpose and audience, analyzing visual characteristics (particularly narrative), and interpreting the significance of images. Lester Faigley, Diana George, Anna Palchik, and Cynthia Selfe's *Picturing Texts* builds on Faigley's own *Brief Penguin Handbook* (2003) to provide a vocabulary for analyzing visual texts; it structures the book around photographic analysis, with special stress on composition (element balance and patterning, interrelations of emphasis, unity, or contrast) and context (purpose, argument, institutions). Less adventurous than *Picturing Texts* in what it's willing to consider visual culture (restricting itself largely to the image), Donald and Christine McQuades' *Seeing and Writing* remains intriguing in the parallels it draws between verbal and visual rhetorical strategies. Their appendix devoted to "Reading Visual and Verbal Texts" (661–77) is a useful complement to the "Thirteen Ways" approach I present here.

This problematic of visual representation has a long and distinguished pedigree within photography's own history. Since its invention in 1839 (the technology was developed more or less simultaneously by Louis Jacques Mandé Daguerre in France and William Henry Fox Talbot in England), the photograph's uniquely indexical relation to the world has been a vexed question for both photographers and their critics. As photography historian Beaumont Newhall writes, "The camera records what is focused upon the ground glass. If we had been there, we would have seen it so. We could have touched it, counted the pebbles, noted the wrinkles, no more, no less. However, we have been shown again and again that this is pure illusion. Subjects can be misrepresented, distorted, faked," a fact that we occasionally "even delight in" (94). Indeed, Newhall's *History of Photography from 1839 to the Present* (first published for a Museum of Modern Art exhibit in 1937 and revised and enlarged several times between then and 1982) can be read as a veritable catalogue of observations on this ebb and flow between the dream of "eliminating the hand of man in the reproduction of pictures of all kinds" (14) and the recognition and even embrace of photography's inevitable shaping of the object of its representation.

On the one hand, Talbot recounted having produced in 1835 "the first instance on record, of a house having painted its own portrait" (qtd. in Newhall 20); he also titled his 1844–1846 collection of calotype photographs *The Pencil of Nature.* In contrast, his contemporaries David Octavius Hill and Robert Adamson made a virtue of the distinct reminders of human intervention expressed in the calotype process, noting in 1848 that with "[t]he rough surface, and unequal texture throughout of the paper [. . .] [t]hey look like the imperfect work of a man—and not the much diminished perfect work of God" (qtd. in Newhall 48). Talbot's faith in the photograph as an unaided "pencil of nature" has continued to resound since.[4] Meanwhile, a counterbalance has been struck throughout photography's history by a self-conscious sense of the constructedness of the photograph's reality and the continuing presence of the human hand in shaping its image.[5]

Within this dynamic, photojournalism has largely stuck to the "pencil of nature" story, rather than the "human hand" admission, in articulating its material engagement with what Roland Barthes called "the Occasion, the Encounter, the Real" (4). News photography has from its beginnings lived at the busy intersection of multiple authorial, editorial, textual, and visual decisions, struggles, agreements, and antagonisms. Though scattered earlier examples of the genre might be pointed out, news photography depended for its effective genesis and subsequent development on the convergence of a number of technological and institutional happenings: the development of a halftone printing process that made it possible to produce, mechanically, facsimile reproductions of photographs alongside text; the economy of scale and mass dissemination made possible by the penny press and a rail (and later road) network increasingly national in scope and depth; and the development and later proliferation of portable hand cameras and celluloid roll film (see Newhall 130–33; 217–33; 248–67). Current photojournalism continues to respond to the economic and institutional forces of today's news market, in particular to competition with televisual media, the demands and possibilities of digital formats and distribution, and the concentration of increasingly for-hire, non-royalty work in news photo agencies such as Magnum and Sygma or wire services such as Reuters and the Associated Press (Roskis 43–45). Such forces have a significant visible effect on the shape that news photographs take (see, for example, John Taylor's cogent reading of war and disaster photography in *Body Horror*). Yet news photography most often represents itself as utterly transparent: simply delivering up the day's happenings, too quickly produced and put to work to warrant or to reward sustained analysis.

"Thirteen Ways" sands against this grain, asking students to read news photography for effects of selection and emphasis that arise through cropping, blocking, and aestheticization; for characteristic tropes of setting, costume, and objects in the mise-en-scène; for the formal/ideological conjunctions of camera distance, angle, and lighting; for issues of representation raised by the photographer/photographed relation, genre and tradition, and the re-presentation within the frame of others' acts of visual-textual representation; and for the shaping effect of the institutions of dissemination and reading through which news photographs are mediated. To begin with news photography out of all possible genres—as I do in my first-year writing course designed around the theme of visual culture and the usable past—is to ask students to look at something very familiar and re-imagine it as something quite strange. Working through the constructedness of this quotidian, casual form, we learn—at least this is the idea—to see and speak the visual rhetoric of other dialogic cultural forms as well.

This baker's dozen of approaches is meant to signify not as holy writ but rather as a set of tools for prying open further discussion, a list of heuristically useful but ultimately insufficient points of reference for other kinds of visual culture. Indeed, thirteen is my magic number precisely due to the aura of arbitrariness that (I hope) attaches to it. The joke of my handout's title plays on this contingency, lifted as it is somewhat unceremoniously from Wallace Stevens's "Thirteen Ways of Looking at a Blackbird" (a classic case study in the modernist practice of making representation and perception themselves the object of perception and representation). The handout's introduction explicitly invites students (and instructors) to remake these approaches in and for their own images and other visual genres. Indeed, the handout as presented here has been adapted, with the input of many students, from its initial appearance in a social texts course in which it served to introduce 1930s American documentary photography. Further revision of it might, in this light, drop #12, "Representing Representation"—a holdover concept crucial to the characteristic irony of the 1930s (see James Guimond's "The Signs of Hard Times"), but not one that many students have taken to in the context of twenty-first-century news photography. Other possible, but untested, ways of looking could include the potential for knowing, ironic digital manipulation (à la *The Onion* or *The Daily Show*), the representation of cultural otherness (see Faigley, et al. 228–48), page design and layout, or the supporting, resisting, or complicating relations that a photograph can bear to the story (or stories) it accompanies.

Thirteen Ways of Looking at a Classroom

As a matter of classroom practice, I begin by bringing in a single, especially rich photograph with which to spend a couple of days—say, August Sander's snapshot of three young German farmers on their way to a dance on the eve of World War I, Gordon Parks's confrontational 1942 portrait of federal government charwoman Ella Watson (paid for by the federal government), or Ken Lambert's double-edged rendering of a George W. Bush presidential photo-op at Mount Rushmore in 2002. As a class, students offer their initial reactions concerning the composition, meaning, or cultural/historical impact of such a photograph. Then, again as a class, we dive into a point-by-point interrogation of the photograph in each of the handout's thirteen ways. That this initial step usually takes two full class periods sends a strong (and delightfully excruciating) signal about the level of surgical depth at which the analytical dissection of visual texts might operate.

Students next work in smaller groups to produce informal presentations that run one way of looking through each of the photographs they have scavenged from that week's newspapers. This initial group work sets the students up for the first half of the individual writing project by 1) enabling them as peers to distinguish iconic but uninteresting images—photographs selected due primarily to an interest in the subject matter—from images rich enough to stand up to extended analysis; and 2) providing a forum in which to test their sense of how material choices in the photograph might be linked to interpretive effects. (This stage also offers an opportunity to explore paragraph construction and relations of warrants, claims, and evidence.)

From each student, I ask for an individual written analysis of a single photograph in the form of thirteen independent paragraphs, each to be crafted as a small jewel of 100–150 words. I do so because of the inevitable redundancy this approach generates across their document as a whole. This redundancy can then be exploited in a next, synthetic stage in which the student pulls together these scattered observations into a complex discussion of overall effects—whether writing about a candidate on the campaign trail, NASA scientists in a nondescript room celebrating the Mars Rover landing, the Superbowl halftime show, a California anti-avocado theft sign, a lone U.S. soldier on a deserted street, a child soldier carrying an assault rifle, or a Daoist fortune-teller plying his trade on the streets of Beijing (all actual student essay topics from a recent semester).

To take a more extended example, we might consider one of the defining images of its decade—a hooded, caped Iraqi prisoner on a small box, dummy wires attached to his fingers and genitals (see Hersh 42).[6] As students have suggested, insightfully, absent the explicit violence or sexualized humiliation of many of the other images of torture from Abu Ghraib, the dehumanization effected in this particular photograph is perhaps best realized when looked at through the prism of genre ("Ways" #11). Whatever other visual traditions the image calls up—Christian iconography of supplication, JPEG S/M, the vast twentieth-century photographic record of lynching, genocide, and torture—it is especially remarkable for adopting and confounding the conventions of the posed portrait. Like the portrait, it depicts a single figure, directly addressing the camera, aware of its presence. Yet it stands on its head the complicity and self-possession that a posed portrait is supposed to enact: the subject's agency is not only denied here, that denial is itself the subject of the image. As a class discussing this image, we were able to suggest that a student writing about this photograph could follow up on this particular moment of generic analysis through a move toward synthesizing evidence from other ways of looking to make his or her claim to genre as a key to the photograph's power. To begin, the student might point to the contribution that *blocking* (#6) and *cropping* (#1) make to this effect of the subverted portrait: the figure might have been centered as the primary focus of our interest, but here is framed and positioned to include the whole body rather than just the face or bust, thus visually surrounding the figure within the prison-wall background and calling attention to the humiliating detail of the small box. (Indeed, the image as it most often appears bolsters this effect through cropping out much of the contextualizing empty space and a partially visible American with a camera [see Sontag "Regarding" 27]). In making this back-and-forth movement, the student can experience analysis and synthesis as modes of thought and writing that are complementary (one can help generate the other), if not entirely coherent (there's bound to be leftover, unassimilable parts).

The handout closes with "The Photograph's Setting." This category of analysis is given its privileged spot (and its own subsection) in order to emphasize it as a springboard to further thinking about context: that is, how images reflect, affect, and reconnect with the world of viewers and institutions from which they emerge. It is worth emphasizing here that contexts of production and dissemination are multiple and multipliable. With respect to the Abu Ghraib images, for example, Susan Sontag has argued (in "Regarding the Torture of Others") that the photographs' digital provenance is a key to their meaning, one reflecting a basic "shift in the use made of pictures" (27). These were not simply soldiers' souvenirs, a recognizable if disturbing version of the thumbs-up tourist photography described in Sontag's earlier *On Photography* as "indisputable evidence that the trip was made, that the program was carried out, that fun was had" (9).[7] These were, instead, "less objects to be saved than messages to be disseminated, circulated" ("Regarding" 27)—a difference of potential access that, "unstoppable" ("Regarding" 42), would play a key role in their eventual public discovery. And the photographs took on very different meanings when they began appearing in newspaper stories exposing the abuses at Abu Ghraib or before the Congressional committee investigating them, than when they had functioned as email attachments or screen savers shared among coalition personnel. As the scene of representation and *the camera's presence* (#10) became the object of interest—the backstory of power relations between photographer and photographed, and within the chain of military, intelligence, and privately subcontracted command linking those on this side of the lens—the photographs could be read as much for evidence of the dehumanizing effect of the situation on American captors as on their Iraqi prisoners. There is no necessary outside to the photographic text looked at in this way, and students can be encouraged to consider how these photographs might also mean differently when viewed late at night on the dorm room PC, over a public terminal in the campus computer lab, or as part of a writing course focused on visual culture.

Thirteen Ways of Looking Ahead

Finally, in addition to all the "Thirteen Ways" handout does in terms of introducing grammars of analysis, rhetorics of synthesis, or symbolics of context, it is most crucially intended as a generative model for approaching other types of visual culture, from the interior design of justice at the International Criminal Tribunal for the former Yugoslavia in The Hague to the ritual of destiny made manifest at a halftime show in Urbana, Illinois. In preparation for a project on the ways the visual self-presentation of urban spaces both reveals and conceals those spaces' history and the tensions currently underwriting them, for example, I've found it useful to have students as a class build their own "Thirteen Ways of Looking at a City Block" handout—which came to include things like aesthetic or functional coherence; the level and kind of activity and motion; function in relation to neighboring blocks or the rest of the city; the difference in function or appearance produced by time of day, week, or year; sanitation; the prominence and impact of text; and the assumption of relative anonymity/familiarity of those on the block. And, to close in the spirit with which I began, students could be challenged to turn this vision-splitting approach back on the work they themselves are producing: on their own work's choice of fonts and typefaces; punctuation and paragraph/sentence lengths; margins, indentations, headings, and bulleted lists; white space; incorporated graphics; and documentation understood not only as a guide to access or the production of intellectual credit, but as a visual act of interpellation designed to make a certain kind of disciplinary reader feel at home. "Thirteen Ways of Looking at Your Own Writing," anyone?

Appendix: Thirteen Ways of Looking at a Black-and-White Photograph

Like other cultural artifacts, news photographs can be read for the choices made in taking, developing, and publishing them. Many of the concepts discussed below could be applied to art, film, candid, portrait, or commercial photography as well. But I focus here on news photography: a style that generally claims to record events exactly as they really happened. If nothing else, this handout is meant to suggest the degree to which news photography's "reality" is a carefully-constructed effect: an illusion of factuality shaped by narrative devices, rhetorical figures, and institutional expectations.

These ways of looking are not equally important to all photographs, and there are other possible perspectives I've left untouched that might be especially important to particular photos—for example, color, depth-of-focus, or digital manipulation.

Subject Matter

1. Cropping—how the photograph's reality is framed

   Photographers create exclusionary borders in deciding where to point their cameras. But the photograph can also be physically cropped later to edit out unwanted material. As with the other concepts on this handout, the single most important question you might ask of a particular photograph is how things might be different. How would it change the photograph to include what is excluded (imagine, for example, the same shot shifted five feet higher, or 90 degrees to the right), and what is gained by its exclusion?

2. Visual cues—how the photograph directs the eye within the frame

   Photographs direct the eye through a number of well-tested techniques. These include blocking (see below), depth-of-focus, color contrast, the rule of thirds (which assumes four privileged points at the intersecting lines of an imaginary tic-tac-toe board laid across the photo), and the tendency to read in a "Z" pattern: horizontally from top left to top right, diagonally from top right to bottom left, and horizontally again from bottom left to bottom right. Some photographs will make use of virtual arrows or frames within the photograph created by doorways, guns, gazes, the horizon, etc.

3. Aestheticization—the effect of art as opposed to the effect of fact

   I've suggested that news photography presents itself as a transparent window onto reality, simply recording and passing on the day's happenings to us. But, on occasion, news photographers aim for more artistic, aesthetic effects: blocking, cropping, or posing their subjects to create patterns, repetitions, frames, dramatic visual imbalances, color harmonies, etc. This aestheticization can exist in tension with the illusion of reality. Simply to freeze a moment—as all photographs do—is to aestheticize it, taking its subject out of its social and historical context. (Theorist Walter Benjamin once criticized photography's inability to say anything other than "What a beautiful world!" ["Author" 262.])

4. Characterization—the photographed subject's surrounding environment

   Surroundings imply the social world of the photograph, suggesting a relation between the figures and their neighborhood, workplace, leisure activities, natural environment, etc. That relation might be friendly, conflict-ridden, indifferent—moods that can be emphasized through such things as blocking, relative size and distance, and color (warm, bright, filthy, high contrast, infinite shades of grey, etc.).

5. Costume

   Even more directly, subjects are characterized by their neat suits, glamorous gowns, ragged overalls, ironically worn hats, etc. Costume (and its absence) provides a wealth of information about occupation, class, age, regional origins, religion, and political attitudes. Consider also how figures are characterized and typed by the objects (props) that surround them: work tools, furniture, food, animals, wallpaper, protest signs, etc.

6. Framing—how the photograph's subjects are positioned within the frame and in relation to one another

   Each given figure or object in the shot might be centered (or not), solidly in the foreground, out of focus in the background, partly obscured, isolated or interacting with other figures, visually balanced against other elements of the photograph. As in theater, staging often works as a kind of metaphor: the figure at center stage (frame) is presumed to be central to the action and its cultural significance. This likewise can work for photographically/culturally marginal, isolated, or obscured figures.

Camera Work

7. Camera Distance—where the camera is located on a horizontal axis in relation to the subject

   Importance is often implied by the percentage of the total frame taken up by a given figure or object. A human figure is a small part of an extreme long shot, a full body fits in a long shot, knees-up in a medium long shot, waist-up in a medium shot, chest-up in a medium close-up, face-up in a close-up, a single feature in extreme close-up. Closer shots emphasize individuals; longer shots emphasize surroundings.

8. Camera angle—where the camera is located on a vertical axis in relation to the subject

   A shot taken from the same height as the subject is a straight-on shot; a shot from below, a low-angle shot; a shot from above, a high-angle shot; a shot from straight above, a bird's-eye view. High-angle shots can suggest the subject's vulnerability; low-angle shots can suggest power (this is, of course, not always the case).

9. Lighting

   Whether natural (sun) or artificial (flash), the lighting in news photography generally aims at realism, as though simply presenting the subject as we ourselves might find it. But lighting—particularly shadows—can aim also at expressionist or presentational effects, suggesting the subject's or scene's psychological state or social condition.

The Scene of Representation

10. The camera's presence—the camera as narrator

    News photography generally takes a third-person stance: an outsider's eye viewing the scene objectively, unnoticed by the subjects (who look at each other or somewhere off-camera). Occasionally, the camera might take a first-person stance: a character in the scene acknowledged by the subjects, whose attitude toward the camera—friendly, hostile, humorous, indifferent—then becomes an important part of what's represented.

11. Genre—the type of image, as recognized by the viewer

    News photography will sometimes use traditional images or types of scenes, sometimes from the news photography tradition (e.g., mass demonstration, head-shot with microphone and podium, political handshake, dead child with a grieving parent, etc.) and sometimes from another visual arts tradition (e.g., painting, film). Genres include landscapes, still lifes, family portraits, madonna and child images, stereotypes, and others.

12. Representing representation

    News photographs will sometimes turn the camera on other acts of representation: billboard advertisements, painted signs, other photographs, a subject's performance, etc. Often the point is ironic, a montage (juxtaposition) of two visions of the world: the one the photographer sees versus the world depicted in this "found art."

Photographs in Their Institutional Place

13. The photograph's setting—where and how the photograph is viewed

    A photograph derives much of its meaning from its physical context. It may or may not appear with a caption, a byline credit, a headline, its own or other news stories (and other photographs), advertising, etc.—all contexts which can reinforce, qualify, or even contradict the meaning of the photograph alone. Consider the photograph's size and placement (what page or section, above or below the fold, etc.). And consider the effect of a viewer's interaction with the photo: over breakfast, online at work, behind the vending machine glass, in a respected weekly newsmagazine, in a less-respected daily tabloid, within a "best of" archive of news photos, in a museum, in a textbook, etc.

Notes

1. For undergraduate-appropriate overviews of this pictorial turn and of the visual event as our cultural dominant, see the introductions to Nicholas Mirzoeff's *An Introduction to Visual Culture* (1999), Marita Sturken and Lisa Cartwright's *Practices of Looking: An Introduction to Visual Culture* (2001), Donald McQuade and Cristine McQuade's *Seeing and Writing 2* (2003), and Lester Faigley, Diana George, Anna Palchik, and Cynthia Selfe's *Picturing Texts* (2004). For a recent overview of the field at large, see Cara A. Finnegan's "Visual Studies and Visual Rhetoric."

2. For Bourke-White's account of taking this picture, see her 1949 study of post-Partition India, *Halfway to Freedom* (81–90). For the image as it appears in various print ads from the Apple "Think Different" campaign, see Apple Computer, Inc., "'Think Different' Ad Campaign Photography." For the "false note" struck by Apple's use of the Bourke-White image, see Michael Richards's 1997 brief for the *History News Service* ("Thinking Differently" par. 1).

3. Such questions might even have included a self-reflexive look at those historical forces and social antagonisms that had brought these students and this image together within this uncritical pastiche in the first place: a look, for example, at the structuring tension between the global, instantaneous access to such images that is promised by networked technologies (I was teaching at the time at a university in Ankara, Turkey, but the students' images came almost entirely from U.S.-based websites) and the restrictive counterclaims staked by proprietary interests gobbling up ever more of the intellectual landscape. By this, I mean, most simply, that copyright and marketing pressures make it easier to find and use the ad than the original. For example, if you attempt to download the Bourke-White photograph as it appears on, say, *Gallery M* (an art market site, and the first site that comes up on a Google search of <Bourke-White AND Gandhi>), right-clicking on the image in Internet Explorer generates a pop-up error box and the message "All Rights Reserved"—to which you can only reply "OK." Meanwhile, Apple, who has a stake in seeing its image disseminated as widely as possible, makes the images from its "Think Different" campaign broadly available, on its website granting "full permission to reproduce or otherwise utilize entire photographs or part" for noncommercial purposes (though, not surprisingly, the publishable-quality uncompressed version of the image is made available

only in the proprietary Apple PICT format) (Apple Computer, Inc. "'Think Different' Ad Campaign Photography").

4. For instance, in 1860s critic Alphonse de Lamartine's characterization of photography as a "plagiarism of nature" (qtd. in Newhall 69), in the New York *World*'s trumpeting of Matthew Brady's Civil War photographs (some, it turns out, staged) as "truthful as the records of heaven" (qtd. in Newhall 89), in Eadweard Muybridge's stop-motion studies of human and animal locomotion in the 1870s and 1880s, in manufacturer George Eastman's description of the amateur-ready Kodak camera of the 1890s as "a photographic notebook" (qtd. in Newhall 129), in the *British Journal of Photography*'s 1889 vision of a vast photographic archive of reality that would provide "a record as complete as it can be made [. . .] of the present state of the world" (qtd. in Newhall 235, ellipsis in source), in August Sander's similarly imagined project (begun in 1910, never completed) to exhaustively catalogue German types in a study to be called "Man in the 20th Century," in the Straight Photography movement of the first decades of the 20th Century, in Roy Stryker's hope that his photography unit with the New Deal's Farm Security Administration would provide a comprehensive document of American life for the 1930s present and the future, in Jean-Luc Godard's epigrammatic statement that "Photography is truth. And cinema is truth 24 times a second."

5. For instance, in the ready acceptance even by the 1850s of retouching portrait negatives, in the admission by the same Lamartine quoted above that photography represented a site "where the artist collaborates with the sun" (qtd. in Newhall 69), in the painterly Art-photography movement of the 1850s, in the impressionist Pictorial movement of the 1880s and 1890s, in the avant-gardist Photo-Secessionist movement of the 1900s, in the cut-and-paste photo collages of Alexander Rodchenko, Laszlo Moholy-Nagy and others in the 1910s and 1920s, in the almost cubist aestheticism of Edward Weston or Margaret Bourke-White in the 1920s and 1930s, in Walter Benjamin's argument from "The Work of Art in the Age of Mechanical Reproduction" (1936) that photography had abandoned the wholeness of reality in favor of a surgical carving up "of multiple fragments which are assembled under a new law" (234), in Pierre Bourdieu's 1960s account of the structural and systematic middle-browness asserted by (especially amateur) photography, and in the work of a whole host of twentieth-century photographers with aesthetic or political agendas as disparate as those of Alfred Stieglitz, Man Ray, Walker Evans, Ansel Adams, Cindy Sherman, or William Wegman, but all working to highlight the constructedness of their images.

6. Or see just about any news source published in or around May 2004. To get a sense of this photograph's iconicity, see Francoise Mouly's image for the cover of the 18 October 2004 "Politics" issue of the *New Yorker,* in which the hooded prisoner, recognizable even in silhouette, haunts the red-

and-white striped background against which it is figured ("A Shadow Over the Election").

7. I could probably better serve Sontag's argument in *On Photography* by citing her account, entirely apropos events at Abu Ghraib, of photography's role in sustaining regimes of power through performing "essentially an act of non-intervention" (11), voyeuristically "at least tacitly, often explicitly, encouraging whatever is going on to keep on happening. [. . .] to be in complicity with whatever makes a subject interesting, worth photographing—including, when that is the interest, another person's pain or misfortune" (12).

Works Cited

Apple Computer, Inc. "Think Different." *New Yorker* 13 Oct. 1997: back cover.

—. 'Think Different' Ad Campaign Photography." *Apple.* 2005. 27 Jan. 2005 <http://www.apple.com/pr/pics/thinkdiffads.html>.

Barthes, Roland. *Camera Lucida: Reflections on Photography.* 1980. Trans. Richard Howard. New York: Hill and Wang, 1981.

Benjamin, Walter. "The Author as Producer." 1937. Rpt. in *The Essential Frankfurt School Reader.* Ed. Andrew Arato and Eike Gebhardt. New York: Continuum, 1992. 254–69.

—"The Work of Art in the Age of Mechanical Reproduction." 1936. *Illuminations.* Ed. Hannah Arendt. Trans. Harry Zohn. New York: Schocken Books, 1969. 217–51.

Bourdieu, Pierre. *Photography: A Middle-Brow Art.* Trans. Shaun Whiteside. Stanford: Stanford UP, 1990.

Bourke-White, Margaret. "Gandhi." Photograph. 1946. Rpt. in *Gallery M.* 1996. 27 January 2005 <http://www.gallerym.com/work.cfm?ID=91>.

—*Halfway to Freedom: Report on the New India in the Words and Photographs of Margaret Bourke-White.* New York: Simon and Schuster, 1949.

Faigley, Lester. *The Brief Penguin Handbook.* New York: Pearson-Longman, 2003.

Faigley, Lester, Diana George, Anna Palchik, and Cynthia Selfe. *Picturing Texts.* New York: Norton, 2004.

Finnegan, Cara A. "Visual Studies and Visual Rhetoric." *Quarterly Journal of Speech* 90.2 (May 2004): 234–56.

Godard, Jean-Luc, dir. *Le Petit Soldat.* 1960. Wellspring DVD FLV5267, 2001.

Guimond, James. "The Signs of Hard Times." *American Photography and the American Dream.* Chapel Hill: U of North Carolina P, 1991. 99–148.

Hersh, Seymour M. "Annals of National Security: Torture at Abu Ghraib." *The New Yorker.* 10 May 2004: 42–47.

Lambert, Ken. "President Bush Speaks about Homeland Security and the Budget at the Base of Mount Rushmore National Memorial, in Background, Thursday, Aug. 15, 2002, in South Dakota." Photograph. Associated Press. *Dodge Globe.* 16 Aug. 2002. 27 Jan. 2005 <http://www.dodgeglobe.com/stories/081602/nat_bush.shtml>.

McQuade, Donald and Christine McQuade. *Seeing and Writing 2.* Boston: Bedford/St. Martin's, 2003.

Mirzoeff, Nicholas. *An Introduction to Visual Culture.* New York: Routledge, 1999.

Mitchell, W. J. T. *Picture Theory: Essays on Verbal and Visual Representation.* Chicago: U of Chicago P, 1994.

—. "The Surplus Value of Images." *Mosaic: A Journal for the Interdisciplinary Study of Literature* 35.3 (Sept. 2002): 1–23.

Mouly, Françoise. "A Shadow Over the Election." Illustration. *The New Yorker.* 18 Oct. 2004: cover.

Muth, Marcia F., and Karla Saari Kitalong. *Getting the Picture: A Brief Guide to Understanding and Creating Visual Texts.* Boston: Bedford/St. Martin's, 2004.

Newhall, Beaumont. *The History of Photography from 1839 to the Present.* New York: Museum of Modern Art, 1997.

Parks, Gordon. "Washington, D.C. Government Charwoman." Photograph. United States. Office of War Information. Aug. 1942. Library of Congress Prints and Photographs Division. LC–USF34–013407–C. Rpt. in "Documenting America: Photographers on Assignment." *America from the Great Depression to World War II: Black-and-White Photographs from the FSA–OWI, 1935–1945.* Library of Congress. *American Memory.* Digital ID: fsa 8b14845. 27 Jan. 2005 <http://memory.loc.gov/ammem/fsahtml/fadocamer.html>.

Richards, Michael. "Thinking Differently about 'Think Different.'" *History News Service* 23 Oct. 1997. 27 Jan. 2005 <http://www.h-net.msu.edu/~hns/articles/1997/102397a.html>.

Roskis, Edgar. "Photojournalism: The Last Lap?" *The Unesco Courier* 52.10 (Oct. 1999): 43–45.

Sander, August. "Young Farmers." Photograph. c. 1913. Rpt. in "The Suit and the Photograph." John Berger. *About Looking.* New York: Pantheon, 1980. 28.

Sontag, Susan. *On Photography.* New York: Farrar, Straus and Giroux, 1973.

—. "Regarding the Torture of Others." *New York Times Magazine* 23 May 2004: 24–29+.

Sturken, Marita, and Lisa Cartwright. *Practices of Looking: An Introduction to Visual Culture.* Cambridge: Oxford UP, 2001.

Taylor, John. *Body Horror: Photojournalism, Catastrophe, and War.* The Critical Image. New York: New York UP, 1998.

12 Collapsing Floors and Disappearing Walls: Teaching Visual and Cultural Intertexts in Electronic Games

Mark Mullen

Dreadful Wonder

In December 2000, multimedia publisher Electronic Arts released *American McGee's Alice,* a dark and disturbing game for the PC conceived as a third installment in the adventures of Charles Dodgson's classic heroine. In the cinematic sequence that opens the game, the player learns that Alice's family dies in a fire shortly after the conclusion of her trip to Looking Glass Land; Alice survives but remains in a coma and eventually is hospitalized in the Rutledge Asylum. When the player meets Alice, she has begun to emerge from the coma; she is now, however, in her late teens/early twenties, a traumatized child trapped in a battered adult's body. Retreating from the world of the institution, Alice returns to Wonderland only to find it horribly disfigured. As is clear from Will Brooker's extensive catalog of adaptations of Lewis Carroll's work in *Alice's Adventures,* McGee's vision of a corrupted Wonderland may be extreme (arguably matched only by Jan Svankmajer's 1987 film version), but its representation of Carroll's work as incorporating dark thematic elements is nothing new. And for all its evident delight in destroying every dear childhood memory one may have of Wonderland, the game also faithfully represents the core dilemma in Carroll's original tales: is Wonderland a place of escape for Alice from the bizarre and alien logic of the adult world? Or is it a truer version of that world that ends up reinforcing its underlying principles?

Like other games in the shooter mode, *Alice* features numerous levels, each of which has to be completed by the player before advancing to the next; the levels themselves are organized into chapters that are linked graphically and thematically. The second chapter, "The Fortress of Doors," in fact represents the start of the game proper, with the first chapter, "The Village of the Damned," functioning largely as a tutorial familiarizing the player with basic movement and combat controls. This second chapter also is distinctive in terms of the overall game because the laws of physics and dimensional coherence seem to have been suspended. In subsequent levels, Alice encounters bizarre landscapes that tease the senses with sudden shocks and flashes of vertigo. All these landscapes, however, still "make sense"; they do not provide so aggressively disorienting and alienating an environment as the first levels. Visually, the spaces in the Fortress of Doors section tend to rely on certain repeated elements: what should be solid floors, ceilings, and walls are broken and fragmentary; the skies are made up of whirling clouds that often give the impression of being formed from both spirals and interlocking planes; floors tend to form and disintegrate unpredictably; furniture that should be fixed rotates statically in space or, grotesquely enlarged, whirls through the sky. The visual design of these early levels accomplishes several things from a narrative point of view. First, it reinforces what seems to be the basic premise of the game: that one needs to read the contours of Wonderland as a series of shifting metaphors for Alice's psychological state. Second, it establishes a powerful sense of the fragility of conventional boundaries as well as other conceptual frameworks that are used to make sense of the world. Finally, the design emphasizes the importance of thinking beyond these conventional constraints, looking for alternative pathways, explanations, ways of making sense of the world. The sophisticated visual design of *Alice* is a useful example of the complexity of which electronic games are capable, a complexity that often is overlooked because it does not correspond to conventional expectations concerning plotting, characterization, etc. The game also stands as an injunction to look for alternative conceptions of visual rhetoric and to explore new pathways toward interaction with the world of electronic games.

Electronic Games in the Writing Classroom

Composition and rhetoric classes are, in many ways, the ideal venue for an engagement with the complexity of electronic games and with their visual density in particular. Introducing electronic games as a domain of study also creates the opportunity for achieving a number of goals that are central to an engaged writing pedagogy. In the first place, as Mary Hocks notes, "Critiquing and producing writing in digital environments actually offers a welcome return to rhetorical principles and an important new pedagogy of writing design" (632). Lev Manovich has argued that our age participates in the "continuing decline of the field of rhetoric in the modern era," a decline in which the hundreds of rhetorical devices detailed by classical and medieval authors were reduced to just two by the middle of this century (metaphor and metonymy) and have collapsed now to a single device (the metonymic relation established by linking pages on the Web, for example) (77). However, if one does not confine analysis of rhetorical devices solely to those describing the navigational relation between new media texts, as Manovich tends to do, but focuses instead on the texts themselves, the field of rhetoric remains as rich as ever when applied to new media.[1] Hocks, for example, proposes three analytical frameworks as a starting point for an understanding of visual rhetoric: audience stance (how the audience is invited to participate in the reading, how interactive, what kind of interactivity, etc.), transparency (the extent to which the document borrows the conventions of other media), and hybridity (the deployment of visual and verbal designs). One can imagine, then, within those categories the deployment of a host of rhetorical devices. Manovich's own five constitutive principles of new media—numerical representation, modularity, automation, variability, and transcoding—themselves offer us ways of thinking about the rhetorical structures associated with new media, and new ways of thinking about the larger cultural and interpersonal functions of rhetoric.

Second, writing about electronic games gives students a chance to enter a relatively new critical discussion; games thereby offer the chance to develop meaningful projects of real intellectual inquiry as opposed to the essentially simulative assignments required in most other kinds of writing classrooms. Third, students are able to use writing to do what cannot effectively be done by other means. One of the paradoxes of gaming is that gameplay experiences are often very difficult to represent in any other way than through the written accounts of players: screenshots don't cut it, and in-game movies don't do the experience justice. This is why many gaming communities are also active and intensive writing communities. The bulletin boards of communities surrounding online combat simulations (*Aces High, World War II Online*) feature extensive After Action Reports (AARs) detailing mission exploits; communities associated with multiplayer roleplaying games create elaborate fan fictions based on the gaming universe; players of many different kinds of games are often involved in discussing the strengths and weaknesses of the game, writing requests to game developers, organizing clans/guilds/squadrons, writing website documents, etc. Fourth, in tackling analysis of electronic games, students are forced to use writing to connect disparate phenomena and to concentrate especially on the intersections between object, experience, and culture. Finally, a writing course based around electronic games has the chance to ground students in a number of different genres of writing, ranging from the more familiar humanities-based analytical and critical styles, to approaches that involve the technical, scientific, and journalistic.

Seeing and Disbelieving

While critics may admit grudgingly that the visuals in electronic games are compelling, they seldom acknowledge the sophistication of the visual design of many games. Therefore, let me briefly highlight the five core elements that constitute *Alice's* visual design in order to demonstrate the kinds of terrain that can be explored in a class devoted to electronic games. Most obviously, the game adopts an oppositional stance toward that which has become, in terms of visual representations at least, the canonical Alice: the 1951 Disney film. McGee's version is influenced heavily by the visual conventions of classic and modern Gothic, with Disney's cast of lovable eccentrics replaced by the psychotic and sociopathic, and Disney's soft-focus pastels replaced with an alternation between dark and brooding earth tones, the stark contrasts of the Pale Realm chessboard levels, and saturated primary colors.[2] Second, in contrast to Disney's portrayal of Wonderland as a compensatory escape for Alice, McGee's version emphasizes the confrontational nature of the original stories by offering a series of environments that oscillate between the claustral (the factory in "Dementia," or the caves in "Rolling Stones" and "Icy Reception") and the vertiginous and expansive (the Fortress of Doors chapter, the "Airborne Terror" level)—an oscillation that is in itself quintessentially Gothic. McGee's game thus restores the sense from the novels that Alice's encounter with these strange worlds is an interactive, participatory process, a sense that is all the more appropriate in the environment of an electronic game. The third component of the game's visual design is its repeated allusions to the work of other Alice illustrators; more commonly they are the artists working at the more extreme end of the spectrum, like Salvador Dali, but elements from more mainstream artists such as Arthur Rackham are also present.[3] The self-consciousness of these allusions often is manifested in small details (like the photographic self-portrait of Dodgson visible in the mirror behind Alice in the game's "Settings" screen) but also appears forcefully within the game itself as, for example, when Alice in the "Castling" level walks through a hallway filled with images of characters from Dodgson's books, including portraits of herself, drawn by several different artists.

The visual elements in *Alice* also serve to mount a strong critique of institutionalized education. When the player first encounters the "Skoolhouse," for example, it is swaying unsteadily. Upon entering one finds that the building contains numerous gaps in the floor, through which one can see that the entire building is supported upon towering, unsteady columns of books that stretch down into the void. The building itself is filled with children, but they are clearly insane; with their heads encased in iron cages they march around aimlessly, bumping into walls, sometimes crowing like roosters. This critique is developed at a later point in the game when the children are encountered again, in the "Crazed Clockwork" level, the domain of the Mad Hatter. Here it becomes evident that the source of the killer robots that keep leaping out at the player from behind mirrors all through this level is a giant factory where the Hatter is turning the crazed children into machines. McGee thus picks up on the obsession of Carroll's Hatter with time, and renders it as a larger obsession with the order, discipline, and control produced by the mechanization that gave rise to our modern sense of time.[4] Modern education, then, is presented rather forcefully in McGee's game as an outgrowth of the rage for order and standardization.

The final element that makes up the visual design of *Alice* is an emphasis upon the game experience itself as an altered reality, faithful to the (il)logic of dream worlds. For example, when the player dies in the game, s/he is taken back to the initial loading screen that features a wide-eyed Alice, sitting upright in her bed in the asylum, clutching her stuffed rabbit: "Each time we play and 'die' our return to the real Alice shows that it wasn't a real death but a broken dream" (Brooker 233). Establishing the sense of this world as an alternative reality is also behind McGee's decision to design the game to be played from a third-person point of view rather than from the more typical (for a shooter) first-person view. This choice fosters a different kind of identification on the part of players than that usually associated with the first-person mode. Brooker notes that, in playing *Alice,* he felt

> an empathetic fear for Alice as a character. This sense arose specifically from the third-person display, from being able to see the comparatively small and fragile avatar—a teenage girl, despite her weapons—in a large, threatening, often vertiginous environment. It depended on this dual dynamic of being and watching at the same time, of seeing a version of "yourself" who is also "her," not a sexual object but a vulnerable figure. (241)

While I am not at all sure that vulnerability isn't sexualized here (would players respond to the figure of a waif-like boy in the same way?), Brooker's point about the dual nature of the identification—a product of being and watching—is a useful one. However, in his choice of a third-person perspective McGee notes that he was going for something a little more specific: "People often see their worlds from a third-person perspective when going through traumatic stress disorder. Alice has suffered from pretty severe mental stress, so it fits" (Salqado). This emphasis upon Wonderland as a space of traumatic re-enactment also lies behind the game's very linear gameplay: there is only one path through each level, and it is usually pretty well marked. The inability to depart from a path that seems to have been laid out is perfectly in keeping with the game's thematics of compulsion and re-enactment.

In its examination of such weighty concepts as the nature of reality, the construction of identity, and the familial/cultural pressures on the individual, *American McGee's Alice* is, therefore, at least as sophisticated as many other cultural products. This fact, however, raises an important question: Why is a discussion of this game (or virtually any electronic game, for that matter) as embodying these kinds of philosophical speculations so unlikely? In the popular media, a sophisticated conversation about the interpretative richness of particular games is almost always derailed by an obsession with discussing the supposed violence of the medium as a whole. In a larger sense, the lack of sophistication in critical analyses of electronic games (in the scholarly realm as much as the popular one) has everything to do with limitations in our current critical approaches to visual rhetoric in general and visual rhetorical analysis as it is applied to electronic games in particular. On the rare occasions where electronic games are treated as worthy of sustained critical analysis, they are often treated only as a visual phenomenon, with an unproblematic reliance on modes of analysis derived from cinema. Thus, what limits our appreciation of the sophistication of the visual rhetoric employed in electronic games is, paradoxically, too great an emphasis upon the visual, where games are understood primarily as occasions for an absorptive rather than a critical seeing.

Manovich's *The Language of New Media* provides the most comprehensive formulation of a theory that privileges the visual sense:

> Cinematic means of perception, of connecting space and time, of representing human memory, thinking, and emotion have become a way of work and life for millions in the computer age. Cinema's aesthetic strategies have become basic organizational principles of computer software. The window into a fictional world of a cinematic narrative has become a window into a datascape. (86)

Manovich has argued that while one can approach the history of cinema "as a succession of distinct and equally expressive languages, each with its own aesthetic variables," a situation in which "cinema was developing toward the still open horizon of many possibilities," the goals of the computer/entertainment industry are a lot more straightforward: "the exact duplication of cinematic realism" ("What is Digital Cinema?" 187). With regard to electronic games specifically, he sees the same drive toward realism as being in evidence during the 1990s (83).

Manovich's argument, however, ignores the fact that many of the best-selling games during this period adopted aesthetics that were non-naturalistic: *Grim Fandango* (1998) and the *Thief* (1998, 2000, 2004) series for the PC, for example, or the long-running Super Mario series for consoles, not to mention the explosion of anime-inspired titles. More to the point, as Richard Rouse points out, the gaming industry as a whole began to recognize that the obsession with cinematic representation created an additional set of problems by introducing a passive distancing into a medium predicated upon immersive engagement (17–18). Do electronic games exploit the visual language of cinema? Of course, but they are hardly defined by it; and while much of the discourse of gamers and industry alike centers on realism, such a concept is meaningful only if one adopts a considerably expanded and problematized notion of "realism." Such a conception must acknowledge, for example, that the criterion most often at stake for gamers is consistent and challenging behavior (of the environment, of the AI characters, etc.) rather than simply the naturalism of the game's appearance.

However, a critical attempt to respond to the valorization of the visual by emphasizing the immersive, kinesthetic qualities of electronic games often produces the impression that gamers simply play "through" the visuals. The visual elements are, essentially, not noticed in any meaningful sense; this approach is particularly evident in discussions of first-person shooters. The visuals, like other elements of the game world, are understood to exist essentially as props to the quality of the immersion: they are absorbed, not contemplated; experienced, not analyzed. While game criticism is to an extent moving beyond some of the early enthusiastic but laughable invocations of the "virtual" and the "interactive," a no-less superficial understanding of "immersion" and "participation" is threatening to take their place. *Alice* offers a useful challenge to this view, and it was not easy for many critics to adjust to the game's insistence upon reading its visual elements.[5] In *Alice,* as is the case with the illustrations in Carroll's novels, the visual elements are not incidental to the gameplay but integral to the player's enjoyment. We are constantly being asked not simply to play but to look as we play, to analyze what we are seeing, and to make connections with other texts outside the game world.

We need a way of understanding electronic games not simply as a highly visual form, or as a participatory experience, but as a place where those two activities coincide and reinforce one another. More specifically, any understanding of how games work shouldn't exclude an understanding of the role of their visual environments as objects of contemplation. Even where a game doesn't solicit contemplation as aggressively as *Alice* does, we need to allow for the possibility of the visual design of the environment shaping the player's experience without him or her being aware of it, in much the same way that we allow for a work of literature shaping readers' responses without their necessarily being conscious of that process at every moment. The focus of our teaching of the visual rhetoric of games, then, needs to be on moving from simple contemplation or unconscious assimilation, to an understanding of the way in which those are analytically complex tasks. We play. While we play we look. While we play and look we think.

The Mad Hatter's Tea-Party: Syllabus Design in the (Partially) Wired Academy

Those who have taught electronic games know that incorporating them into the classroom is challenging on a number of levels. Many of these challenges are not unique to electronic games but are familiar to any teacher who attempts to employ popular media in institutions that—despite marketing pronouncements to the contrary—are still organized around the study of print or print-based texts. However, even in an institution like my own, where a moderately high level of computer and audio-visual resources supports both the teaching of film specifically and the incorporation of multimedia elements more generally, an attempt to teach electronic games runs into some unique conceptual and logistical challenges. If institutions (in the sense of both brick and mortar establishments, and organizational and professional bodies) consider certain activities valuable in an educational context, those activities are, generally speaking, granted the necessary logistical wherewithal. By contrast, any class predicated upon the claim that electronic games are a useful and meaningful object of study, not simply for a niche population (students in electronic media majors, for example), but for everyone, is embedded in cultural and institutional matrices that either explicitly or implicitly communicate to students that such a claim is invalid and—quite literally in many institutions—cannot be supported.

Teachers of film, for example, do not have to deal with the problem of proprietary platforms. If I want to teach *The Good, the Bad, and the Ugly,* my biggest headache is whether or not to use the VHS or the DVD version; regardless of which format I choose, it is fairly easy to find the necessary display technology. Once that basic decision is made, every member of the class has access to the same basic text; more importantly, whether they watch the film on a projection screen, on a TV in our classroom, or on a computer in their dorm, my students will be familiar with the basic mechanism of accessing the visual text (sophisticated interpretation is, of course, another matter). With electronic games, however, the task is more complex: games are designed for Windows PC, Mac PC, X–box, and/or Playstation 2, not to mention older models of console that still attract legions of fans (Nintendo 64, Sega Genesis). Rarely are games released across all these platforms, and those that are crossplatform compatible are not the kind of games that would be terribly interesting to make the subject of a class (Checkers, anyone?). In practical terms, especially if I want to incorporate live playing sessions in the class, I will have to default to games made for the PC (Windows and Mac) while recognizing that this is not the format of choice for the majority of my students.

The platform affiliation of players has enormous consequences when it comes to the analysis of electronic games. When teaching film one rarely finds people who are so partisan about celluloid, VHS, or DVD that they will not watch a film in another format. And while film critics do pay attention to the context of the viewing experience in their scholarly articles and in some of their classroom discourse, in functional terms when they teach film they tend to foster the illusion of the fundamental portability of the film-viewing experience. Viewing is viewing whatever the context. In the world of electronic games, however, players often have decided platform preferences, not least because games require a substantial level of investment in titles and peripherals that militates against employing multiple platforms. Thus, the vast majority of players tend to play their games on one or at most two kinds of platform. The most significant divide is between computer and console gamers; console players are a little more likely to play across multiple platforms, but this is because upgrading technology in the console world is not simply a matter of replacing one platform with a bigger and better version but requires instead buying a whole new set-up.

Even if a game has been released for different platforms, the experience of playing it will not be the same in all cases. It doesn't look the same, it doesn't sound the same, and one doesn't interact with it in the same way in terms of the basic input devices or the location of the machine. Similarly, many players find it difficult, either as a result of familiarity or of personal preference, to play even the same game on a different platform; someone used to the highly mobile and responsive controller of a console finds playing the same game using a computer keyboard (or even a joystick) a bewildering and frustrating experience. More importantly, the choice of platform limits the kinds of games one can play. Although first-person shooter games, with their simple control structure, tend to be the most portable across platforms (and this portability accounts in no small degree for their popularity), games that require a large array of controls (like sophisticated combat simulations or complex massively multiplayer online role-playing games [MMORPGs]) rarely appear in the console world.

The implications of basic text choice are therefore much greater than in other kinds of classes. If I want students to purchase those texts in the same way I would for any other class materials, I am facing a number of problems. First, I need to choose a game that is available (and stable) in both Mac and Windows formats. Second, as much as I might want to, I need to resist the urge to focus on bleeding-edge games because not every student will have a computer capable of handling the most recent games; in practical terms, teachers need to build their classes around titles that are at least two years old. To add to the challenge, that game cannot appear too dated graphically, since for even some of the most game-savvy students (especially for them, perhaps) the problem of outdated graphics can become an initial and sometimes insurmountable hurdle. Assuming that I manage to find the ideal game, I may well face another set of problems based on the fact that many students will arrive in college with laptops: a sensible choice for other areas of their academic life but an awkward device upon which to play the majority of games (and which now may even lack such essential gaming features as a CD drive).

Let us assume, however, that I press on regardless and settle upon the major texts that I want students to purchase; like any teacher dealing with conventional subject matter, I want to make the core texts, and perhaps additional resources, available via the library's reserve system. I'm fortunate to have a section of our library that deals exclusively with multimedia reserve items, so they are used to the handling, storage, and tracking problems (making sure the disc is in the case when it is handed back in, for example, or that the manuals are still in the box). Obviously I would have to purchase the necessary texts myself and, once again, to select older games and to purchase Mac and PC copies. Regrettably, the increasing emphasis on copy protection means that most CD-based games will not play unless one has the CD in the drive; such a measure effectively works against the whole idea of putting material on reserve. It is relatively easy for a seasoned Web-searcher to locate hacks that can be installed over some games and which will disable copyright protection of various kinds; these things can be hard to locate for students who aren't in the know, and since they are illegal (and players are faced with an increasingly litigious entertainment-industrial complex), I'm not eager to expose myself and/or the university to potential legal problems by pointing out that these solutions exist.

Even asking students to buy the games for the class is not without its perils. For all the vaunted multimedia literacy of the current generation of students, they also tend to resent being asked to purchase anything other than conventional print texts. This resentment has different causes, ranging from the financial (such items don't have much semester's-end buy-back value from a bookstore's point of view) to the disciplinary (why are students looking at something like this in a writing class?) and the cultural (while students may, if pressed, stretch their understanding of film to grant it some educational or aesthetic component, even dedicated gamers share their culture's prejudice in thinking of electronic games as "mere" entertainment). Experienced teachers might see this resistance as an insignificant problem. After all, teachers routinely make students purchase texts that they wouldn't have chosen for themselves, but that we, in our teacherly wisdom, have determined will be good for them. However, the resistance here is derived from the deep-seated cultural expectations that surround games as a species of new media product:

> New media objects assure users that their choices—and therefore, their underlying thoughts and desires—are unique, rather than preprogrammed and shared with others. As though trying to compensate for their earlier role in making us all the same, descendants of the Jacquard loom, the Hollerith tabulator, and Zuse's cinema-computer are now working to convince us that we are all unique. (Manovich, *New Media* 42)

Thus, the generation that has come of purchasing age in a world of iPods, customizable cell phone faceplates, and ringtones, individualized Web-profiles and instant messenger avatars associates information-rich media itself and, moreover, purchasing such items, with entertainment, freedom of choice, and individuality. Electronic games, then, are for students definitively not part of the educational domain, which they often associate in no uncertain terms with duty, constraint, and groupthink.[6]

I have spent time discussing a few of the logistical issues that accompany any attempt to teach games because it's precisely the constraints of the material teaching situation that often drop out of discussions of visual rhetoric. Mary Hocks, for example, argues that

> Whenever students look at artifacts such as online games or Web sites, we can begin by teaching them to "read" critically assumptions about gender, age, nationality, or other identity categories. Visual communication theories, however, tend to draw too easy a parallel between visual grammar and verbal grammar or to posit visual literacy as easier or more holistic than verbal literacy. We need to recognize that these new media and the literacy they require are hybrid forms [. . .] at once verbal, spatial, and visual. (630–31)

Hocks's point concerning the frequent confusion between notions of visual and verbal grammars is a good one, as is the way in which she draws attention to the often facile, but culturally embedded assumptions about the ease of interpreting visual culture. Teachers often assume students possess just this kind of visual literacy in remarks that are usually prefatory to bemoaning their lack of other, more substantial, supposedly more important skills. However, the way in which Hocks indiscriminately combines Web sites and online games points to a larger problem with her approach to visual rhetoric: lack of attention both to the cultural situatedness of the form, and its position within an analytical and educational setting. While for many critics the Internet still heralds the decline of civilization as we know it, websites now have a substantial degree of cultural authority if only because of their utility for business, communication, and research processes. They are also fixtures in college classrooms, either as a supplement to instructional needs or as a problematic content (as when, for example, in my own classes we talk about strategies for locating useful research materials online and authenticating that information). Most colleges therefore provide support for access to and study of Web sources in the form of appropriately equipped computer labs, many offer online courseware packages that ease the incorporation of Web content, and a few even make software available for building and hosting Web pages. Electronic games, on the other hand, generally are not regarded as culturally valuable. Consequently, for the purposes of teaching visual rhetoric, we need to be cognizant of the ways in which any analytical or instructional occasion will be shaped by our students' (and our own) attitudes toward entire classes of media objects, as well as how attitudes are being reinforced or countered by the larger institutional environment (over which teachers have very little control) and our own teaching approaches and practices.

These logistical and cultural constraints, then, form the background against which a teacher designing assignments for a games-centered writing class must operate. As far as the assignments themselves are concerned, if students are to be partners in developing increasingly sophisticated frameworks for understanding electronic games, assignments must move beyond the simplistic "compare and contrast" or the only slightly more ambitious "describe a pop cultural phenomenon." Diana George puts her finger on this problem when she notes that

> the terms of debate typical in our discussions of visual literacy and the teaching of writing have limited the kinds of assignments we might imagine for composition [. . .]. Instead, I would argue that if we are ever to move beyond a basic and somewhat vague call for attention to "visual literacy" in the writing class, it is crucial to understand how very complicated and sophisticated is visual communication to students who have grown up in what by all accounts is an aggressively visual culture. (14–15)

What I have been arguing throughout this piece is that the best way of fostering creative and effective analysis of visual rhetoric is, in fact, to reconsider the appropriateness of terms such as *visual literacy*. The New London Group, for example, argues that if pedagogy is to be based around a "teaching and learning relationship that creates the potential for building learning conditions leading to full and equitable social participation," teachers need to expand the notion of literacy itself (9). In particular, this conception of literacy must "account for the context of our culturally and linguistically diverse and increasingly globalized societies [. . .] [and] account for the burgeoning variety of text forms associated with information and multimedia technologies" (9). While such an approach represents my larger goal, two specific strategies can be brought into play in terms of focusing on games themselves as analytical objects: "we must offer students experiences both in the analytic process of critique, which scrutinizes conventional expectations and power relations, and in the transformative process of design, which can change power relations by creating a new vision of knowledge" (Hocks 644–45).

Building on Hocks's point concerning the integration of both critical and design elements into writing assignments, teaching a writing class around electronic games involves four distinct challenges, all of which can be met over the course of the semester with at least four different kinds of assignments. My intention here is less to provide templates for particular assignments although I will describe the specifics of the assignments that have worked for me. I am, rather, more interested in describing an approach to designing a writing-intensive syllabus around electronic games that clarifies the goals the course as a whole is trying to accomplish and outlines how different writing tasks might work together to achieve those goals. Because the logistical concerns I have discussed will be different for every campus, specific assignments will also look very different (a school bookstore may have no mechanism for ordering electronic games, for example, or an institution may not provide the computer support necessary to integrate such games effectively into a curriculum). In addition, I would argue that whatever the opportunities and constraints afforded by one's campus, there is a real pedagogical value to making students partners in the design and execution of the assignments upon which they will be working.

The first challenge in designing a writing-intensive, game-focused syllabus is to enable students to see that games are in fact externally referential—that they are shaped by larger cultural conversations and in turn help shape those conversations. The task is to undo the dependency upon the "mere entertainment" narrative, a standard strategy by which students (and not only students by any means) attempt to avoid engaging in nuanced critique of popular culture. The way around this problem is not by denying the entertainment value, but rather by exploring the political dimension of collective and individual pleasure. Why is it that specific games are entertaining in a specific time and place for a specific audience? The easiest way to begin such a conversation is an assignment that focuses on games that employ a nonnaturalistic visual design, thus allowing students to explore the ways that aesthetic choices are integral to the thematic and experiential components of games. Games such as *American McGee's Alice* or Lucasarts's *Grim Fandango,* with its *El dia de los Muerto*s iconography, are excellent choices; games that employ cell-shaded graphics typical of anime would also work well (the *Final Fantasy* series, for example). The kind of assignment that is useful in this respect asks for the same kind of scene analysis that one would ask for in an assignment based around a novel, for example, or a film: such an assignment usually involves scene description, discussion of the way in which the scene connects with the argument(s) implicit in the larger work, and the significance of the scene-work relation in terms of larger cultural codes. In the same way that teaching the visual conventions of cinema is sometimes best done by starting with films that flout those conventions, looking at games where the visual design is obviously out of the mainstream tradition of superficial naturalism allows students to begin to talk about how these pieces are the product of choices and how those choices affect the gameplay experience. A slightly harder task, in many ways, is to move beyond attention to the visual and to engage more closely and carefully with the idea of visual rhetoric: the idea that selecting among design elements creates, by implication at least, an argument.

The second challenge is to enable students to see games as designed—that is, to see how certain options flow from initial choices that have been made in the design stage and have foreclosed other options. The issue of design has already been raised in the first assignment I have described above, but I think the larger issue here is to help students understand games as the product of a design culture. One assignment I've employed successfully in my own classes is to ask students to prepare a design proposal based upon a game they would like to see realized. Given that within the industry such documents are usually more concept documents than actual programming blueprints, this is a task well within the capabilities of every student.

I set up this assignment by asking students to read some sample game design documents and a number of articles in which well-known game designers discuss a variety of design issues; the assignment itself is undertaken by teams of two or by small groups, depending on the size of the class. The assignment also gives students valuable experience at technical writing, a kind of writing that poses the challenge of how to be innovative within a highly regulated and constrained format. I require students to develop the criteria they will use to evaluate the proposals, develop the worksheets that we as a group will use to score the proposals and provide feedback, and establish some kind of rubric for converting our numerical assessments into letter grades for class purposes. Each person then reads all the group projects (as I do), grades them, and provides feedback; I collect it all, average the scores (so that mine ends up being one voice among the others), and hand the project back. Though demanding, this assignment is one that students have thoroughly enjoyed. One reason for their enjoyment is, I think, that the form of the project is adapted perfectly to the content of the class. More to the point, it gives students experience working in exactly the kind of team environments (both creative and evaluative) that characterize the gaming industry and allows them to recognize how those structures influence game design. Students put much more effort into examining questions concerning the kinds of visuals they recommend for their games, the impacts on gameplay, and the overall meanings they are trying to convey than if the assignment had taken a more analytical approach. The assignment also gives students a glimpse into the kind of creative differences that are effectively masked by the glossy marketing of individual games and the anonymity of a team. I do, however, have an additional agenda with this assignment, one that is made explicit in my insistence that students come up with a means of converting their numerical scores into letter grades for the assignment. This assignment is, for me, a useful way of beginning to demystify some of the educational processes in which they are enmeshed. As we talk about grading scales, students are at first disturbed and then often intrigued by the discovery that not only is there no inherent link between numerical scores and the grade of a B, for example, but there is little standardization across the campus, with the fundamental use of any grading scale being to establish consistency only within the course. The extended discussions we have had concerning this element of the assignment help gradually undo some of the mystification surrounding the question of evaluation and are entirely appropriate to incorporate into a first-year course.

The game design assignment flows into a third area of challenge which is, as I see it (and neither Hocks's nor George's work mentions this), to analyze the issue of new media in general and games in particular as educational instruments and to explore their role (or lack thereof) within a designed educational apparatus. Focusing explicitly on the educational arena allows students to explore some of the interesting contradictions in which electronic games are caught and which bear directly on the web of cultural assumptions within which students themselves are enmeshed. While students are often resistant to the idea of analytical reading, they will nevertheless acknowledge that literature can, on occasion, teach us useful knowledge concerning character, culture, psychology, and the world. Similarly, our culture constantly stresses the valuable lessons that can be learned from participating in games: this argument is a staple of sports metacommentary, for example. And yet the idea that electronic games, with their strong focus on narrative and play, can offer learning occasions appears somehow ridiculous. A starting point for such an assignment is James Gee's thought-provoking book *What Video Games Have to Teach Us About Learning and Literacy* (2003). Again, the choice here is strategic, in that Gee's book not only contains intriguing analyses of some of the better-known games, but proceeds from a more thoroughgoing critique of current educational theories, institutions, and practices. Such a critique helps set the stage for an assignment requiring students to analyze their current educational environment, how well that environment supports learning about electronic games, and how this influences the kinds of analyses we are able to produce concerning these objects.

Finally, all these elements need to come together to give us a way of talking about the vast majority of games, in which a nominal adherence to visual realism, or a patently nonrealistic setting (horror, sci-fi, etc.) seems to afford very little room to talk about either design choices or the connection with larger cultural values and narratives. Here too, however, there are many useful titles. For example, *Medal of Honor: Allied Assault* (2002), with its strong visual and aural connections with *Saving Private Ryan,* opens up the chance to explore the contemporary cultural marketing of WWII and the attempt to enshrine the political righteousness of the "greatest generation." *Deus Ex* (2000) and its sequel enable us to talk about the role of conspiracy narratives and to bring the contemporary discourse of terrorism into focus; the parody of B-grade movies in the *Max Payne* (2001) games allows us to begin to examine gender attitudes and the representations of inner-city space as they are encapsulated in visual design.

Closer attention to games as spaces that invite contemplation and reflection in conjunction with often frenzied activity, where the influence of design elements can be teased apart by subsequent analysis is, I think, essential for establishing electronic games as a sophisticated part of our cultural landscape. Teachers do not, after all, let novel readers off the hook simply because they burn through a novel from cover to cover; our working assumption with film and print literature has always been that the structure of the text, in conjunction with cultural influences, helps shape readers' or viewers' experiences of the text in ways they may not be aware of at the time of reading or viewing. I see no reason why writing teachers should let players and critics of electronic games get away with an entirely different, and more reductive, set of assumptions concerning the question of how electronic texts work.

Notes

1. After having argued for the metonymic nature of the Web, Manovich continues:

> The hypertext of the World Wide Web leads the reader from one text to another, ad infinitum. Contrary to popular images of computer media as collapsing all human culture into a single giant library (which implies the existence of some ordering system), or a single giant book (which implies a narrative progression) it is perhaps more accurate to think of the new media culture as an infinite flat surface where individual texts are placed in no particular order [. . .]. (77)

Invoking this kind of comparison allows him to move smoothly, à la Jameson, to an invocation of a postmodern culture of surfaces. However, focusing on the metonymic access structure of the Web succinctly bypasses all issues of rhetoric associated with content, ethos (some sites have a different level of cultural authority than others), user intent and response, and so on. Functionally, his argument here is the same as if we were to describe print as representing a decline in the field of rhetoric because each page is implicated even more closely in a metonymy of recto and verso.

2. Not surprisingly, McGee declares that he is a fan of Tim Burton's work and "readily admit[s] that *Alice* was hugely influenced by movies like *Sleepy Hollow* and *Edward Scissorhands*" (Sluganski). McGee also notes that the opposition to the Disney version was quite deliberate: "This dark Victorian look and feel to the characters I think is more what Wonderland was supposed to be than, say, what the Disney version was" (quoted in Brooker 249).

3. While many critics of Carroll's work have tended to approach Wonderland as a self-contained, nonreferential entity, thereby foregrounding Carroll's attempts to build a world entirely bounded by its own logical (im)proprieties, Carroll employed the visual design elements of the text to set up a referential framework between Wonderland and the larger text of Victorian politics and culture. Dodgson considered Tenniel's original illustrations central to the effectiveness of the text as a whole and oversaw their execution with an obsessive, exacting attention to detail. While some critics have seen this collaboration as representing the genius of the moment (see Lull, for example), Tenniel in fact both drew on a stock of imagery from his work as a cartoonist for *Punch* prior to the collaboration with Dodgson (Tweedledum and Tweedledee are almost identical with his representation of a young version of John Bull), and then went on to employ some of his Alice figures in future work in *Punch* (most noticeably the figure of Alice herself) (Hancher 27–29).

4. This point is made succinctly in Rebecca Solnit's analysis of Muybridge's photographic motion studies, *River of Shadows:*

> Tightly enforced schedules came in with the factories whose owners sought to calibrate human labor to machine labor, the machine labor that was speeding up the production of goods, thereby speeding up the raking in of profits, the consumption of raw materials, and on and on—a runaway train of consumption driving production driving consumption. It was these factories and railroads that made knowing the exact time important, that launched the modern world of schedules and bustle. (19)

5. While the game was generally reviewed positively, several critics pointed to its relentlessly linear nature. For examples, one reviewer singled out the linearity of the game in terms that conflate types of interactivity with levels of complexity:

> Alice is a fairly standard shooter wrapped in a very attractive package. It offers none of the complexity of a non-linear 3D platform action game with vast environments, and it offers none of the fast, intense action of a first-rate shooter [. . .]. Alice is completely linear, and it has no mul-

> tiplayer option, let alone any additional challenges that would help keep you involved in the game after you finish the main quest [. . .]. So while you'll undoubtedly enjoy the imaginative artwork, you might end up disappointed with just how straightforward the underlying game really is. (Wolpaw)

6. In my most recent class that focused on games, we established a workable option (suggested by the students themselves) whereby we pooled our resources. Each of us made available a list of all the games in our collection so that other students could have a broad selection from which to choose. This system worked well, but the downside from an educational point of view was that students tended to choose games from genres and sub-genres with which they were already familiar. As a teacher, I want to be able to push my students out of their comfort zones to help them discover new and exciting things in novel situations, to make connections between what they already know and what they have not yet experienced.

Works Cited

Aces High. Developed by HiTech Creations. 2004.

American McGee's Alice. Developed by Rogue Entertainment. Electronic Arts, 2000.

Brooker, Will. *Alice's Adventures: Lewis Carroll in Popular Culture.* New York: Continuum, 2004.

Deus Ex. Developed by Ion Storm. Eidos Interactive, 2000.

Gee, James Paul. *What Video Games Have to Teach Us About Learning and Literacy.* New York: Palgrave Macmillan, 2003.

George, Diana. "From Analysis to Design: Visual Communication in the Teaching of Writing." *College Composition and Communication* 54.1 (Sept 2002): 11–39.

The Good, the Bad, and the Ugly. Dir. Sergio Leone. Perf. Clint Eastwood, Lee Van Cleef, and Eli Wallach. United Artists, 1967 (U.S.).

Grim Fandango. Developed by LucasArts. LucasArts, 1998.

Hancher, Michael. "*Punch* and *Alice:* Through Tenniel's Looking Glass." *Lewis Carroll: A Celebration: Essays on the Occasion of the 150th Anniversary of the Birth of Chrarles Lutwidge Dodgson.* New York: Clarkson N. Potter, Inc., 1982. 26–49.

Hocks, Mary E. "Understanding Visual Rhetoric in Digital Writing Environments." *College Composition and Communication* 54.4 (June 2003): 626–56.

Jameson, Frederic. *Postmodernism, or, The Cultural Logic of Late Capitalism.* Durham, NC.: Duke University Press, 1992.

Lull, Janis. "The Appliances of Art: The Carroll-Tenniel Collaboration in *Through the Looking Glass*." Ed. Edward Guillano. *Lewis Carroll: A Celebration: Essays on the Occasion of the 150th Anniversary of the Birth of Charles Lutwidge Dodgson.* New York: Clarkson N. Potter, 1982.

Manovich, Lev. *The Language of New Media.* Cambridge, MA: Massachusetts Institute of Technology P, 2001.

—. "What is Digital Cinema?" *The Digital Dialectic: New Essays on New Media.* Peter Lunenfeld. Cambridge, MA: Massachusetts Institute of Technology P, 1999. 172–92.

Max Payne. Developed by Remedy Entertainment. Gathering, 2001.

Medal of Honor: Allied Assault. Developed by 2015. EA Games, 2002.

The New London Group. "A Pedagogy of Multiliteracies: Designing Social Futures." *Multiliteracies: Literacy Learning and the Design of Social Futures.* Ed. Bill Cope and Mary Kalantzis. London: Routledge, 2000. 9–37.

Rouse, Richard. *Game Design: Theory & Practice.* Worldware Game Developers Library. Plano, TX: Worldware Publishing, 2001.

Saving Private Ryan. Dir. Stephen Spielberg. Perf. Tom Hanks, Tom Sizemore, and Edward Burns. Paramount Pictures. 1998.

Salqado, Carlos "dr. angryman." "GameSpy Interviews: American McGee." *GameSpy* Oct 2000. (31 July 2004) <http://archive.gamespy.com/interviews/october00/alice/>.

Sluganski, Randy. "Cleaning up after the White Rabbit: An Intimate Interview with American McGee." *Just Adventure.* n.d. 5 Aug. 2004 <http://www.justadventure.com/Interviews/American_McGee/American_McGee.shtm>.

Solnit, Rebecca. *River of Shadows: Eadweard Muybridge and the Technological Wild West.* New York: Viking Penguin, 2003.

Thief: The Dark Project. Dev. Looking Glass Studios. Eidos Interactive. 1998.

Thief II: The Metal Age. Dev. Looking Glass Studios. Eidos Interactive. 2000.

Thief: Deadly Shadows. Dev. Ion Storm. Eidos Interactive. 2000.

Wolpaw, Erik. Review of *American McGee's Alice. Gamespot.* 8 Dec. 2000. 31 July 2004 <http://www.gamespot.com/pc/action/americanmcgeesalice/review.html>.

World War II Online: Blitzkrieg. Dev. Cornered Rat Software. Strategy First. 2004.

13 Revising for Activity Purposes: Improving Document Design for Reader-Oriented Activities

Kristin Walker Pickering

With thorough processing and rapid application of vital information essential for many users of technical documents, writers must ensure that their documents apply effective rhetorical principles. In fact, scholars such as Paul Dombrowski ("Haeckel," "Ethics") and Dorothy Winsor ("Communication") argue that professional communicators have an ethical obligation to help readers avoid misinterpretations that might lead to physical or other harm. Ethical communication in this sense often depends, at least in part, on the successful integration of visual and verbal texts that reflects readers' activity purposes.

This paper expands the idea of reader-oriented document design by introducing activity theory as a foundation for examining graphics both as culturally oriented visuals and as tools for successful completion of activities. The document revision assignment discussed is taken from an upper-level professional communication course entitled Professional Communication I, a course concentrating mainly on technical writing, document design, and oral communication skills. The assignment focuses on student revisions of documents that either do not incorporate text and graphics or do so ineffectively. Among those examples discussed in this chapter is a student's revision that incorporates maps and a timeline to help address a culturally sensitive highway construction project in a semi-rural area. The revision, along with the theoretical background supplied by activity theory, suggests ways that teachers can encourage student efforts to design effective technical documents.

Activity Theory and Culturally Oriented Graphic Tools

Activity theory provides opportunities for holistic study of socially dynamic environments. The theory is complicated, and scholars have defined activity systems in various ways to suit their research purposes (Artemeva and Freedman; Chaiklin and Lave; Engestrom, Miettinen, and Punamaki; Russell "Looking Beyond" and "Rethinking"; Walker "Activity Systems" and "Theoretical Foundations"; Winsor "Communication," "Genre and Activity Systems," and *Writing*). The abstract nature of the theory allows researchers to isolate particular activities within a system and study them while relating them to the broader activity of the system as a whole. For example, a low-voltage assembly area located in an electrical plant's production facility has a specified location for manufacturing instruction sheets. The assemblers on the plant floor use these sheets in the product assembly process. Researchers studying the communicative effectiveness of these sheets might study one assembler as he or she reads the instructions and studies the graphics; this process would provide one picture of the activity involved in processing written/graphical information and assembling the product. A broader look might focus on ways that the assembler interacts with other assemblers in that same area during the reading and assembling process, or ways that the assembler interacts with the manufacturing engineer who wrote the instructions. The ability to narrow the research focus and to relate one's research to a larger (or smaller) whole is a benefit of applying activity theory to such a broad process as textual/visual communication and activity.

Activity theory stresses the importance of cultural situatedness and the use of tools as cultural artifacts (Cole and Engestrom; Cole, Engestrom and Vasquez), especially as these concepts relate to situated learning (Lave and Wenger). These two concepts are useful for studying the connections between text, graphics, and activity purposes because graphics and written texts are tools working together to communicate through a culturally approved medium in a workplace/community environment.

Sometimes, the cultural aspects of activity can inhibit change because they have become institutionalized (Cole and Engestrom):

> [a]ctivity systems such as those that take place in schools and doctors' offices, for example, appear to

> reproduce similar actions and outcomes over and over again in a seemingly monotonous and repetitive manner that gives cultural constraints on action a seemingly overpowering quality. However, closer analysis of apparently unchanging activity systems reveals that transitions and reorganizations are constantly going on within and between activity systems as a fundamental part of the dynamics of human evolution. (8)

Tools within activity systems become cultural artifacts that can be analyzed to determine what effects they are having on the activity system as a whole. Cole and Engestrom explain that "Cultural artifacts are both material and symbolic; they regulate interaction with one's environment and oneself. In this respect, they are 'tools' broadly conceived" (9). In addition, the impact of technology on tools carries special significance because technology itself is tied up in the historical practice of culture (Lave and Wenger 101). Activity theory presents researchers with the opportunity to choose which tools to analyze and connect to the evolving social environment.

In the teaching of the complexities of integrating written texts and graphics, specific document design principles are useful as well, including Karen Schriver's five principles of integrating visual and verbal elements (complementary, supplementary, juxtapositional, stage-setting, and redundant). These principles can provide a bridge between the theoretical concepts of activity theory, culture, and tool use and the application of effective document design principles.

The Assignment

The assignment sketched in Appendix A asks students to find a document needing revision and to revise its images and written texts. Students understand that the document may be effective in general but still may be revised to address another audience more effectively. The class has already studied ways that visual aids can assist readers in performing tasks, so students are aware of the complexities surrounding activity and visuals. The course does not cover many specifics about activity theory itself, but it does encourage students to consider how visual aids coordinate with activities that people are trying to perform, especially in workplace or community contexts.

Jennifer Cloud, a student in this class, chose a timely and culturally relevant document to revise: the "Tennessee Department of Transportation 15 Project Case Study: Project Assessment Final Report State Route 451 in Cookeville Area." In an online discussion posting addressed to her classmates, Jennifer described her interaction with this document and her motivation for choosing it for the final project revision:

> I actually came across this document in May, before the semester began; I had been looking at the Tennessee Dept. of Transportation's webpage to find out about construction projects that could impede a trip I was planning. I noticed a small link about "15 Projects Report," which listed the "Cookeville area" for a potential project. I go to school in Cookeville so of course was interested in where this new road would be, so I started reading the report. And then started skimming, and more skimming, more skimming, [. . .] and finally on page 10 (out of 20 pages) I found a description of *where* this road would be! There were no diagrams or maps in the document, so I had to pull out my Tennessee road map to find where the project would be.
>
> When it was time to do the final project, this immediately came to mind, and in my critique of the report, I noticed several areas that needed improvement: document organization, lack of visual aids, some excess words (like a general history of TDOT projects??), and a lack of usability for the secondary audience.
>
> I have identified a secondary audience that the original document might not have addressed; this study was written for the TDOT Commissioner and gives enough information for those officials who are familiar with the project. However, this document needs some quick-reference visuals and charts for people who do not have time to read the whole report or just want the answer to one question, such as news reporters or concerned citizens like me. Through my revision, I will be working to make this document

> useful for its secondary audiences. The most major overhauls I will make are to the organization and to the visual layout of the document.

After reading the original document, Jennifer recognized that it wasn't as effective as it might have been in helping readers perform several activities, including understanding the document, identifying the areas affected, and determining how the Tennessee Department of Transportation's (TDOT) activities affected readers in the community. Jennifer's position as a temporary resident (student) in the area, as well as her need to gather information for her traveling purposes, designated her a member of the audience this document might affect and motivated her to transform this artifact to better serve its audiences' needs.

I will focus on the two main changes that Jennifer made to the TDOT document: her additions of maps and a timeline. In making the decisions to include these visual elements, Jennifer also assessed the cultural context of the document, as activity theory promotes. This context included the fact that the project had been rejected by the public. After reading the original report, Jennifer realized that the TDOT had not addressed the community's need to know certain details. The report states that

> A TDOT feasibility study was prepared in 1996 and an Advanced Planning Report (APR) was approved (12/00). In conjunction with these activities three TDOT public meetings were held 7/99; 2/00; and 5/00. At these meeting [sic] there were much negative citizen comments against the project. Concerns voiced at the "Listening Session" (5/03) stated the TDOT public participation process for project SR–451; [sic] was deficient. The hearing included the following citizen comments:
>
> - TDOT officials showed insensitivity to citizens during public meetings. There were no chairs in which to sit, poor maps and no consistent meeting place.
> - TDOT ignored public input. There was a lot of input into this project but the current plan is essentially the same one originally proposed with very minor modifications.

- There has been overwhelming opposition to this project but TDOT didn't hear it.
- There was almost no investigations process.
- TDOT was listening to elected officials using the rationale that they represent the people. The public felt shut out of the process.
- TDOT should bring senior officials to public sessions and listen to dialogue, not have people walk around to tables.
- Information at the public meetings was confusing with upside down maps. (Richards 14–15)

Part of the context of this document, then, was the absence of information, some of it visual. The citizens of the community wanted to know exactly where this highway was going to go, and they did not receive the information during the public discussion. The context that produced this document was one that clearly related to citizens' needs for certain types of tools with which to complete the activity of understanding the project: accurate and clear maps.

Also connected to the history of this meeting was the document itself, for citizens wanting to know how the TDOT followed up on the public meeting might have searched for the updated information on the TDOT website. The document lacked the visual tools the public needed to access this information. Jennifer recognized this lack and decided to include two maps to indicate two different perspectives on where the highway would be located. In the original document no maps were included. Below are the two maps that Jennifer included, along with the text that referred to them:

> This project involves the construction of State Route 451 (SR 451), a limited access, four-lane, divided highway on a new right-of-way connecting SR 111 to SR 56 north of Cookeville, Tennessee, in Putnam and Jackson Counties. The eastern terminus of the proposed new roadway is at SR 111 immediately north of Gibbons Road and northwest of the community of Algood in Putnam County, as shown in Figure 1. The western terminus is at SR 56 north of Baxter in Jackson County. The approximate road length is 9.7 miles, although the actual length will depend on which of several alternative alignments is chosen.

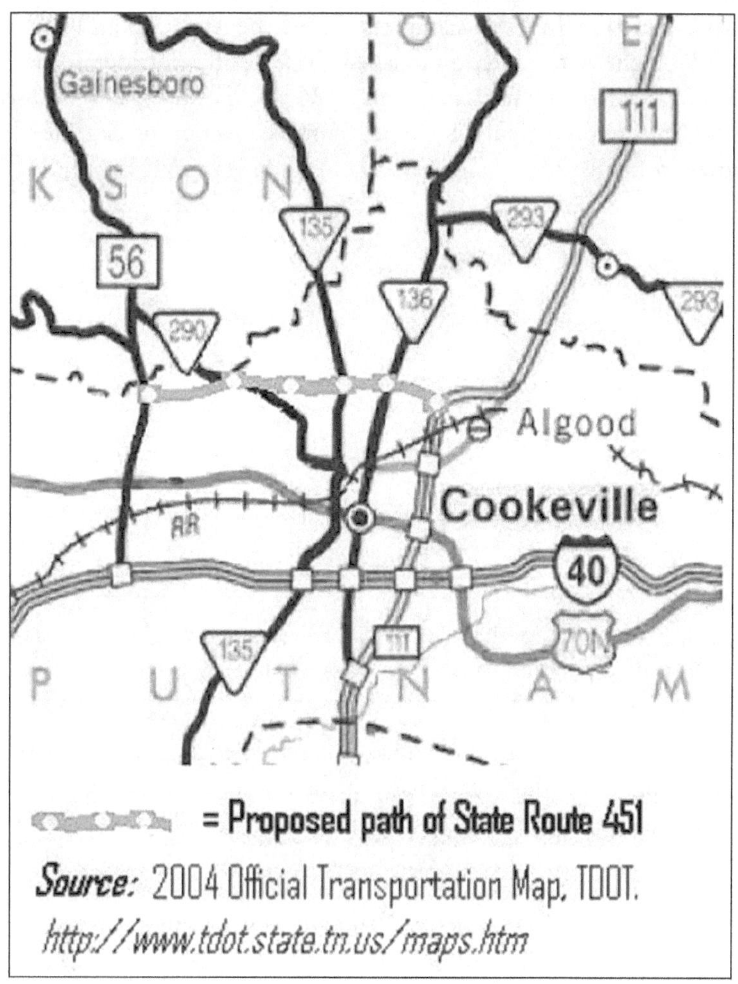

Figure 1. Location of proposed route for SR 451 in Cookeville area. (Used by permission of the Tennessee Department of Transportation.)

Most of the text from the paragraph above was from the original, but an important visual had been added. This map was the first visual aid that readers would encounter. It highlighted in yellow and red the exact route the new highway would take. This holistic view gave the readers a color perspective of the highway, something they had not encountered up to this point. The fact that Jennifer had obtained the map from an official TDOT site lent credibility to this visual aid for anyone reading the document. Jennifer discussed the second map as follows: "In 1965, Congress passed the Appalachian Regional Development Act, which established the ADHS. Corridor J, one of 26 ADHS corridors, stretches from I-124 at Chattanooga, Tennessee, to I-75 at London, Kentucky. The Tennessee section of Corridor J is shown in Figure 2."

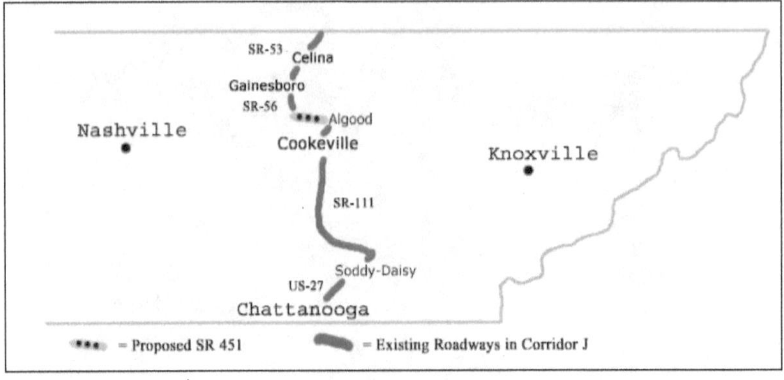

Figure 2. Corridor J of the Appalachian Development Highway System (ADHS). (Used by permission of Jennifer Cloud.)

The second map Jennifer included was one she had designed: a state map highlighting the overall path of the highway, including parts already constructed. This map gave readers a statewide perspective of the highway and what parts of the state had been affected and might be affected in the future.

The final visual aid Jennifer included was a timeline that concisely outlined the progress made on the project from its inception to the present (See Appendix B). Although this timeline presented information that was contained within the original document in a more narrative and expanded form, Jennifer presented the information in a more visually appealing and readable way so that readers could assess information more quickly. This timeline might, at some time in the future, replace the more extended text provided in the document, for revisions can continue to take place as readers' needs become better understood.

As Jean Lave and Etienne Wenger point out, cultural artifacts develop during communication. These artifacts are essential parts of developing activity systems, and a history develops in which certain tools can facilitate or hinder communication. In the case studied by Jennifer, community members in Cookeville who were attending public meetings about the highway project might have been said to constitute an activity system. The TDOT report was a cultural artifact that had reinforced the negative reactions most community members felt towards the proposed project. Although these reactions stemmed from more than simply the document and the poorly constructed maps presented by the TDOT at public meetings, Jennifer's additions to the report created new cultural artifacts: two maps outlining the highway and a timeline encapsulating the processes that had occurred regarding the project. Because citizens rejected the project in part because of a lack of information, the addition of maps likely would have served as useful tools for understanding. The inclusion of maps at this stage might even have promoted the use of additional maps in future documents/reports from the TDOT, as the process of highway development continued.

Activity theory provides a framework for studying not only physical activities but also mental and psychological ones. Although studying the latter is certainly more abstract, learning about the mental activities that precede physical activities can provide insights into communication processes and their scope. Regarding the TDOT project, one positive activity resulting from this document might have been an informed public willing to consider the highway project once the necessary environmental testing had been completed and required location information had been provided. But before that activity could take place at another public forum, the activity of actually understanding the document and the information the TDOT was presenting needed to take place. Although the activity Jennifer addressed in her revision is more abstract than technical or physical (e.g., she did not provide instructions for a task to be completed), the activity still was crucial if the public were to feel that it had participated in the highway construction decision-making process. And even though the activities Jennifer encouraged through her revision were abstract, the changes she made to the document were tangible.

Jennifer's project addressed ways that a workplace document related to community participation in a culturally sensitive construction project; other students from the same class chose revision projects reflecting a knowledge of how readers interact with visuals as they performed activities in the workplace. For example, Susan worked in an admissions office at a community college, where employees followed detailed steps in the processing of student applications. An outdated instruction sheet—absent graphics—was available for new employees, but Susan saw the need to integrate screen shots into the instructions to help readers verify that they were processing information accurately. Because Susan was an employee, she was familiar with the need to verify at various stages whether data had been entered accurately. The screen shots she added to the document helped workers ensure that they had performed tasks correctly by providing a visual they could use to compare to their computer screens. The visually enhanced revision was the result of an evolutionary process initiated by the needs of a changing work environment: before, employees had been more likely to communicate orally and could ask each other questions and receive verification as they worked side by side. But as a result of changing work schedules and greater turnover in the office, the original instruction sheet was no longer performing its function because its reliance on experienced employee explanation and support was no longer practical. The revision constituted a more culturally relevant tool, one that would probably continue to change based on the needs of its users as they participated in the evolving admissions processing activity.

Another student, John, revised instructions for a group of assembly line workers exposed to harmful paint fumes related to products they were assembling. The instructions explained that the workers should face in a certain direction while assembling so that large fans at one end of the line would blow the harmful fumes away from them. No graphics were included to clarify the workers' positions, however, and John believed that graphics would benefit the instructions. The workers likely would be more receptive to a visual description because their assembly work didn't allow them time to read and interpret verbal instructions.

John photographed the line at the plant, including workers facing the appropriate direction in relation to the fans. Then he included that photograph in the instructions, with the written indications of how the workers needed to stand as they worked on the products. While John didn't report any results of user tests with the new instructions, he believed that the revised instructions would address workers' safety needs better than the original. Again, because the original instructions no longer seemed relevant to workers' experiences and required excessive motivation/time to be read, a new, more culturally relevant tool needed to be adapted from the original.

This process is indicative of what often occurs within a system when approved communicative forms and activities cease to accomplish their desired objectives: an evolution begins to introduce other tools into the system. Rather than being a neat and orderly process, evolution within activity systems is often messy (Russell "Looking Beyond").

Activity Theory and Effective Document Design Formulation

Teachers of professional communication can encourage students to be aware of certain aspects of activity theory as they determine the most effective ways to include graphics and other visual aids into technical and professional documents. First, students can be encouraged to analyze readers' needs within the current culture of practice. Emphasizing knowledge of such a culture highlights for students the importance of context in document design. Emerging from the culture of practice are the tools used within an activity system. Documents themselves can be tools. But because technology plays such an important role in workplace communication, the technological tools used to communicate should also be analyzed as part of the context that produces documents. Students don't have to be trained in all the specifics of ethnographic research to develop an awareness of an environment's culture; often, interviewing participants and observing can reveal much about ways that an activity system operates. And if the observer is also a participant in workplace/community culture (as all the students discussed were), even more complex information can be gathered.

Because activity systems evolve and change, students can learn much about a workplace culture's history of communication by studying previous documents produced in that environment and determining what may or may not be working in those documents. The visual and verbal elements incorporated into such documents should reflect basic document-design principles (such as Schriver's) and should have purpose within the broader context of the specific activity system. Susan, who worked in the admissions office of the community college, demonstrated knowledge of her readers' need to verify that the correct information had been entered before continuing on to the next screen, indicating in turn her knowledge that accuracy and thoroughness are essential for successful data entry. The screen shots that she included addressed that need and reinforced its importance.

A final suggestion for students as they consider revising for activity purposes is to realize that the communication process is evolving and that changes often need to be tested and adapted to meet the needs of people within the system. This process requires an awareness of how different people and technologies work together. Involving people who are part of the activity and learning from their attempts to use documents and graphics can suggest means for improving future document drafts. As suggested by the student projects described in this chapter, activity theory's focus on tools and their means of effecting social action makes it a useful framework in which to examine both the uses of visual texts and the effects of visual design.

Appendix A: Document Design Revision Assignment

This assignment requires you to choose a document that you feel could be revised and improved. The document might be a manual or pamphlet, some sort of sales literature, instructions, or a website that is technical in nature. These documents might be present in your home or workplace. If you have any questions about the suitability of your documents for revision, please let me know.

The goals of the assignment are for you to familiarize yourself with the process of revising a document created by someone else, to assess the effectiveness of the graphics used, and to revise where necessary. When revising, consider ways the documents might be improved to help readers accomplish specific activities and goals.

Prerequisites

- Your revised document should be approximately 10 pages long. The original document might not be that long. In that case, you would add sections to make it longer.
- The document should have problematic features that you can address through revision. (In other words, you should not simply re-copy the document and call that a revision.)

Requirements

- Obviously, you should be careful to have your document saved in various stages of the revision process.
- Text should be re-typed to reflect revisions.

- You may make typed notes regarding how you would revise graphics if you do not have the software capabilities to revise the graphics. You should attempt to improve the graphics, however.
- Consider elements and topics you wrote about in your individual document assessment even if you do not choose to revise that document. You can still use your ideas for revision.
- Turn in your revision with a copy of the original document, which will be returned to you at your request. If your document is a website, simply refer to the URL in your revision.

Appendix B. Timeline of SR 451 Cookeville Area Project History

Timeline of SR 451-Cookeville Area Project History

1965 Congress passed the Appalachian Regional Development Act, establishing the Appalachian Development Highway System (ADHS).

1973 The first ADHS-improved sections of Corridor J were opened to traffic in Tennessee.

1998 Congress passed The Transportation Equity Act for the 21st Century (TEA-21), significantly boosting the availability of funding for the ADHS.

1999 TDOT conducted an initial field review of the SR 451 corridor on January 14.

1999 The first public meeting on the SR 451 project was held at Cookeville High School on July 27, with 561 persons attending. TDOT presented two alternate alignments, designated A and B, for public review and comment. Of the 511 persons submitting comments to TDOT, 438 (86 percent) expressed opposition to the project, while five people were undecided.

1999 TDOT conducted a second field review of the SR 451 corridor on October 14.

2000 TDOT held a second public meeting at the Hyder-Burks Agricultural Pavilion in Cookeville, on February 15. The 555 meeting attendees were shown an alternative alignment labeled

B1. Of the 557 people who gave comments to TDOT at this meeting, 512 (92.3 percent) were opposed to the project.

2000 TDOT conducted a third public meeting on the SR 451 project on May 25. The 439 meeting attendees were shown three new alternative alignments, labeled D1, D2, and E. Opposition to the project was still very high as 450 (92 percent) of the 490 people who submitted comments expressed disapproval.

2000 On September 7, TDOT issued a press release announcing a proposal for an access-controlled alignment of Corridor J through the Cookeville area. Then-TDOT Commissioner J. Bruce Saltsman directed TDOT staff to immediately begin environmental studies.

2000 The Advance Planning Report (APR) was approved on December 13. It was subsequently revised and reapproved on March 16, 2001. The APR discussed only two of the alternative alignments—B, presented at the first public meeting, and B1, presented at the second public meeting.

2002 TDOT discovered caves inhabited by gray bats, an endangered species, that could be adversely affected by the proposed alignments for SR 451. A study of the bats' habitat and range was initiated on March 12, and a draft report was submitted on August 14. TDOT decided on October 17 to extend the study to document the bats' range during the winter season.

2003 At the time TDOT put the SR 451 project on hold for review, the bat study was still in progress. The consultant subsequently submitted a second draft report for this study on March 25. An Environmental Impact Statement (EIS) was under development.

Works Cited

Artemeva, Natasha, and Aviva Freedman. "'Just the Boys Playing on Computers': An Activity Theory Analysis of Differences in the Cultures of Two Engineering Firms." *Journal of Business and Technical Communication* 15.2 (2001): 164–94.

Chaiklin, Seth, and Jean Lave. *Understanding Practice: Perspectives on Activity and Context.* New York: Cambridge UP, 1996.

Cloud, Jennifer. "Corridor J of the Appalachian Development Highway System (ADHS). (Graphic used by permission, 2004).

Cole, Michael, and Yrjo. Engestrom. "A Cultural-Historical Approach to Distributed Cognition." *Distributed Cognitions.* Ed. Gavriel Salomon. New York: Cambridge UP, 1993. 1–46.

Cole, Michael, Yrjo Engestrom, and Olga Vasquez. *Mind, Culture, and Activity.* New York: Cambridge UP, 1997.

Dombrowski, Paul. "Ernst Haeckel's Controversial Visual Rhetoric." *Technical Communication Quarterly* 12.3 (2003): 303–19.

—. *Ethics in Technical Communication.* Boston: Allyn and Bacon, 2000.

Engestrom, Yrjo, Reijo Miettinen, and Raija-Leena Punamaki, eds. *Perspectives on Activity Theory.* New York: Cambridge UP, 1999.

Lave, Jean, and Etienne Wenger. *Situated Learning: Legitimate Peripheral Participation.* New York: Cambridge UP, 1991.

Richards, Stephen, et al. "Tennessee Department of Transportation 15 Project Case Study: Project Assessment Final Report State Route 451 in Cookeville Area." Aug. 2003. Center for Transportation Research, University of Tennessee. 2004. 20 July 2004 <http://www.tdot.state.tn.us/information-office/2003pr/listening/State%20Route%20451%20in%20the%20Cookeville%20Area.pdf>.

Russell, David. "Looking Beyond the Interface: Activity Theory and Distributed Learning." *Distributed Learning: Social and Cultural Approaches to Practice.* Ed. Mary Lea and Kathy Nicoll. London: Routledge/Falmer, 2002. 64–82.

—. "Rethinking Genre in School and Society." *Written Communication* 14.4 (1997): 504–54.

Schriver, Karen. *Dynamics in Document Design.* New York: John Wiley and Sons, 1997.

Walker, Kristin. "Activity Systems and Conflict Resolution in an Online Professional Communication Course." *Business Communication Quarterly* 67.2 (2004): 182–97.

—. "Theoretical Foundations for Website Design Courses." *Technical Communication Quarterly* 11.1 (2002): 61–83.

Winsor, Dorothy. "Communication Failures Contributing to the *Challenger* Accident: An Example for Technical Communicators." *IEEE Transactions on Professional Communication* 31.3 (1988): 101–7.

—. "Genre and Activity Systems." *Written Communication* 16.2 (1999): 200–24.

—. *Writing Like an Engineer: A Rhetorical Education.* Mahwah, NJ: Lawrence Erlbaum Associates, 1996.

Contributors

Nancy J. Allen is Professor of English at Eastern Michigan University, where she teaches rhetoric and professional communication courses at the graduate and undergraduate levels. She has published on collaborative writing and a variety of topics on visual and writing relationships, including subjects such as ethics, visual narratives, and visual meaning.

Jean Darcy is Assistant Professor at Queensborough Community College, where she teaches in the composition program of the English Department. She has specialized on the use of visuals in distance learning and has participated in the "Learning to Look" project and the Georgetown "Crossroads" project on visual education.

Carol David is Professor Emerita in the Rhetoric and Professional Communication Program at Iowa State University, where she taught a variety of undergraduate and graduate courses in composition and served as Director of Advanced Communication. She has published articles on the visual in professional communication and on management writing.

Jane Davis is Associate Professor of English at Iowa State University, where she has served as Director of Curriculum for the Multicultural Learning Community. She studies nineteenth- and twentieth-century American literature, black literature, film, and modernism. Her book *The White Image in the Black Mind* was named one of the best books of 2000 by *Choice,* the leading review journal for academic and research libraries.

Ryan Jerving is an Assistant Professor of Writing at The George Washington University, where he has taught writing courses centered on issues of visual rhetoric, the cultural role of the 21st-century university, and intellectual property. His research concerns writing's place within the culture industries, with a focus on early jazz literature; popular poetry, film, and theater; and documentary modernism.

C. Richard King is an Associate Professor of comparative ethnic studies at Washington State University, where he teaches anthropology. He has written extensively on the changing contours of race in post-civil rights America, the colonial legacies and postcolonial predicaments of American culture, and struggles over Indianness in public culture.

Mark Mullen is Assistant Professor and Deputy Director of First-year Writing at The George Washington University. He has published articles and presented papers on electronic media in composition and coordinated programs in the training and development of new teachers.

L. J. Nicoletti teaches visual studies and English at Centenary College of Louisiana and chairs the Department of Art and Visual Culture, while researching the cultural reception, perception, and representation of victims in the nineteenth through twentiy-first centuries.

Alyssa J. O'Brien lectures in the Writing and Rhetoric Program at Stanford University, where she has taught numerous courses on visual rhetoric, including The Persuasive Power of Visual Rhetoric in Contemporary Society, and Multimedia Autobiographies: Visual Rhetoric of Self and Community. She has published articles on feminist theory, film studies, and James Joyce. She is co-author of the recent Longman title *Envision: Persuasive Writing in a Visual World.*

Iraj Omidvar is an Assistant Professor of English, Technical Communication, and Media Arts at Southern Polytechnic State University and a recent Fulbright Fellow. In addition to authoring articles on the visual rhetoric of online interfaces and on critical thinking in engineering classrooms, he is a widely published translator of modern Persian poetry. In spring 2007, his translation of Ahmad Shamlu's "I Am Still Thinking about This Crow," originally published in *New Letters*, was featured by *Poetry Daily.*

Deborah Rard is a Lecturer in English Composition at California State University, Hayward, where she teaches a variety of composition courses and specializes in curriculum design and writing center instruction. She has presented workshops and papers on writing-across-the-curriculum and developmental writing.

Anne R. Richards is an Assistant Professor of English at Kennesaw State University, where she teaches with the Master of Arts in Professional Writing Program. Recently returned from a year as a Fulbright Fellow in Tunisia, she is completing a study of medical illustrations from the Early Islamic Empire. She publishes and presents on gaming communities and video and sound design in hypermedia.

Kristin Walker Pickering received the Ph.D in English-Composition and Rhetoric from the University of South Carolina in 1997. Currently, she is an Assistant Professor of English and Director of the Professional Communication Program at Tennessee Technological University. She teaches courses in first-year composition and professional communication. She has published on activity theory, genre theory, and website design.

Yong-Kang Wei is Assistant Professor of English and Communication at the University of Texas–Brownsville. His research interests include classical and cross-cultural rhetoric. Wei has spoken internationally on the topic of the panopticon, media and the Chinese face and has recently published on corporate image as collective ethos, in *Corporate Communications: An International Journal.*

Barbara Worthington is a full-time English Instructor at Chabot College in Hayward, California. Barbara earned a Masters degree at California State University, East Bay, where she worked as an Assistant English Professor for eight years. She has presented at conferences and conducted several workshops on methods for using visual rhetoric to enhance classroom instruction.

Index

www.ingramcontent.com/pod-product-compliance
Lightning Source LLC
LaVergne TN
LVHW091033080826
845145LV00002B/470

* 9 7 8 1 6 0 2 3 5 0 4 6 5 *